Gameplay and design

Kevin Oxland

ADDISON-WESLEY

An imprint of **Pearson Education**

London • Boston • Indianapolis • New York • Mexico City
Toronto • Sydney • Tokyo • Singapore • Hong Kong • Cape Town
New Delhi • Madrid • Paris • Amsterdam • Munich • Milan

To Emma, Rebecca and Jessica

Pearson Education Limited
Edinburgh Gate
Harlow
Essex CM20 2JE
England

and Associated Companies throughout the world

Visit us on the World Wide Web at:
www.pearsoned.co.uk
First published 2004

ISBN 0 321 20467 0

British Library Cataloguing-in-Publication Data

A catalogue record for this book is available from the British Library

Library of Congress Cataloging-in-Publication Data

Oxland, Kevin.
  GAMEplay and design / by Kevin Oxland.
    p. cm.
  Includes bibliographical references and index.
  ISBN 0-321-20467-0
    1. Computer games--Programming. I. Title.

  QA76.76.C672095 2004
  794.8--dc22

                                                            2003069503

10 9 8 7 6 5 4 3 2 1
08 07 06 05 04

Typeset in 10/12pt Century Schoolbook BT by 30
Printed and bound in Great Britain by Biddles Ltd, Guildford and King's Lynn

The publisher's policy is to use paper manufactured from sustainable forests.

Contents

Foreword

People that succeed in making their living doing something they enjoy are very lucky; for me, if you can count yourself in that category, you've already won the lottery! Like me, Kevin Oxland has managed to turn his hobby into his living, and the joy he has had along the way shines through in this book. Rather than talk from on high, like so many designers tend to, as they bombard you with rhetoric and buzzwords, Kevin takes you step by fascinating step, through all of the ins-and-outs of life as a game designer.

Games have been designed and played since man first discovered boredom. It is known that games like Mancala were being played in Egypt around 1400 BC. The author will introduce you to a game in common usage today that was being played, again in Egypt, some 1600 years before Mancala was designed! I wonder if Tetris will still be being played in 5000 years' time.

Mancala is an elegant game of skill that is usually played between two players. The most common version of the game sees players moving game-pieces or tokens around two rows of indents or hollows as they attempt to capture as many of the tokens as possible. While modern versions of the game in Western countries use perfectly formed wooden or plastic trays to hold coloured glass pieces, the game would have been played in a series of scooped-out hollows in the ground and with readily available seeds acting as tokens. I find it fascinating to imagine the design processes that the game's early originators would have followed.

Some games such as Snakes and Ladders are solely based on luck while others, like Chess, are solely based on skill. Most commercially successful games incorporate variable amounts of both. Indeed, it could be argued that games involving both luck and skill usually provide the players with more enjoyment than those games that rely on luck or skill alone.

In essence, all games are a means of passing time as enjoyably as possible; beyond that they fulfil many desires including those of social interaction and personal challenge. As children, most of us grew up with that special pleasure that can only be found in the act of taking part in, or the 'playing' of a game.

When you stop to think about the range of things that we precede with the term 'play', you realise that they include such things as music, films, sports and, of course, games; all of them are forms of entertainment and providers of fun and enjoyment. In computer games we've come to understand this magical component as gameplay; an important component that it is often impossible to know precisely why it is right when it is, but one that reveals itself so much more readily when it is wrong.

I encourage you to keep reminding yourself of this thought about gameplay and entertainment during your career as a game designer; for a variety of reasons, some games appear as if the need to entertain was an optional extra. It is that commodity, enjoyment, which we use to gauge how good one game is when compared to another and ultimately, therefore, which games will get played most and which will go on to sell the most.

You might be wondering why I've been banging on about traditional games in a book about the design and creation of computer games. Well, the simple answer is that the computer is a new medium that makes it easier and sometimes more enjoyable for us to play our games. Like me, you probably remember those irritating frustrations when as a child you struggled to find willing opponents with whom to play a game. Your computer will always provide that willing opponent, which is one of the main reasons for their explosive success over the last three decades.

The only attribute that the critics of this wonderful pastime will claim has been sacrificed is that of human interaction; but even this criticism is about to be diluted with the advent of accessible on-line, multi-player games. Access to such games is now being provided for platforms like Microsoft's Xbox® and Sony's PlayStation®2 in addition to the good old PC, and many more people are enjoying games with opponents from all areas of the globe; something that has, until fairly recently, not been possible.

The first trap that is waiting to ensnare the novice game designer is best summed up by the following statement: 'A great concept does not alone maketh the game'. All games evolve from an initial concept. The problem is that it is remarkably easy to come up with a great-sounding concept and remarkably difficult to turn that concept into a top quality game; in fact, I would go as far as to say that for every 100 great-sounding concepts, there results one top-quality game.

Imagine the feeling when you come up with a great-sounding concept, only for the concept to flounder when the going gets tough. This can be a soul-destroying experience and one that all game designers experience at some stage. Even for those games that turn out to be classics, there tend to be phases when everything seems to be wrong and nothing is hanging together properly. This is where the seasoned designer learns to spot the concepts that just need to be looked at from a different perspective or require the addition of a new game mechanic to make them work again and separates them from the flawed concepts that are simply not going to make the grade.

Concepts that fit into the latter category do not always get terminated when they should and they often turn into games that take many years to complete; there's a growing list of games that fit this description all too well; games that were in development for as long as four or even five years before being forced to market by a desperate publisher. If you succeed in becoming an expert at recognising the unpolished diamonds in a pile of useless rocks, you will be one step closer to making it to the top of this great profession.

No one would expect the reading of one book on such a diverse subject as this to magically turn you into a thoroughbred game designer overnight, but in *Gameplay and Design*, Kevin takes you on a journey that will not only point you in the right direction, it will help you to navigate past the obstacles and pitfalls that stand between you and your dream of becoming a successful designer of interactive computer games.

I hope you enjoy reading this excellent book and who knows, I might be playing one of your games in a few years' time!

Kevin Buckner
Game Design Consultant
Design Games Ltd
www.designgames.co.uk

About the author

Kevin Oxland has worked in the games industry for the last twenty years, recently holding a position as creative director/producer for an independent game development studio. He has worked within many aspects of game development, beginning as a freelance programmer, coding games for the Commodore 64 and the Amiga 500, subsequently turning his attention to his true passions, art and design. After many successful developments, he became Creative Director at Virgin Interactive in London UK where he spent five years working on various projects. He spent time working at Westwood Studios in Las Vegas on Disney's 'The Lion King' and 'Pinocchio'. He has also been involved in setting up two successful development studios and creating products for many of the top publishers for global publication.

Author's acknowledgements

It can be a daunting and solitary affair writing a tome such as this. It would not have been possible without the understanding and support of the many great friends, family and colleagues who have helped me compile the contents of this book. Any mistakes left in the book are mine alone.

I would like to thank Chris Taylor and all the folk at Gas Powered Games®, particularly Jeremy Snook and Michelle Lloyd for all their help, and for allowing me to use the excellent Dungeon Siege® as a case study.

I thank Kevin Buckner of Design Games Ltd for his kind words in the Foreward, and his inspiring words of wisdom for budding game designers. John Palmer for his rendition of Norbot, my flagship character that may someday see the three-dimensional world he was intended for.

Thank you to also all the people who have inspired me and helped me through the last twenty years of the industry, particularly those who have contributed to the book in one way or another: Christian Johnson, Louis Castle, Bobby Earl, Robbie Tinman, Sean Millard and Colin Gordon.

Publisher's acknowledgements

We are grateful to the following for permission to reproduce copyright material:

Figures 1.2 and 1.4 from The Tetris Company, LLC; Figure 2.1 from First Star Software, Inc; Figure 2.2, 2.4 from Electronic Arts Inc; Figure 2.3, 2.4, 5.1, 6.1, 6.2, 6.3, 8.2, 8.3, 10.1, 13.1, 14.1, 15.2, 15.5 from Gas Powered Games Corp and Figure 3.1 from www.pegi.info, © 2004, ISFE.

Norbot image (including cover image) published courtesy of John Palmer, copyright © 2003 John Palmer, all rights reserved.

In some instances we have been unable to trace the owners of copyright material, and we would appreciate any information that would enable us to do so.

Trademark notice

Introduction

Before we delve into the murky depths of game design, I feel a brief historical overview of the games industry is necessary for the readers who are not familiar with the rapid growth and current state of our fast-paced industry.

The games industry is relatively young compared to most other industries, but it is one of the fastest growing industries in the world, and revenues are about to exceed that of the movie industry. It's difficult to determine when it truly began. Pong was the first home computer game I can remember – two white blocks, representing bats, that moved up and down the left and right sides of the screen in a desperate attempt to hit a white square, symbolising a ball, that moved horizontally across the screen. The simplicity was bliss! For me however, it truly began with the Commodore 64. I still have my original machine and it still works, although I hesitate to play the games of old and would rather harbour the fond memories I have. Great games such as 'Paradroid', 'Mercenary' and 'Elite', to name but a few, conjure sentimental memories of 24-hour gaming sessions and 30-minute load times. The very first game I bought was for the Commodore 64, entitled 'The Hobbit' by Melbourne House, and it was published on a cassette. It really did take 30 minutes to load! Can you imagine gamers today waiting that long? The worst thing about cassettes was the unreliability of them. You never knew if your game was going to kick in at the end of the 30 minutes; then some bright spark invented flashing borders to inform the player that their game was in fact loading, but that didn't improve the quality of loading from tape!

Technology did what technology does, it evolved at an alarming rate. Over the following twenty years, when the Commodore 64 and Spectrum days were over, came a plethora of game consoles and computers including the Amiga, Atari ST, NES, SNES, Megadrive, Gameboy, Sega Saturn, N64, Playstation, Dreamcast to name but a handful. Today we have the PlayStation2, Nintendo Gamecube, the Xbox, and let's not forget the mighty PC. Today there are growing rumours of a PlayStation3 and Xbox2 on the horizon; technology is relentless.

When I first approached publishers with the idea of writing this book, the first question I was asked was 'Won't you be revealing your secrets?' The answer to that question is no. It's like asking an artist if he can reveal how he paints a masterpiece. He just does it with his innate creative ability. However, as with most skills, you can learn to nurture such a talent. Computer and video game designers do have a set of principles that are used to form and shape the masterpieces you see today.

There is no step-by-step instruction manual for making great games, nor is there a conspiracy to conceal the secrets of great gameplay and game design techniques. The devices and techniques are under your very noses and in abundance; we have been using the same gaming techniques for thousands of years. But the closer you look at these games and break them down into definable pieces, the more you realise that creating games is an art form in its own right – and it's not easy to create a masterpiece. What it does require is passion, imagination, talent, a good understanding of gameplay and game design principles, experience, a dedicated team, efficient project management and good old-fashioned hard work. Every game developed is individual, a different experience both in the playing and the developing, and should be regarded as such.

There are techniques and fundamentals one can learn to understand the creative process of game design, and these will be discussed throughout the book, culminating in a set of techniques used by designers in the industry today. This book is peppered with examples and case studies, from the ancient games of Egypt through to the modern monster-mashing high-tech games of today.

Who this book is for

Most of the books on game design I have seen are targeted at the industry itself, either very technical and requiring the reader to be a programmer of sorts, or they use language that many apprentice designers would find difficult to understand and follow. With this book I wanted instead to offer anybody interested in computer and video games an insight into the world of game design, and provide a solid foundation on which to build from. Whether you are a student or a practitioner working within the games industry and wish to shift your career path, or somebody simply interested in how games are made, then this book is for you. If you are a flourishing designer and want to look at game design from a different perspective, then you too could learn new and varying techniques on the development of many aspects of game design offered in this book.

Terminology

I have tried to keep the terminology as consistent and simple as it can be. Where I have used computer game register, I have included a glossary in the back of the book for your reference.

I have also tried to avoid the irritation of joint pronouns such as him/her and he/she and have simply used 'he' and 'him' when referring to the designer and the game player, for clarity and ease of reading. This in no way reflects my opinion on who should and should not play and design video games. I believe games should be played by everyone, and be designed by any individuals who choose to make their career in game development.

There is one thing I would like to clear up; I have been asked on many occasions; 'what is the difference between computer games and video games?' Well, technically speaking, computer games are designed and played specifically for computers, like a PC for example, whereas video games are designed for arcade machines and game consoles, like the PlayStation2 for example. There are games that are cross-platform, in other words they are specifically designed for both PC and consoles. Occasionally you might find a game that has been designed for the PC, but has been badly ported to a console and vice versa.

Book structure

The book is in two parts: Part I discusses the components that make up a gameplay using case studies and examples, revealing the elements that create fun and absorbing gameplay – game DNA if you like. It discusses each component in detail and includes reference from various games. Part II goes through the stages of creating and formatting design documents and offers tips on how you can approach the industry with the view of starting or developing your career.

I have attempted to write each chapter so it can be read separately, but it is, however, recommended that you start at the beginning of the book and read your way through to the end.

You will *not* be learning anything about:

- Programming techniques
- Programming languages
- Creating beautifully rendered 3D environments and characters
- Artificial intelligence
- Polygons and vertices
- Quantum physics

So if you are wanting to learn about these subjects, this is not the book for you. However, you *will* learn about:

- The art form in creating fun and absorbing gameplay
- Recognising and creating the components of a game
- Creating coherent game design documents

An attractive feature of this book is the full colour plate section. Images flagged with a camera icon in the text can be found in colour in the plate section.

Follow my design

Making games is hard work, but at the same time it can be fun and rewarding. To make things a little more interesting for you, the reader, I have included a template design, called Norbot, which you can follow through to concept and beyond. These are clearly identified with the use of a Norbot icon.

I do not claim this design to be a potential blockbuster, or contain state-of-the-art game ideas. In fact the structure and feature set come from the more traditional action adventure game and can be found, in a different form, in many other games. No matter how great my concept might appear, it will still need proving and this is the job of the designer. The concept will, however, give you first-hand experience of putting a design together from an idea to a full design spec. However, time does not permit me to include a complete set of design documents, therefore I am going to allow you to fill in the blanks and make your own version of 'Norbot', using the techniques you will learn from reading this book.

Myths

There are various myths surrounding game designers and the prestige of working within the games industry. So, before we delve into the magical world of game design, I would like to clear the air and dispel some of those myths.

The first myth is that if you make games you become rich beyond your wildest dreams. I'm not going to lie to you, it can happen, but no more so than in any other industry. If it were going to happen to you, you would have to be so incredibly talented that any developer or publisher will pay you extortionate amounts of money in order for you to work for them. It rarely happens! You will go to work in the morning, just like any other job. You will get paid a salary, and on most nights, you will even get to go home. You can earn a great living making games, and perhaps after fifteen or twenty years, when you have five or six top-ten games to your name, you can begin to make some serious money, even build your own company, but learn to walk first!

Myth number two is the idea that working on games is going to be great fun. If I had a dollar for every time somebody said to me, 'you're so lucky, what a brilliant job', I would have achieved myth number one. The truth is, it is great fun but it is also incredibly hard work and you have to be prepared to put up with some serious pain. The long hours and late nights can be soul destroying and can put relationships under severe pressure. If you're currently working in the industry and you're finding it easy, then look behind you, somebody is watching. Making games is most fun when it is well planned, organised and on schedule. The real fun happens when you see your work come alive and the ecstasy comes when you see your first title on the shelf of your local game store.

And finally …

Once you have completed reading this book, don't expect to be an expert games designer who can demand hundreds of thousands of dollars a year from a design studio. Game design is an ongoing process that takes years of practice to master.

PART I

Design DNA

CHAPTER 1

Introduction to game design

'Gameplay' – what exactly is this elusive magical ingredient that developers strive to embed into their games? Can it be the tension from Attic Attack™? The rip-roaring scream of Daytona™, the kill thrill of Quake™ or perhaps it's the entrancing escapade of Dungeon Siege™? Some believe you have to create a symbolic character like Lara Croft™ or Mario™ for great gameplay to exist. Others believe that if you lack state-of-the-art technology, awesome graphics and high-level **AI**, your game will end up in the bargain bucket in record time.

All of these things are very important elements of computer and video games, but it is simply not true that they are the nutritive components of gameplay. It does not come from a great visual character, nor does it come from state-of-the-art technology and beautifully rendered art. However, these elements are required as a conduit for gameplay feedback and are used as tools to convey the style in which the gameplay is presented and executed by the player.

I believe gameplay is the components that make up a rewarding, absorbing, challenging experience that compels the player to return for more, time and time again. It sits at the heart of a game that cannot be seen as a dimensional entity, but only felt from a superbly woven and captivating world of interactive challenges that stimulates your every sense.

Back to basics

Before we delve deep into the depths of game design and the ingredients that command the compulsion of gameplay, I want to take you back in time, back to the very basics of game design and gameplay and show you, in its simplest form, some of the components that make up gameplay.

In a computer or video game, gameplay is presented through many strands and is an amalgamation of many elements that present challenges to the player. Therefore, it cannot easily be identified as an individual unit. I am going to present these strands in their simplest form, which will provide you with a solid grounding and prepare you for the rest of the book.

This chapter discusses the very basics of game design and game mechanics. Each topic discussed here will be scrutinised in greater detail in subsequent chapters, which also includes case studies from various games. But if you think you know how to make games, or have already been involved in making games, you can skip this chapter. For the beginners, this chapter will provide a solid foundation for the chapters ahead.

History lesson

Even the Egyptians knew how to make games. As far as we know, they couldn't make video games, but they certainly knew how to use the mechanics of games to create interactive entertainment. Now, you might be thinking, what has that got to do with computer and video games? Well, showing you the techniques used in games like Draughts that are thousands of years old will substantiate the methods we use in video games today. Of course there are additional features of video games to discuss, but the heart and soul of every game is gameplay. It is this place we will venture first.

Draughts, or Checkers as it is known in the United States, is one of the earliest games created by man. Obviously Draughts is not a video game, but it is a good example of how gameplay can be created using a few simple rules and boundaries that underline and present the challenges.

Almost everything in life has a history and games are no different. Draughts as we know it today has been around since 1400 BC but a board game that appeared very similar to Draughts was discovered in the ruins of the ancient city of Ur, in Iraq and dated around 3000 BC. In Egypt, the game was called 'Alquerque', and early forms of it, Draughts' venerable ancestor, have been found in Egypt dating as early as 6000 BC. Alquerque boards can be seen carved into stone slabs, which form the roof of the great ancient temple at Kurna, Egypt, built in 1400 BC. The game of Alquerque was played, like Draughts, on a 5 × 5 point board with pieces starting in a non-symmetrical pattern. The game clearly had staying power – it is mentioned under the name of Quirkat in the Arabic work *Kitab-al Aghani*, the author of which died in 976 AD. Quirkat was first brought to Europe by the Moors during their invasion of Spain. It was recorded as Alquerque (Spanish form of El-Quirkat) in the Alfonso X Manuscript, which was written between 1251–82 at the command of Alfonso X, King of Leon and Castile.

Sometime later, somebody decided to play Alquerque on a chessboard instead of the standard Alquerque board. The compulsory rule, forcing players to 'take' whenever possible, was introduced in France around 1535, the resulting new game being called Jeu Force. Jeu Force is the game played in England today under the name of Draughts and which at some stage was taken to America and called Checkers.

Draughts is a good example of simplistic gameplay that has rules and boundaries that can be easily broken down and labelled. A similarly simple game that uses technology and computers and uses simple boxes and shapes to create gameplay is Tetris.

Simple rules and boundaries

Video games can be very complex indeed, but at this stage we will keep it simple. Rules and boundaries are important for gameplay to exist. They govern the player's actions and they define what he can and cannot do in the gaming world. A rule is a device used to control, govern and circumscribe. A boundary, in game terms, defines limitations. This limitation could be a constraint on the world space, or a game feature such as health or magic power. These two elements, rules and boundaries, will shape and mould your gaming world more than anything else. You will apply rules and boundaries to every element of your game design. Some rules and boundaries may be invisible to the player, but for clarity, they are mostly revealed through playing the game. Occasionally, rules and boundaries are defined by technical limitations and some might say by producers brandishing schedules. Whatever the source of your rules and boundaries, they are very important to your game design.

To illustrate my point I am going to use Draughts as my case study. The reason for using this game is because it is a very old game and it has clear and simple rules.

An example of a boundary is visually evident and clear in standard Draughts. The game is played on a square board, divided into 64 smaller

FIGURE 1.1   Draughts playing field

squares of equal size, alternately coloured light and dark, technically described as black and white. That description describes the playing field of Draughts where the battle is fought. If your game design requires that your environment be restricted in any way, then it needs to be clearly defined, just as it is here.

Let's begin by forming the shape of the game of Draughts by defining the rules and boundaries that govern it.

Draughts rules

1 When playing Draughts, the players must only use the black squares, and they must remain on them for the duration of the game. No piece can venture onto the white squares or outside the arena unless a player's piece has been taken, in which case it is removed from play.

Immediately, you can see that the game universe has a finite, well-defined *boundary*, and with a couple of *rules* applied, they encapsulate the playing space. As in chess, the effect of this limited space forces the player to think about tactics and long-term strategic planning, which of course is the intention. Not all games are like that, but the point is that this game, like a lot of video games, has environment boundaries that affect the way in which the game is played.

FIGURE 1.2   Tetris boundaries

The original Tetris is very similar in that respect. The game arena is deliberately restricted and you cannot, even if you wanted to, venture outside of the pre-defined space. The gameplay forces the player to stay within the pre-defined boundaries. Tetris has the same effect on the player as Draughts, in that the restricted boundaries force the player to think about what is coming next and consider where the player will place the next piece for maximum effect.

FIGURE 1.3   Draughts players' pieces

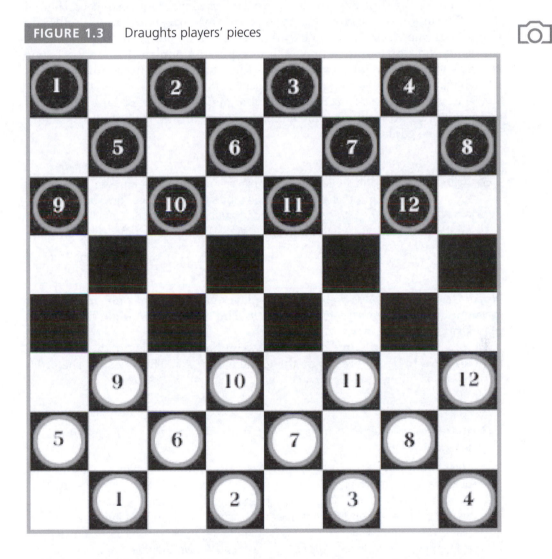

The player components of Draughts are very clearly defined, and each of the player's pieces can clearly be seen and identified when placed in the arena. There is no confusion as to who is who on the board. At the start of the game, each player has twelve pieces each and can choose, or is chosen by a flip of a coin, to be black or white. Most video games have components that are manipulated by the player, but it is important to know and clearly depict which pieces are the player's and which pieces are the enemy. The components, or playing pieces in Tetris, are identified using two methods. There are a set number of pieces, all of which are different shapes, but made up of four squares, which is one important rule for the gameplay to exist in Tetris. The shape is the first method of identifying a piece. The second method of identification is that each piece type is a different colour, which helps the player to acknowledge them quickly – at a glance. If your game requires quick thinking and immediate action, like role-playing games (RPGs), real-time strategy games (RTS) and action games, the player won't have time to examine who is who in the world, it has to be clear.

We now have the *boundaries* and the gaming pieces of Draughts well defined. Let us now look at some simple *rules* governing the pieces that allow us to play the game.

> **2** At the start of a game of Draughts, the players must place their pieces in the arena. The pieces must *always be* placed in the same positions. The black pieces are placed on the first twelve spaces and invariably the white pieces are placed on the last twelve squares. It's always the same. The only thing that can change at this point is the colour of pieces each player has chosen.

Note: Draughts has always been a two-player game. There is no single-player version; the rules simply don't permit it. The only way a single human can play Draughts is against a computer.

Before you begin a game of Draughts you have to know *all* the rules and they all have to be adhered to or the game will break. The rules for the order of play are as follows.

> **3** The player, who has chosen black always makes the first move, after which the players move alternately.
>
> **4** The player whose turn it is to move proceeds by advancing one of his pieces diagonally forward to an adjacent square. However, several possible scenarios could be presented to the player at this point. If an opponents' piece occupies an adjacent square, and there is a *vacant* square immediately behind it, the player *must* capture that piece. This is compulsory. The player achieves this by leaping over his opponent's piece and removing it from the board. If possible, the player *must* continue capturing pieces, without removing his hand, until all pieces are captured along the chosen path, at which point his turn is over. The exception to this rule is if there are several pieces that could be caught that are

not chained, the player has to choose which of the opponent's pieces he would like to take. He cannot have multiple turns.

5 If a player fails to recognise that an opponent's piece can be taken, the opponent, as a penalty, can then remove the piece that should have captured.

You can see how the rules provoke strategy and planning while playing this game, just by adding a few simple rules. Further rules expand the game and make it more challenging and ultimately more fun.

6 If a player reaches the opposite edge of the board, to a space that was originally occupied by his opponent, without being captured, then that piece becomes a King and is crowned by placing a captured piece on top of the piece in play.

In video game jargon, this is where the pieces in Draughts become 'powered up' and adds a new dimension to the game, which is always good. In essence, the King in Draughts has gained 'special powers'.

Video games often award special items, abilities and special powers to player-characters, just as Draughts awards the King. Allowing the King to possess special powers could also be perceived as a reward for reaching the other side of the arena. To activate the special powers of the King, we have to introduce additional rules.

7 The King can move and capture both backwards *and* forwards across the board. All other rules still apply.

The effect of having a King on the board is staggering in terms of what it does to the game. It induces a sense of urgency into both players and alters the players' strategy when moving their pieces around the board. One simple addition has modified the game and added a greater challenge. This is exactly what games and gameplay is all about.

Video games can induce urgency on many levels and in different ways. Quake, for example, is adrenaline-pumping fast furious action, and a state of urgency is evoked 90 per cent of the time, particularly if you have a large multi-player game in progress. Different games provoke people in different ways. Draughts might be as dull as a drizzly day to somebody who experiences the rush of Quake. However, there are many people in this world who play Draughts, take it very seriously and can get their heart racing from playing it.

8. Draughts' victory condition is achieved when a player captures all the opponent's pieces, or renders him immobile, forcing surrender.

If you play Draughts professionally, you will know there are additional rules that can make the game more complex than this, but for a fun game, the above will suffice. For many experienced designers, what I have just described may be totally obvious. For others, it may light the way for a greater understanding of what makes games work and what makes them fun. Rules and boundaries police the gaming experience, enabling it to take place in a controlled well-defined environment. They define how the game begins, how the game ends, and what takes place in between, like a beautifully crafted story. This is gameplay in its most basic form, but computer and video games can be much more than this.

Feedback

We wander through life, busy as bees, downloading an enormous amount of information without even realising it. When driving, we look at road signs and traffic lights. When shopping we look at products and prices, and we are constantly bombarded with subliminal advertising, from TV, milk cartons and from our banner-filled streets. The world around us is feeding us information; all you have to do is sit back and take notice. I can almost guarantee that something will be feeding you information right now, informative or otherwise. Perhaps you have the TV or radio on in the background or your computer is beeping at you for conformation. This is a form of **feedback** in the real world, both directly from asking for it or indirectly by just receiving it because it's there.

Feedback is such an important part of video games. Without it, games would be very dull. For this reason, I have dedicated a whole chapter to it later in the book. In this section I am going to skim the surface of feedback to give you a basic understanding of what is meant by feedback in the context of games, and why we as developers frivolously wallow in it, in abundance.

Feedback is exactly what the word implies. When a player inputs to the game, the game should provide feedback to the player. Input to the game is instigated through handheld devices, which in turn could activate anything from the movement of your character through the environments, to a missile launched at your enemy. Whatever the input, the player will require feedback. It is presented in many forms from a simple animation when you move your character, to big explosions when your missile hits the target. It's not just visual feedback we require, audio feedback plays a very important part to games also.

Feedback generally falls into two categories. The first is explicit feedback, which is activated when the player performs an action, and implicit feedback, which is presented informatively i.e. a signpost or a well-trodden path are good examples of implicit feedback. In Table 1.1 I have identified which types fall into which categories.

TABLE 1.1   Feedback types

Feedback type	Feedback description	E	I
Visual feedback	This is what the player is seeing on the screen both directly and indirectly.	✓	✓
Audio feedback	What the player is hearing both directly and indirectly.	✓	✓
Action feedback	A reaction from the player's actions. This could be a combination of visual and audio, and is explicit feedback.	✓	
NPC feedback	Feedback from non-controlled characters that populate the game world.	✓	✓
Accumulative feedback	As the player progresses through the game he is going to require progression or accumulative feedback.		✓
Emotional feedback	This is feedback that provokes an emotion in the player.	✓	✓
Fulfilment feedback	Feedback that stimulates a sense of fulfilment, it is important for games to recognise the need for fulfilment.	✓	✓
Informative feedback	Feeding information to the player. A context-sensitive control mechanism does this.	✓	✓

Within each category there are several types, which I like to label. Some designers do it differently and some just do it without even realising it. But I feel it is good practice to know what they are and identify them as an entity or a piece of work that has to be implemented into the game. It is this type of work that often gets neglected or overlooked in schedules. If it is not identified it will be omitted and could spoil an otherwise great game. It could also cause the game to run over time and budget if they have not been identified as a block of work. All types of feedback can fall into both categories – so you can have explicit visual feedback and implicit visual feedback. This will be explained in detail in Chapter 6.

Some types of feedback may seem obvious, but if you study games, you will notice that many of them do not communicate to the player adequately and the player is left wondering what he supposed to be doing.

The first two types of feedback in the list are self-explanatory. They are what I would call generic feedback, comprising the obvious animations and sounds that you would naturally expect to find in a game. The other forms of feedback are most likely to be a combination of audio and visual but it is the context and the way in which they are delivered to the player that is important here. Action feedback is the information a player receives as a result of his actions. You might be thinking, 'that's audio and visual feedback', and you'd be right, but you get audio and visual feedback constantly whatever you are doing in a game. You need to be able to label the feedback pertinent to the player's actions. A game is after all, a series of actions, decisions and challenges executed by the player.

When you label feedback, not only does it make for a better game, it becomes clear to all involved in the development of the game, what is required for the *game* to exist. Think about what information you want to communicate when a player performs an action in the game!

Action–Reaction–Feedback or, as some people say, 'Cause and effect'.

Feedback should be embedded into the gameplay, not simply used as a visual and audio tool for effects purposes. When the player is playing the game, he needs to be informed of how he is performing, particularly at key stages throughout the game.

With more of the mass-market playing games today, players often need to be taught how to play the game from the start. This is known as the mentor, or informative type of feedback. A good example of the mentor can be seen in Black and White™. The two characters that float across the screen, toying with the player to take different paths into the game, while at the same time teaching the player how to play the game, represent the good and the bad mentor. The great thing about this is that it's done in a jovial way, which makes it fun to be taught.

Many hardcore, die-hard gamers demand that they be dumped straight into the action, and frown upon this type of handholding. For this reason, the 'mentor' approach for teaching has to be an option for the player.

A simple and perhaps perfect example of feedback that triggers an emotion can be found in Tetris. If you have never played Tetris then you've probably been living on Mars for the past twenty years! The 'core objective' of Tetris is to stop the arena from filling up with blocks, by erasing strips of fallen blocks. The blocks, which are various shapes and colour, fall from the top of the arena to the bottom. The player has to guide the blocks into position, locking the shapes together. Once you have built a solid strip across the arena, from wall to wall, they disappear, allowing the blocks above to drop down. The player has to keep the wall as low as possible, for as long as possible and prevent it from reaching the top of the player arena.

Tetris uses a now tried and tested method for delivering tension, panic and a sense of urgency, which ultimately creates an emotional response. If the player allows the wall to get close to the top of the arena, the tempo of gameplay and music increases to convey a sense of urgency. This informs the player that something must be done to avoid inevitable doom and stimulates

FIGURE 1.4 Tertis players' pieces

'panic' in the player. If the player manages to fix the wall and force it down again, the music slows, the player feels a great sense of achievement and the urgency is removed.

Emotional feedback creates an emotional reaction in the player, and if you want to be a designer, you should always strive to achieve emotional feedback within your games. Many games, past, present and future, use similar techniques and I will be looking at them in more detail in Chapter 6.

When a player is playing an adventure game, players will want feedback in regards to their location along the timeline of the adventure. Maps have always been a good reference point and indication of where you have been and where you still need to go. In games of old, designers would include a simple percentage progression meter. This was great because you knew how close to the end you were and the closer you got, the more you wanted to play. Even when the player completed a game, the meter would often read less than 100 per cent, encouraging the player to play again.

As time moves on and technology advances, the traditional map appears to be a fading format and different devices are used. For example, in an adventure game I saw recently, the player character grew old as the adventure unfolded. At the beginning of the game the player character appeared very young, but by the time he reaches the end, he would be visually much older. This is the same principle as a percentage indicator, but presented in such a way that the player is looking at it constantly, being fed the information subliminally.

Chapter 6 discusses feedback in great detail and uses many games, both old and new, to give examples of the various types of feedback designers should consider putting into their games.

Interface

Once again, there are interfaces all around us. We interface with our cars, our kitchen appliances and our vacuum cleaners. The designers make these interfaces easy and subliminal. They want you to use their products, but generally they don't want you to be disappointed and not return for the next instalment.

So what is an interface? It is a method in which the user can interact with a secondary device. It normally exists between two entities passing information from one to another. A light switch is probably the simplest form of interface. On and off! A switch is positioned to interface between a human and a light bulb.

Board games are often designed as the interface to the rules of the game. Humans physically touch the pieces and move them around according to the rules and boundaries. We cannot put our hands into the world of a video game and physically touch the components; we have to design a **graphical user interface (GUI)** or control mechanism, which is accessed by an input device.

Without an interface, the player would have no control and subsequently render the game useless. An interface is more of a necessity than a design option. However, the interface has to be implemented in such a way that the player does not struggle with it. Also, if the design of the input is interpreted badly by the programmer, the player could have a negative and unrewarding experience. Therefore, it is imperative that a transparent and intuitive interface is designed and programmed with the target audience in mind.

> **TIP**
>
> Study the way other designers have designed their interfaces. Write down the things you like about the interface and things that irritate you, and why you think they are either good or bad. If you do this for every game you play, and solely concentrate on the interface, you will slowly begin to get a feel of what is good and what is bad. You will know if it is a good interface because the game will drag you away from the physical world and plunge your consciousness into the game. If something works particularly well, use it. There is no point in reinventing the wheel.

Game designers should venture beyond games for their interface research and look at other industries for inspiration. Within a car, there are two great examples of different interfaces, that are targeted at different audiences but perform the same function. I am of course referring to the gearbox – manual and automatic. They both perform the same function and both can be as much fun to drive. For some, however, the task of actually driving the car is made simpler by the automation of the gear stick as it eliminates the possibility that the driver could struggle with the car and places more emphasis on the road and surroundings. When you purchase a car, you have the option to buy the one that suits your driving preferences.

Cars can be complex machines and car designers are always experimenting with ways to simplify the act of actually driving the car. A hardcore gamer might go for the gear stick while the non-hardcore gamer (mass-market) may opt for automatic. The choice should be designed into the game to allow the user to choose how they want to interact from the outset.

So, how can you be sure that the interface you design is intuitive and friendly? Unless you have felt what it is you want to achieve, you will not know if it's going to work until it has been implemented into your game. Once it has been implemented, play it, play it until the handheld device breaks, let everyone play it. Make sure you include your target audience. Stand and watch them as they play it, take notes and listen to what they are saying. If they are commenting on the game content then it's likely the interface is working. If the player is struggling with the control mechanism, then he will never get to see the game itself and you will undoubtedly know about it.

At the start I mentioned the difference between video games and computer games. The interface should be designed specifically around the target platform. An interface for a computer game is, more often than not, designed around a mouse and a keyboard. However, a controller device usually interfaces most video games consoles. There are exceptions, like Disney's Jungle Book on the PlayStation® where the player has to dance on a mat to interact with the game, which is very cool, although exhausting!

When a successful game is converted from one platform to work on another, the interface is the one part of the game that is most likely to let it down. This is largely because the game has already been designed for a specific platform, and developers and publishers are reluctant to spend extra money and time on redesigning the interface for a new platform. Therefore it is often left up to the programmer to hack it in until something works, good or bad!

In Chapter 15, we will study interfaces from many games, from different genres and on different platforms. I will also go through, step by step, the initial interface design for Norbot.

Context sensitivity

So what is context sensitivity? We are all after a simpler, less complicated life in one way or another, and the car example above is evidence of that. Some people are calling it the dumbing-down process, while others feel it creates diversity in game design. I believe it does the latter.

I recently watched a documentary about the future of technology and I was staggered to discover that 'context-sensitive' control mechanisms have been around for quite some time. A good example of this is fighter jets. When in the air, they are practically controlled by three main computers. The computers constantly monitor what the pilot is doing and modifies the jet to stop the plane from crashing or spinning out of control. In a combat situation, this allows the pilot to concentrate on fighting rather than actually flying the plane.

A similar thing is taking place in Formula 1 racing cars: these days they are loaded with computers, which transparently modify the car's intricacies as the driver guides it around the track. Traction control is just one example, as it helps control excess wheel spin and allows the driver to think about other things without the worry of spinning the car. They say the computers allow the driver to be creative and explore the track and the car, pushing the boundaries and applying pressure on the rules. Now, obviously I am not a F1 driver but if that is the case, that's fantastic because you have the opportunity for progression and originality to take place.

Both are examples of a context-sensitive environment – it basically frees up the processing power of the brain, allowing the user to concentrate on other things, without losing any functionality.

The context-sensitive control mechanism has caused much controversy amongst hardened gamers in recent years. Today, there is a greater challenge for designers to create an interface that is both intuitive enough to attract new gamers, whilst avoiding the alienation of hardcore gamers. It is a tough challenge but one that must be overcome.

Context sensitivity is essentially part of the interface, and I have included a detailed section, with an example, in Chapter 15.

Goals, quests and challenges

When you get up out of your bed in the morning, what is your 'core objective'? It would most likely be to go to school, or go to work, but diversifying that day with a series of mini-tasks. Most of us conform to this, but some may try something different and skip school or work and bend the rules. Now I am not suggesting for one moment that you do that, but if you did, your day would be different and it would most likely create negative feedback from your colleagues. Your 'core objective' would change and the feedback you receive throughout the day would be different.

The point is, as we live our lives, most of us have immediate, short- and long-term goals that we want to achieve one way or another. However, we all need a break from the monotonous forward motion of goal seeking and try something different in order to make life more interesting. If you tirelessly chase your goal, it would like being stuck on a perpetual train, moving forwards until you reach it. Let's face it; trains can be boring places to be!

Game design is no different. All games have a 'core objective', but designers break the monotony of chasing that objective with sub-goals punctuated in the gameplay on the road to achieve that core objective. These sub-goals should be related to the core objective and play a significant part in the game's design. A game is like a complex spider's web, all linked and related to the central point. Take a piece away and it will weaken or possibly break the game altogether.

In video games, goals, quests and challenges are your targets and your motivation for playing, no matter how big or small. Goals, quests and challenges can be a complex string of events, or they can be one simple 'core objective', like in Tetris. They are also the elements of a game that define its gameplay.

Environment design

The term 'level' is a flimsy description considering what it refers to. 'Level' is almost certainly inherent from days of old where games used to be level-based and progression was measured in levels. Games like the 2D 8-bit Donkey Kong™ and Mario, for example, were typical level-based games.

Today, however, game worlds are far more complex in quantity and structure, than anything previously. We also have to consider other games like racing, fighting and role-playing games. Dungeon Siege doesn't have levels. It depicts a unique, seamless, perpetual world that unfolds and swells as the player progresses. It has different locations, towns and villages etc. but certainly not levels. I prefer to call them environments. After all, that's what they are.

When you're designing games, you need to think about the whole world in relation to progression and balance. You also need to break down that world into bite-sized manageable pieces. Sections of game should be punctuated by sub-goals that break the game down into small challenging objectives. It is this structure that defines gameplay areas of your world, previously known as levels. The structure is obviously different for every genre and I will show this in later chapters.

As hardware capabilities evolve, character development and animation techniques improve, and game content intensifies, therefore the manner in which we design and create richer worlds for players must also evolve. As I said before, making games is a team effort and environment design is an art form that requires a special talent. A development team will most likely have among them several designers whose sole job is to create interesting and fun environments.

The majority of today's environments are constructed in **3D** using off-the-shelf applications and, occasionally, custom software developed by the developers to manipulate their worlds specifically for game content.

If you are building a realistic city, it might be a good idea to study the basics of architecture. I am not suggesting you approach your environments in the same way as an architect might, but we can learn from some of their proven methods on how to create believable, well-balanced worlds. Game worlds are limited to our imaginations, platform specifications and artistic licence. Architects design environments for functionality, interactivity and they know how to get the most from the space available. Architects also design for the customer. They know who the user will be and their designs reflect the needs and ability of the end user.

Before you begin designing your environments, be sure of your audience and their needs for the product you are designing. An architect will consider how the user will enter and leave the environment, travel through it and interact with it. They will also consider what feedback is required for the user in regards to an entrance lobby, signposts, door signs, painted lines etc. This consideration should be applied to your environment design.

One of the trickiest environments to design is a realistic one. The reason for this is simple. Anybody, architect or not, can simply *see* if it looks wrong. If the doors and windows are the wrong scale or the building is architecturally unsound, or the textures are not real, the player will notice instantly. This is because the player lives in that world and unwittingly becomes a critic the moment he enters your virtual environment.

Environment design is an art form in its own right. A badly designed environment can destroy a game, particularly if it was rushed at the end of the game, which does happen.

The role of an environment designer will generally take all the building blocks that have been pre-defined, and construct new sections of the game. He does not have the authority to create new elements of a game or features, but must constrict his creativity inside the pre-defined parameters.

Balance

When I began writing this book, everybody said I must include a section on balancing gameplay. They say there aren't many books that have a good section just on this. I have a theory on this. Balancing gameplay can only happen when you can play the game. Not before. Also, the team have to balance every element of the game and therefore, it isn't a straightforward process. Balancing is not a singular entity you can point a finger at, therefore it is a little difficult to present and explain the concept of balancing.

Balancing begins when you can play your game. Once all the elements are together, you, your colleagues and focus testers will push and pull elements of the game until they bond and blend like a finely tuned car. A painter will begin with a foundation and apply layer after layer until he has a finished painting. He will craft it and shape it until he reaches perfection. A similar process happens with video games – or at least some of the time!

I always believe that playability needs to begin as quickly as possible. The programmers should use placement graphics, and work with box maps, box men or boxy cars to get the feel of the game and the balance of the gameplay just right. Art can slot in and consequently the quality will be better because it will be designed to fit exactly. It will also be highly cost-effective by reducing needless art and animation to begin with.

Summary

I have merely skimmed the surface of game design, bringing to light some of the more important components that go into making a 'game'. The following chapters will take you through the many elements of game design in greater detail, looking at games past and present to show how designers make a living from game design using tried and tested techniques.

If you are a budding designer, you must be prepared to work harder and longer than you ever have before. Every element of game design discussed in this book requires 100 per cent effort from you and your team if your game is to hit a top ten slot and make money. Every topic covered in the book is complex and takes many years of practice to master. It's not just about doing it; it's about feeling it and knowing when it feels and looks right. Many designers can come up with ideas and implement them, but the mastery is in the arduous task of following through, getting it to feel right.

Just by buying this book and reading this far, you have already taken the first steps to becoming a game designer, with the potential to make it into the games industry.

CHAPTER 2

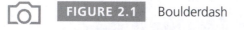

Genre

To know where to position your game, you first need to understand what defines a genre. Identifying what constitutes a genre has been fraught with ambiguity, mainly due to the creative flux our industry induces, the overlap of genres, and the constant churn of technology and ideas. Therefore, different people will have varying ideas of the different kinds of genre and the elements that define them.

Why do we need genres? There were many games in the **8-bit** era that could not be categorised. Some were ridiculously outlandish and yet wealthy in imagination and creativity – Wheeling Wally™, Gribbly's Day Out™, and Boulderdash™ to name but a few.

FIGURE 2.1   Boulderdash

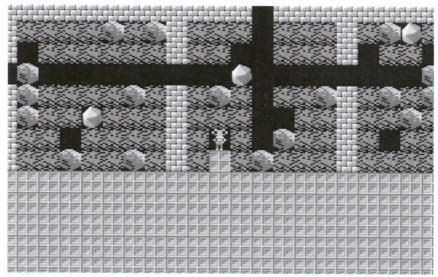

So what happened? The industry started as an over-active creative child and is currently blossoming into adolescence. Today's games have to make sense and appeal to the mass market for them to be successful. Or at least that is the perceived notion by many people within the industry. The stakes are too high for any risk taking and, therefore, we follow the tried and tested movie and music route of franchise building and genre defining. Genre definition enables the market to understand what it is they are buying.

Defining genre

What does genre actually mean? **Genre** is the French word for type. Like most things in life, games are loosely categorised by various types. The closest comparison you could make are movies because they too are a visual medium, and just like movies, there are only so many different types of games. It's highly unlikely you will ever invent a new core genre. That's not to say you will never invent a new idea, but that idea will most likely fall into one of the genres or sub-genres that already exist.

There is some overlap of genres, and subsequently sub-genres have emerged. This is the result of designers attempting to mix two core genres together, like action with adventure, or sports and simulation, for example. These hybrids can be just as popular as the core genres, and have spawned many new ideas in the past.

The make-up

A singular core genre is a collective type of game from all games that exist in the marketplace, that have the same narrow definition of its contents. That is to say, at the heart of each genre exist fundamental components that make it what it is. A core genre can usually be described using just one word as the following list depicts.

Core genres
■ Sports
■ Adventure
■ Action
■ Simulation
■ Strategy
■ Puzzle
■ Role-play
■ Management
■ Uncategorised

They all speak for themselves, except the last one perhaps, and you might be inclined to think it's a conveniently placed safety net for any potentially new genre, but I will discuss this in more detail later.

On compiling this text, I asked many colleagues to provide a list of game genres as they saw them. I was surprised at what I received! Included in the lists I received, defined as core genres by several people, were racing, shoot em up's and others. Although racing games are popular and could be conceived as a genre, they do in fact come under the 'sports' heading and exist as a sub-genre. For as long as I can remember, racing has always been a sport, whether in a motor vehicle, using animals or on foot. If, within a racing game, the primary challenges for the player are to race, then it is a sports game.

Let's look at some other aspects of games that one might imagine go some way to defining its genre. A lot of designers will have differing ideas, but I believe we have to strip back the layers and get to the heart of a game to reveal its genre.

Theme

Let's examine the top-most layer of any game – the graphical theme and setting. Contrary to popular belief, the graphical theme does not define its genre. Although the majority of **role-playing game (RPGs)** are set in a fantasy world full of wizards and warlocks, it doesn't have to be. You can have an RPG set in space, for example. The words 'role-playing game' conjure images of dungeons and dragons, but even these are not exclusive to RPGs – they exist in other games also. The graphical themes of **real-time strategy (RTS)** games vary enormously, therefore we cannot rely on the graphical theme for genre identification.

FIGURE 2.2   Command and Conquer

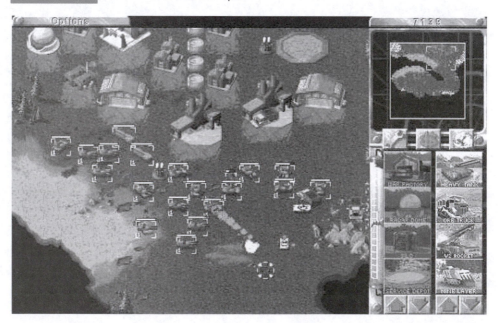

As you will discover in Chapter 4, we can apply a theme to almost any component of a game. The gaming theme of RTS games is fairly consistent. Command and Conquer™, for example is themed around war and set in a traditional war scenario. Starcraft® is also themed around war, but is set in space. Age of Empires™ is an epic real-time strategy game, set in a historical context and also involves war between various civilisations. But you can also have war in an RPG. Therefore, the game theme cannot be genre defining.

Structure

Can the structure of a game contribute to genre positioning? Games of a particular genre often follow a similar structure although many sports games have varying forms. So does the structure form the sub-genres? Most racing games have a similar structure. They are section based; whether it's around a track or through a city, the challenges tends to go from A to B and push the player on to the next section. The player is generally in control of a vehicle or avatar of some kind, from a Formula 1 car to a 100-metre sprinter. But are all sports games structured like racing games? No, they're not. Soccer is played in two halves, or more if the resulting score does not determine the winner. Therefore we can determine that the structure of games does not define the genre.

Game mechanics

Now we are getting to the heart, the moving parts of a game. Game mechanics is one of the more significant contributors to defining the genre. The mechanics define the types of challenges in a game. The mechanics also determine how the player interacts and controls the challenges. I believe it is the challenges that define the genre and sub-genre of any game.

To illustrate this supposition, we will discuss some of the genres and examine the ingredients that characterise them. I'm not going to delve too deep into the structure and design of each genre; I couldn't possibly do all types in a single chapter, but I can discuss the fundamental elements that define them as a genre.

I am using Dungeon Siege as a case study throughout the book, so it seems pertinent to begin with RPGs.

Role-playing game (RPG)

Role-playing games are unmistakable. They have evolved from the **MUDs (Multi User Dungeon)** and text-based **MMORPGs (Massive-Multiplayer On-line Role Playing Games)** of yesteryear. There seems to be some confusion with on-line games as to whether they are a genre in their own right. Many of them are perpetual, like Everquest® for example, but I don't believe existing on-line constitutes a new genre. On-line games are after all, derivatives of off-line games, but with potentially massive multi-player capability and social interaction.

Some have argued that an RPG is an adventure game, but RPGs go way beyond adventure games in design complexity and sheer scope and they also have an element of strategy about them.

So what constitutes an RPG? There is one fundamental element to an RPG that makes it what it is, and that is character development and growth. I don't mean character development in a story sense. For a novelist or scriptwriter, character development is something different to that of an RPG. In a story, characters are defined by the choices they make in their lives. A novelist will cover their back-story and how they change and evolve emotionally and physically as human beings rather than as a symbolic avatar. Well-rounded, in-depth characters with personalities are the stuff of adventure games, not RPGs.

FIGURE 2.3   Dungeon Siege characters

In an RPG the player can generally institute everything about their character's persona, from their gender, race and physical prowess, to the colour of their hair, skin and the clothes they wear. Once the player has defined his character, or characters, he will take them on an epic journey of character evolution.

The evolution is the mechanical structure of character growth applied by journeying through the game itself by overcoming the many challenges. The characters are endowed with attributes that when influenced, will determine whether the challenges of the game can be overcome, subsequently allowing the characters to grow. RPGs exist in a finely balanced unwavering game loop. The attributes vary slightly from one RPG to another, but define a character's strength, dexterity, intelligence, damage and armour rating, to name but a handful. A character's class will determine what skills a particular character is good at. A wizard for example will be particularly excellent with magic, but not so good at close arm-to-arm combat.

Some RPGs go into more depth and complexity than this, by giving characters special abilities and broader attributes and skills. They may have an immunity to sleep, or be luckier or fearless than other characters. All skills, attributes and abilities can be manipulated and modified when the player nurtures his characters. The clothes they wear, the weapons they carry and the actions performed can all influence the characters' personae. The whole RPG genre is hinged on this stats mechanism and the entire structure of the game is built around it.

Another element that tends to play a major role in an RPG is the inventory system; this is because of its boundaries. What I mean by this is that the player can usually collect an overwhelming amount of objects, but has limited space in his inventory and therefore cannot carry them all – unlike Zelda™, for example, which has an inventory system but has the exact number of slots for a pre-defined, non-disposable amount of objects the player can find in the game.

FIGURE 2.4 Dungeon Siege inventory

The RPG inventory system becomes a major part of the gameplay because the player has to make choices as to what to leave behind and what to take with him. The choice is forced upon the player through using several means. Firstly, the size of the objects has to fit into a limited amount of slots, and if they become full then choices have to be made. Also the weight of the objects the player is carrying can potentially become a burden for your character, and have adverse affects on other attributes. The final reason is the class of your character will only require certain items. Therefore the player could either leave the redundant items behind, or bring them along to trade. These choices alone can have players clicking around their inventory for hours.

The core challenge for the player is to guide his character(s) successfully through to the end of the game and to build them up to their ultimate state of being. But the end does not necessarily mean the end of the game. It could mean to bring the characters up to a certain level and sustain it, as in Everquest, for example. But the player can only do this by modifying his characters' attributes and components as he moves through his quest. That is the heart of an RPG.

It takes major commitment on behalf of the player to actually sit down and play these games. The biggest and most consuming thing of all is time. RPGs can take months, sometimes years to complete. With some RPGs, it can take hours or even days of character creation before you even begin your journey. But this is a major element of RPGs and character creation is a prerequisite for the people that play them. The players often project themselves into the characters they create, or at least what they would like to be. This is usually reflected in the physical appearance of the character and the way the player commands the game. This is clearly evident in on-line RPGs when players have to interact with other players.

RPG summary

So are characters what RPGs are about? Well, fundamentally yes. Of course the designer usually mixes it up with quests, an interactive story, combat and adventure, but essentially it is character evolution that is the defining feature. Take that away from an RPG and you remove the primary challenge of all RPGs. Some fine examples of RPGs are Dungeon Siege, Ultima™ series, Diablo® (I and II) and Neverwinter Nights™, to name just a few.

RPG components

- Character creation
- Character evolution
- Character class, attributes and skills
- Inventory management
- Melee
- Quests
- Interactive story
- Adventure

Real-time strategy (RTS)

Next up is the real-time strategy (RTS) game. It has a core substance that makes it what it is, which is fundamental to the way the game is played. Take this one thing away from an RTS and the genre evaporates. The clue is in its title.

When games first appeared, strategy games were turn-based. It was a console game called Herzog Zwei© on the Sega Genesis that put the 'real-time' in strategy games.

War is a consistent theme within RTS games. Commanding units in real time by giving them orders and then letting them go is a clear ingredient of RTS games. But they are far more complex than that. The player has to create his units before any battles can really begin. Harvesting resources is the fuel for RTS games and generally rewards the player with the ability to construct buildings and weapons of some kind and to spawn units of varying capabilities. This diverse variation of unit building allows for some diverse strategic game tactics against your opponent.

The setting can be anything, as the game Warcraft™ shows us. This game drops the player in a fantasy setting reminiscent of an RPG. Another example synonymous with RTS games is Command and Conquer.

FIGURE 2.5   Command and Conquer

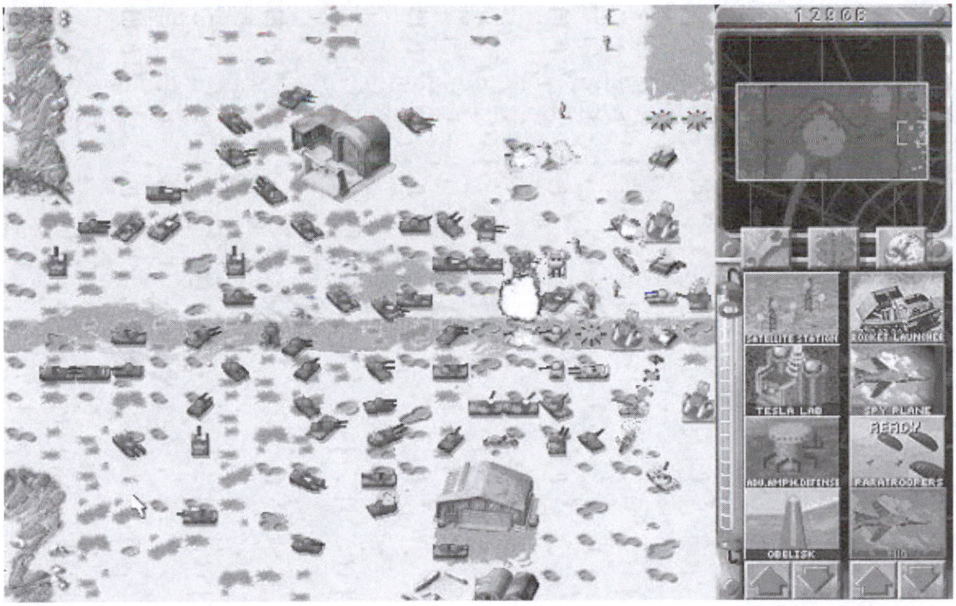

The name 'Command and Conquer' depicts the challenges of the RTS genre perfectly. Then we have Starcraft, which is set in space, but still has all the elements that define an RTS. Therefore it is clear here that the setting does not define a genre.

Another resounding element of RTS games is their multi-player capabilities. Multi-player RTS games come into their own when played by more than one human participant, and the strategy element lends itself to time-consuming multi-player sessions.

So what are the challenges of an RTS? The principal challenges are to harvest resources, build units and subsequently strategically attack and destroy the opponent. This is what defines the RTS genre.

A sub-genre of the RTS is the 'god-game'. Some believe the god-game, like Black and White and Populas™ for example, to be a core genre, but god-games were born out of the strategic elements of the RTS. Within the god-game exist the same elements as an RTS game: harvesting, building and destroying. But there is one additional overriding challenge that defines the god-game and that is the management and caring of your units. There is an economical infrastructure within a god-game and a parental influence that forces you to care for your units and keep them alive – hence the 'god-game' tag. In Black and White for example, you have to gather food for your villagers, or they die. You have to heal them of disease and generally shield them from the many opposing influences within the game. In an RTS, the emphasis is placed on the strategic planning and destruction of your opponent, whereas in the god-game the emphasis shifts to the care and maintenance of your units in order for them to stay alive long enough to achieve the core objective. If you take this caring element out of the god-game, you are left with an RTS.

It is interesting that by simply adding another mechanic or dimension to a genre can shift the focus and the tactics of a game. But this is what game design is all about.

RTS summary

From the discussion above, we can determine that the following elements constitute an RTS game.

RTS components

- Harvesting resources
- Building a community (generally a home base or bases)
- Spawning units with varying capabilities
- Strategic attacks
- Destroying the opponent

Sports games

Along with action games, sports games are one of the biggest of all genres and have a large family of sub-genres. Sports games sift through retail like butter off a hot knife. Sports are universally understood so I don't need to tell you what a sports game is. Sports games sell more units than any other genre and they sell to the masses. Publishers love them – if they're good!

There was a time when the market was flooded with soccer games. You might be thinking, a soccer game has the same rules no matter who develops it, and you would be right. However, it's the execution and presentation of those rules and the delivery of a good intuitive interface that can make or break a soccer game. This applies to most sports games for that matter, because there is little room for creativity and modifications in the game rules and mechanics that define factual sports.

One sports sub-genre that has got flexibility is extreme sports, like Tony Hawk's Pro Skater™ and SSX Tricky™, for example. Extreme sports, like snowboarding and skateboarding, place the participant in extreme conditions involving an element of danger. You could say this about most sports but extreme sports can be potentially fatal in the real world if not performed in a controlled environment. Extreme sports have the flexibility for modification, because the challenges pose the extremities, while maintaining the essence of the sport.

As for the action end of sports, you could take any sport and drop in some action, but you run the risk of diversifying the game and alienating an otherwise ready-made target audience. However, an example of how this has been done well is Speedball™ – a Bitmap Brother's game, which has taken elements from real sports and modified them, turning it into a brutal action fantasy sport game.

Another fine example of an action sport is Wipeout™. At the heart of Wipeout is a racing game, but it is blended neatly into a fantasy environment. It also provides the player with action-based capabilities that can hinder the opponent or enhance the player's capabilities, adding an additional survival challenge to the game.

The fundamental difference between extreme sports and action sports is the realism aspect. Extreme sports are generally real sports taken to the extreme (Tony Hawk's Pro Skater), while action sports provides the player with unrealistic abilities (like weapons) that can give the player an advantage over his opponent. The latter is the riskiest of developments because although the design may say sports game, it is still an unknown quantity and therefore risky for a publisher to fund.

Figure 2.6 shows a hierarchy that can be applied to most core genres, outlining the sub-genres that exist beneath them.

The list of sports games is enormous. For example, there are track and field (Olympic) sports; indoor sports such as basketball and ice hockey; field sports such as football, baseball, rugby and cricket. Within the family of factual

FIGURE 2.6 Sports genre and sub-genre

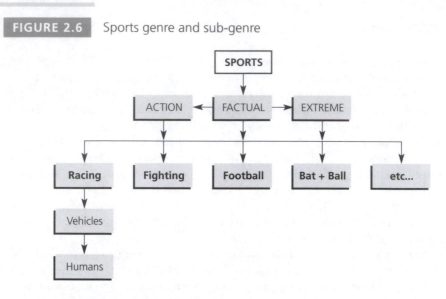

fighting games you have street fighting, boxing and wrestling and the action fighting games such as Tekken™. The list goes on …

Sports summary

All sports require an opponent or competitor, whether they are computer controlled or another human player. The challenge in any sports game is to win, not necessarily by destruction as in many other games but by performance and skill. The player challenges his opponent to compete against him. Then they perform the actions in an attempt to reach the victory condition as quickly and as efficiently as possible in such a way that beats his opponent. That is the fundamental core of sports games.

Sports games sell, there is no doubt about that. If you design a sports game, it has to be better than the best one currently out there. That alone is difficult to do, but it's even harder to prove before any development begins. Designing extreme sports or action sports is not easy, and just because the rules already exist, doesn't make it any easier to develop. In fact it is harder if anything, because you have millions of critics who know their sport before you even begin!

Sports components

- Competition
- Performance challenges
- Quick reflexes

Adventure games

Pure adventure games are a rare breed in today's market and I believe there is one fundamental reason for this, which lies in the elements that define the genre.

Adventure games generally require the player to use his brain more than in any other genre, except RTS games perhaps. It is the thinking person's game. The title suggests that the player embarks on a great adventure, which often he does; this can be a major factor in adventure games but it can also be misleading as many other game types also allow the player to embark on great adventures, particularly RPGs. Therefore, this turns out not to be the defining ingredient that classifies the genre as the title may suggest.

Adventure games often have interactive stories, which are revealed as the player journeys through the game and overcomes the challenges. They are often shrouded in mystery, like The Secret of Monkey Island™ series. They are often multi-threaded plots, but again, many other types of game have stories too and therefore, this too is not the defining requirement for adventure games.

The very first adventure game I played was The Hobbit™ by Melbourne House on the Commodore 64. I would leave my machine on for days at a time, but this was mainly down to the extraordinary long loading times of the first cassette-based game more than anything else. It was a great adventure game in its time and provided a template that echoed throughout the industry. There was no jumping from platform to platform, there was no shooting or combat, in fact there was very little in the way of on-screen movement at all. It was a text-based graphic adventure. The graphics were no more than static, low-resolution pictures that changed as you moved from location to location.

FIGURE 2.7   The Hobbit (C64)

The game allowed the player to perform simple actions using a collection of words. For example, to move around the world, the player would simply type North, Northwest, South, East, etc. It also allowed you to abbreviate the commands by typing N, NW, E, etc. A big part of the game was the ability to perform simple actions like 'use items', 'open door', 'open chest', 'get rope' etc. It also had various states, like night and day which affected the gameplay; for example when dawn broke, the Trolls turned to stone, allowing you to venture among them.

I can remember a particular challenge. I was thrown into a dungeon and I had to figure out how to get out. This challenge, like most challenges in adventure games, was intended as a kind of combination lock and the key was the solution if performed in the right order. Remember, all I had were the words printed on the screen and a crude **2D** backdrop to give me a hint perhaps. The solution was to 'dig' into the ground until you found a trapdoor. Then I had to 'smash' the trapdoor until it was broken. Beneath it I found a curious key, which I gave to Thorin. I then had to command Thorin to unlock the window, pick me up and move in the direction of the window, thus getting me out of the dungeon.

The performance of the actions were all in your imagination and you saw, in your mind's eye, the trapdoor smashing, and the characters climbing through the window. Today however, you would see those things happen on-screen in full 3D, and the game would provide clues and feedback to that end.

The Hobbit was, and still is, a perfect example of an adventure game in its purest and simplest form. It is the challenging situations and puzzle solving that reveal the story and drive the game forward, and it is this that defines the adventure game.

Today we have many sub-genres of adventure game, such as the 'action adventure', which, combined with the defined adventure prerequisites, has plenty of action also. The 'action' elements generally come in the form of combat or shooting, be it fantasy or realistic.

Another sub-genre in the adventure stable is the 'survival horror' game, like the Alone In The Dark™ series, for example. These types of games have the above adventure elements combined with action, but the added element is the intention to frighten the player using traditional scare tactics as seen in most scary movies to date.

Another popular form of adventuring is the 'platform adventure'. There was a time, particularly in the 8-bit days, when the 'platform game' was a core genre. The challenges of platform games were primarily based around lots of jumping and lots of platforms, but people soon realised that jumping is not fun, but in fact very frustrating. I believe jumping from platform to platform and simply collecting items have been diluted and overwhelmed by stronger game mechanics that have rendered the platform game extinct. It has been relegated to a mere sub-genre, if it exists at all.

Platform adventure games still rely on 'jumping' as a feature but it's never so critical, and missing the jump rarely kills the player in today's games. It is even automated in some games and therefore requires little acknowledgement from the player. The 'platform adventure' obviously has many other elements besides jumping and the majority of them include an interactive story, mainly for motivation purposes.

Adventure summary

I believe the adventure game still has much to offer as we career more towards the movie industry, particularly in characterisation, dialogue and story telling. This is why few adventure games are made today, because they require the components of a traditional story to make them stand out. And by definition, games designers are not storytellers – they make games. The components that traditionally make up an adventure game are as follows.

Adventure components

- Puzzle-solving challenges
- A great deal of thought process is generally required from the player
- An interactive story that is tied to the challenges and revealed as the challenges are overcome
- A multi-threaded plot to draw the player through the game
- An adventure – a journey from one location to another
- A central protagonist

Action games

Action is another of the big genres. Action games are really the grandfather of genres, the genre that started it all off. You could add action to any other genre, but would that constitute it an action game? No it wouldn't. It very much depends on what the overriding challenges of the game are.

Let's take the adventure out of 'action adventure' and what do we have? We have a game like Quake, or Doom™, pure adrenalin-pumping action. There are many sub-genres that fall into the action category, however: first- and third- person shooters and shoot 'em ups for example.

Action games flooded the arcades, where the challenges were designed to be quick and satisfying in order to keep the cash slots busy. Action games require few thought processes and rely more on reflexes and quick reactions. There is very little in the way of puzzle solving, and pushing a switch on the wall to open a door on the other side of the world, or using a key to unlock a door does not constitute a puzzle!

One other common element of the action game is the facility to pick up and put down without the need for long hours of play.

Let's take Burnout™, for example. Does it slot into the sports/racing genre or is it an action game? One of the coolest and most dominant features in this game is the ability to crash. It even lets the player play in 'crash' mode where the player is awarded cash for crash, depending on how much damage the player does. It was described by some magazines as an arcade racer and in the manual as 'high-speed driving action' and 'fast racing'. This is an arcade action game mixed with racing, with emphasis placed on the action side. It doesn't have a steep learning curve; it is 'pick up and play' and there is lots of action.

Pure action games have little in the way of interactive stories and are often mission based. These are a series of challenges placed in front of the player and when each one is completed successfully, the game will allow the player to progress. This is often the case in stealth-based action games. The player is usually dropped in a hostile environment, and is given an objective. It usually goes something like this:

> **Objective: Blow up the base**
> **Challenges:**

- Sneak across the river to the facility without being detected (stealth)
- Kill the guards patrolling the outer perimeter (action)
- Destroy the security cameras (action)
- Find the back entrance and make your way to the basement without being spotted (stealth)
- Place explosives in calculated positions (stealth)
- Activate explosive timer (timer)
- Get out before the explosives detonate (time-based–action)
- Victory equals successful escape
- Mission complete

The challenges do not require the player to think too much but do require the player to perform specific functions and complete the objective by giving clear instructions for the challenges.

Action summary

The action game is obviously predominantly action in content, but can also involve other elements, such as racing, fighting and flying, for example. Most games have an element of action because most games have evolved from early games that were successful, particularly arcade games.

Action components

- Action
- Quick reflex movements
- Little thought process required
- Pick up and play
- It doesn't have a steep learning curve

Simulations

There are many simulators on the market, from steam trains to aircraft, that are physically accurate simulations of the real article. This is a genre that I personally have little experience of, either in the creation of or the playing. To me, simulations seem to defy what games are all about, but this is purely subjective. I have a friend who enjoys flight simulators. I watched him one day, incessantly staring at the screen, occasionally jabbing at a button on his keyboard. He would stay like this for hours, as if he was mentally controlling the aircraft from one place to another, eventually mastering a landing at an airport, thus delivering the gratification he was seeking.

The genre is exactly what it says it is – a simulation of a real activity, vehicle, aircraft etc. – and they are generally designed down to the smallest detail. Some racing games attempt to build a simulation mode into the game but often this doesn't work and the player, who was expecting an exhilarating racing game, soon gets bored. The reason for this is that most racing games apply exaggerated physics to deliver something that is not real, but amplifies the excitement and challenges. When the player crashes, it becomes a reward rather than a punishment. Therefore, by adding these elements, it is no longer a simulation.

A simulator is traditionally a teaching tool and was not designed for entertainment purposes. The description of simulator in the *Concise Oxford English Dictionary* (10th edn revised) is:

> **simulator** *n., a machine that simulates the controls and conditions of a real vehicle, process etc. used for training or testing.*

It is for this reason I have problems accepting simulators as a 'game'. By no means am I saying they are not games, but the mechanics, feedback and gratification is limited to a real-life simulation. We live in the real world, we want to play out our fantasies and escape from reality. Simulators tend to attract enthusiasts more so than games players. That's not to say enthusiasts don't play games, as I'm sure they do, but they buy simulators because they simulate their interests.

Perhaps your simulator, if indeed you are designing one, is of a warplane and the user is put into a situation that replicates a war scenario. Now, with extensive research you may very well replicate a warplane in that situation, and it may very well be perceived as fun, but the complexity of controlling such a machine may be too much for your average gamer. It would require a dedicated enthusiast to play this. If you simplified it to appeal to a wider audience, it no longer becomes a simulator in the true explanation of the word.

I remain unconvinced that pure simulators are 'games' and to that end, I will reserve judgement until I can study them in more detail or I am convinced otherwise.

Simulation components

■ Real physics
■ Real vehicles
■ Steep learning curve

Puzzle games

A puzzle game is another rare breed these days. A puzzle game is usually designed to discombobulate the player. A puzzle is a problem that cannot be easily solved, but a puzzle will *always* have a solution otherwise it's not a puzzle. Generally, the challenge for the player is to find the solution to the puzzle.

Tetris is often categorised as a puzzle game, but once you learn the rules the challenge is not to solve any puzzles, but to get the highest score possible. Games that simply have a series of puzzles to solve are being increasingly relegated to mobile phone and Internet downloadable games that can be played in the office behind a word processor. For next-generation technology, it seems no longer acceptable to create a simple puzzle game as it was back in the 8-bit days. Therefore, you will often find puzzle elements embedded into other genres, primarily adventure games.

Management games

Management games are close cousins to god-games and strategy games. Some designers would argue that god-games are management games, but it is the fine detail that separates them.

Management games allow you to construct cities or singular households, and then populate them with inhabitants. Sometimes they let you build football teams and then plunge the player into the world of football team management. They all have an economic and social element that needs monitoring and managing in order for the player to be successful.

For me, the difference between management games and god-games is the lack of action in management games. You do not generally send your population to destroy your opponent or parts of the world like you do in god-games. Therefore, the challenge in management games is to manage your world and make it thrive to the best of your ability.

Uncategorised games

Collectively, the game's theme, structure, mechanics and challenges will almost certainly determine its genre. But what about a game like Tetris: what genre does that fall into? We've already determined that it can't be a puzzle game. It certainly isn't a sports game, nor is it a RPG, RTS, adventure, management or a simulation. Some might say it's an action game with an element of strategy, but it is hard to quantify this. It is certainly a game that challenges the player, and remains one of the most addictive games ever created.

Games like Tetris that cannot be placed do exist but only come along very occasionally. So, it is for this reason we have an uncategorised genre. It would be unwise and very difficult to begin designing a game that didn't fall into a category. Tetris was created in a time when there were few influences and anything went. If it was fun it was a game, it was as simple as that. Today however, if people can't see what they are buying, they don't buy and if they do buy it and don't understand it, they are disappointed.

This genre exists mainly as a museum for games of old, but it has a few remaining slots for the occasional game in the future.

On-line games

On-line games have become the new frontier in game development. They are not the future of gaming, they are here right now and have been for some time. This type of game is yet to penetrate the mass-market and the concept of socialising on-line still frightens many people.

So why am I discussing this here in a chapter about genre? On-line games are regarded as a new genre in some circles, but they're not. The majority of them are on-line multi-player versions of genres that already exist. However, new challenges and innovative ideas are coming through, and this is mostly due to one fundamental element in on-line games that doesn't exist in off-line games: social interaction on a mass scale. Apart from the fact that these games are on-line, i.e. accessed via the Internet, this one element is what separates on-line games and off-line games and it is from this feature that the majority of new game ideas will come from.

Of course you could, and still can, play multi-player games on your console, but the player has been limited to his opponent sitting next to him in the same room. Now he can be anywhere in the world. Instead of the lonely warrior tracking through a vast wilderness, the player can be accompanied by a partner, a team or an army, all controlled by real people from around the world. This element of gaming has only been touched upon in off-line games, and multi-player gaming is constantly scaling new heights and possibilities.

You can apply this social element to any genre of game. The idea of participating in a championship Formula 1 season on-line, with every driver a human opponent and all sitting in the comfort of their own homes, is mindblowing! Action adventure games that require more than one person to combat the challenges present endless possibilities.

The fact that they have this social element does not make them a new genre. Rather, it opens up new avenues and possibilities for designers to exploit existing genres.

Norbot: Genre

If you recall, in the introduction I mentioned I would be compiling a design shell for a game that you could follow throughout the book. Although the chapters are not compiled in the same order you would compile a game design document, I will still include elements of the design as we move through each chapter.

We have established a name, which is not that important at this stage and is simply a label to identify the product. But which genre are we going to place Norbot into? Do I need to decide that now? Well yes, you will be asked this, and if you have no answer the people that question it will immediately see red.

To define our genre, we have to look at the challenges of the game and what the player will actually be doing. Now I have already thought this through, so I know what the player is going to be doing. The challenges are going to involve exploring, puzzle solving, combat and I'm going to send my little robot friend on a journey of self-discovery – quite literally!

Norbot will therefore fall into an 'action adventure' sub-genre.

Summary

Defining genres is one of the most difficult things I have done in this book. I asked many people about genres, and I got a different answer nearly every time. Some people simply didn't want to answer. They were clear about RPG and RTS, and reasonably clear about the action genre but the rest were foggy. When you play a game, simply ask yourself what the overriding features are and what the challenges require the player to do. Are the challenges designed to make the player think a lot, or are they designed for quick reflex reactions or is it a combination?

So, when designing your game, it's always good to know what genre your game falls into. In Chapter 3, we will be discussing 'knowing your audience', which includes defining your game's genre. Games clearly fall into various categories as shown above, but having a clear understanding of its genre prior to development will help you, your team and marketing pitch your product perfectly. Its genre may seem obvious after the game is complete and playable, but it's not always clear at the start of development. When you do your research, this should involve seeking out the very best in the genre of your choice and studying its strengths and weaknesses. By no means copy, but you can learn what works and what doesn't in any particular genre from past games.

WORKSHEET **Genre considerations**

- Decide in which genre your game will exist.
- What gameplay components and challenges do you have in your game that identifies its genre? List them.
- Are there elements overlapping from other genres that slot it into a sub-genre? Be clear what they are.
- Do your research and study the very best of the genre you have placed your game into.
- Determine which games are the best and why they are the best of that particular genre.

Further reading

It is difficult to recommend any text that explores the depths of game genres, because like so much of our industry, genres and their definitions are still to be officially documented. However, there are many books that explore genre in the context of stories and movies, which can be particularly useful if your game has an interactive story or is an adventure game.

CHAPTER 3

Knowing your audience

'Who is your target audience?' This is often one of the first questions you are asked when you walk into a marketing meeting. I feel it's a valid question and one that needs answering as early as possible in the creative process.

It is something that the games industry has traditionally evaded – until recently. So why have we started to acknowledge our audience now? There is one simple explanation: if we didn't, the games industry would not be a viable business. Many other industries target their products at a specific audience. They design them and market them with their audience requirements and desires firmly embedded into the core of the product. An obvious example would be movies. For example, animated and computer-generated movies are invariably targeted at children.

Almost every man-made creation is designed towards a specific audience. Buildings such as houses, hospitals and hotels are all designed to cater for a particular type of person and for a specific purpose. So why is it that some video game designers find it so difficult to share the same mindset?

Most of the quirk factors of game design are inherent from the traditional sole programmer sitting at home creating games. The glimmer of big bucks has lured them from the confines of home and dropped them into the hustling world of big business. But we weren't ready for it. It came bolting towards us like a train from a tunnel and the words 'target audience' were alien to us. However, slowly we are learning – we have to adjust, the train will keep going regardless.

In the past, and to some extent today, designers are guilty of designing games for themselves. This is one of the biggest mistakes a designer can make. *Never* design a game for yourself. *You* are not your audience and *you* are not a typical mass-market gamer. You are most likely to be a hardcore gamer, who owns, or has access to, every type of games console and computer system in the market-place – past and present. If you were to play a multi-player game against a casual gamer, you will most likely find them an easy opponent to beat, which by the way they always find utterly annoying!

It is crucial for a designer to know who he is designing for before embarking on his design. On many occasions, after the initial concept document has been typed, I have asked the designer who his audience is. This meets with raised eyebrows, as if I'm completely insane for asking. 'Gamers' is invariably the answer, and correctly so. 'Ok,' I say, 'so we've narrowed it down to hundreds of millions of people all over the world who play games, great,' I tell them. 'So we're going to sell hundreds of millions of units … it's going to be a record.' That's the moment they start defining their target audience. 'Well … not all gamers,' they usually reply sheepishly.

Some designers believe that restricting the design to a specific audience inhibits the designer and curbs the game, but the opposite is the reality. Designers can design any type of game they like, be it a strategy war game, or a cartoon adventure game, it doesn't really matter. Designers need to stand back and ask themselves, 'If I design this type of game, who will play it?' Once they have answered that crucial question, only then should they continue to design their game. Making and selling video games is a business, and for it to be successful, it needs to make money. If you have no audience, you make no money. Making a game, hoping that somebody will like it, is simply naïve and very risky.

Defining your audience

The audience-defining process is a hard rule to swallow for some designers and many find it difficult to comprehend why they should adhere to it; but there are many reasons why you, the designer, should do this.

> 1 **Product placement.** Marketing can confidently place your product within the market-place. Marketing will know the audience before production is even complete and a marketing campaign can be prepared.

There seems to be some sort of angst between developers and marketing departments that has been dragged up from the depths of game development since its infancy. Developers believed that marketing knew nothing about making games and they should not be involved in the creative process. The ironic thing is, most of them would probably agree with that statement. They work in marketing for a reason – to sell your game. But in order for them to do that, they need to know who they are selling it to.

> 2 **Sales forecasting.** This consequently allows the production costs to be levelled and, provided the planning is done efficiently, the publisher's profit margin can be anticipated.
>
> 3 **Design consistency.** This will help you focus your ideas and interface and tailor it to fit.
>
> 4 **Product focus and direction.** There will be focus and direction in development; marketing and people outside the company will know who the audience are.

Consider this. You work in the games industry, surrounded by games constantly. If you're a designer, you probably play them unyieldingly everyday and get paid for it! Therefore, a designer's perception of gameplay is elevated way above that of the game-buying public. The designer needs to be careful that he does not design and balance the game to his own playing level and interactive desires. The public will be spending lots of money on your game and they want value for money. They don't want a game that they can't play! So what effect does this have on the design process?

Effects of audience defining

When the home games market began to emerge in the early 1980s, the variation in games and gameplay was enormous. Imaginations ran wild, games were innovative and it was the new frontier in entertainment, muscling in on TV, radio and video. Game designers knew no bounds. I believe one of the reasons for this torrent of creativity was the technical limitation imposed on games. The confines of the 8-bit computer system forced designers to look for variation in their designs and delve deep into the bits and bytes of the comparatively limited machines. Today, however, it is very different – we can create semi-realistic three-dimensional cities, worlds and galaxies, and games are getting closer to reality with every generation of hardware.

I believe that imposing restrictions on the design process encourages variation and stimulates imagination, allowing the designer to implement and invent content that might not otherwise be considered. This applies to the process of audience definition as well. When your audience is identified, it slots your product into a snug groove. Some people call this pigeon-holing, but whether designers like it or not, it is an important part of the design process.

> **TIP**
>
> One way to study your audience for real is to begin on the ground floor. Hang out in a game store for a day and study customers, talk to them, ask them what they like and make notes of who is buying what. You might want to inform the store manager that you'll be there or you might get arrested! You could even volunteer to work there for a day for research purposes. Either way, you'll learn something about the real gamers – your audience.

Some examples

Let's look at some games and discuss the projected audience. Let's start with an easy one, Formula 1 on PlayStation2. You can almost see the player in your mind's eye, sitting in front of a monitor with his mates cheering him on. It is very unlikely a 10-year-old girl would play this game. However, it is highly likely that fans of Formula 1 that also own a PS2 *will* play this. If they play this, what other games might they play? In your concept document under 'target audience' you need to list other games that your audience might play, not games that are similar to yours, but games that your audience might play besides your game. You need to substantiate why you think your defined audience will play your game and do some research, otherwise it holds no weight.

Consider Donkey Kong Racing™ on the Nintendo 64! It's a racing game as is Formula 1. Do you think Formula 1 fans are going to rush out and buy Donkey Kong Racing? Perhaps, but I don't think so! It's highly likely that the 10-year-old girl will play this game.

But your audience can be defined more clearly than this. Not only does the age become an issue for the designer, audiences are also fickle about the type and genre of game they play. Not all 10-year-old girls will play a cartoon racing game. In fact, fewer 10-year-old girls play video games than 10-year-old boys.

Remember – you cannot design for all the people … it's just not possible.

When defining your audience, you might want to create a chart that looks something like my example in Table 3.1. You don't have to use my format – you're a designer, invent your own way of presenting your audience.

TABLE 3.1   Audience definition

Game: *Dirt Racer*		*Platform:* *Format*	
Age	*Core audience*	*Other games played*	*Secondary audience*
18–30	Male: Plays realistic racing games. Motor sports fan. Will most likely enjoy extreme sports	Colin McRae Rally™ TOCA Touring Cars™ Burnout 2	Other sports fanatics

Market research:

Motor sports are enjoyed all over the world and is staged and televised in a multitude of different countries. Both men and women, the majority of which are men, enjoy the sport.

Other activities my audience will typically participate in:

My audience might also be found watching and attending football matches, reading car magazines, listening to contemporary music and reading other sports magazines.

Of course, your marketing department will add their own detail to your description, as they will have access to more demographic information than you. But if you do this and stay true to your definition, your marketing department will love you. You will be showered with gifts and they will worship the ground you walk on. This type of insight will be invaluable to them. But not only that, if your design is given the green light, you will be able to steer your design confidently towards a clearly defined goal.

If you are developing a game from a licence, i.e. a movie, life is a little easier for you. You will already have an audience defined by the licence itself. You will still need to take it into consideration when designing your game though.

CASE STUDY

I was working in London for a top publisher within their internal development studio. One day, a fighting game came through the door from an external development team and it immediately grabbed everybody's attention and imagination. The publisher was excited, marketing became ecstatic and it was an awesome game – or so it seemed. It had one major flaw. The visual content went way beyond anything that could ever be publishable. It was so grotesque and violent, that it would have gone beyond the highest rating and would have put *Silence of the Lambs* to shame. So, after much excitement, money spent and a stint at a trade show, the project was pulled and shelved because nobody would allow it to be sold to the general public. This is a perfect example of what could happen if you don't define your target audience. The publisher considered a re-design and to replace all the art work, but decided that it would lose its USP (unique selling point) and would be too similar to many other fighting games.

Legal requirements

In 1994, ELSPA introduced a rating system for interactive entertainment, but has been replaced with a new system from the Interactive Software Federation of Europe (ISFE), in spring 2003 (Figure 3.1). By the time you read this, it will probably be in operation. There will be five age categories, 3+, 7+, 12+, 16+ and 18+. The federation have also designed icons to symbolise the content of the game, such as violence, sex, drugs, fear, discrimination and bad language. Inevitably your game will go through the ISFE and possibly the local country board of film censors. So, if you don't think about your audience, somebody else will!

For more information about video game ratings, visit ELSPA at its website: http://www.elspa.co.uk/

FIGURE 3.1   ISFE rating system

Source: www.pegi.info, © 2004, ISFE

Hardcore versus casual gamer

As if it wasn't hard enough defining your audience age, you have to think about the *type* of gamer that will play your game. The publisher will undoubtedly want to sell as many units of your game as they possibly can. After all, it is a business. This generally means they will want your game targeted at the mass-market, also known as the casual gamer.

So who are these hardcore and casual gamers? I question whether I'm a hardcore gamer. I certainly used to be, but I don't think I am today; I simply don't have the time to devote to actual hardcore gaming. Hardcore gamers enjoy playing games more than any other pastime or entertainment medium. If they're not playing games, they're watching them, reading about them or thinking about them. They sit at work or at school and think how to solve the next puzzle, or how to plot a new strategy for the latest war game. They live for games.

Hardcore gamers have other attributes that can characterise them. They will most likely tolerate flawed software and will often play around it in an attempt to maintain their digital dripfeed. They use the Internet to search out game sites for cheats, hints and tips. They will wait for hours to download the latest patch that will enhance their game and perhaps even fix those flaws and glitches. Casual gamers will only upgrade their computers every year or two for the most part, but hardcore gamers find themselves upgrading far more often. This is due in part to their perceived need to keep their computer on the 'bleeding edge' of technology, but mostly because they really have to if they want to enjoy new and more demanding titles in all of their 3D graphical glory.

Casual gamers are the complete opposite: they will play a game for fun, a form of entertainment, in the same way they watch a movie, or listen to music. Hardcore gamers also play for fun, but for them it has an element of hobby status, a perpetual presence in the gamer's life.

A casual gamer will play for approximately an hour, maybe a little longer, which means you have to grab them immediately and avoid any confusion and complicated interface design. They will not tolerate bugs and crashes, long Internet downloads, ambiguous puzzle design and fuzzy confusing objectives. As soon as the casual gamer switches their system on, they want the game to come and get them and pull them in and they want to be able to *play* immediately.

A casual gamer will purchase only few games in a year, spending little money, and only on games that he is familiar with or has been highly recommended. These games could be a sequel to a previous game they enjoyed, or a game based on a licence, be it a movie, sports personality or a TV show. When they spend their money, they need to know what they will be getting. One of the most successful PC games in the UK is Who Wants To Be a Millionaire and was the first PC game to ship over a million units. This game is a casual gamer's type of game. The format is familiar, they know what they have to do and can interact with it immediately.

Without the casual gamer the games industry would become non-existent – the industry needs them in order to survive. Hardcore gamers spend a lot of money on their favourite pastime, but the problem is, there aren't enough of them to fund the industry. They are a rare species in danger of extinction, being pushed aside by the casual gamers' desires for easy accessible games.

So what does this mean for you, the designer? It doesn't mean you can't develop hardcore games, but your design must convince a publisher that it will make them money. RPGs generally attract hardcore gamers, but even those are changing. On-line games such as Everquest and Asheron's Call© I would consider hardcore games. The casual gamer just isn't ready for this type of game, or maybe this type of game isn't ready for the casual gamer. At the time of writing, Everquest has a player count of around 400,000. In box-shifting terms this is not great, but because it's on-line and the gamers are paying a monthly subscription fee, making the developers a handsome profit, the business model works!

Hardware

We should discuss hardware in relation to the audience. I don't want to give specific details, numbers and charts for demographics, because it differs from one report to the next. Video game consoles and PCs are universal, they don't have an age bracket slapped on the side of the packaging; anybody can buy them. Therefore, we will look at which types of games are developed for each platform, which are more successful and why.

It is evident that each platform certainly attracts a specific type of person, so the platform you are targeting is also an important consideration during the design process.

The PC

PC gamers are predominantly adults. This is evident from the types of games developed specifically for the PC. Children do use the PC, but they are more likely to use it for educational purposes, surfing the Internet or listening to music, and the minority do play games. In today's development community, the PC is generally an afterthought. It is a very powerful medium in which to express your creative talents, but the sales can be very poor in comparison to game console sales. Why? I hear you cry. Long before game development became a mass-market industry, the PC was traditionally designed to do many other things than play games, and for this reason it is not truly regarded as a 'games machine'. Since computers were introduced to the gaming community, they have been gradually shunted from the game development world, from the Commodore 64, to the Amiga, Atari ST and now the PC, and replaced by the compact, affordable and somewhat funky games console.

Another drawback with designing games for the PC is the devices used to interact with the hardware. They have not been designed for games – rather games are designed around them, and of course I am referring to the mouse and keyboard. There are many other peripherals for the PC but the designer can't guarantee that every household will have one, unless it's sold with the game, which is very rare indeed. Consequently, designing for the mouse and keyboard has additional drawbacks in that it becomes difficult to cross-develop the product to a game console. Consoles are designed for games and the console controller is far removed from a mouse and a keyboard.

Consoles

Consoles are far more accessible to the mass-market than the PC because all you have to do is put in a disc, switch it on and it works – every time. Gamers can sit in their living rooms and play them on the TV. There is no need for additional monitors and a big clunky keyboard lying around.

Console controllers are generally very comfortable and simply to use; you don't have to take your eyes off the screen to press a button. The controller is an important element to any console. It is the interface to the hardware and subsequently the player's interpreter to the game.

The Xbox is the first game console to have an onboard hard-drive, which might partially explain the size of the console. This single hardware inclusion offers designers the option to implement elements of PC gaming inside a console environment.

Consoles are getting connected to the Internet for the next tier of interactive entertainment. One of the concerns for on-line gaming is security, particularly for kids. Using consoles eliminates this concern for many reasons. The most obvious is the lack of a keyboard, and therefore designers are forced to design other ways of communicating to players. Of course keyboards can be purchased for consoles, but they are not associated with consoles and therefore are not common. They cannot be considered a viable console input device.

Consoles are also more affordable than PCs, making them more attractive as gifts and to the younger population. Because of this, there are more of them in the market-place and subsequently, publishers need to develop for game consoles. This makes your audience definition slightly biased, but if you are realigning your game for cross-platform development, then there should be no problem and you should define two audiences.

Handhelds

Don't you just love them! You can play them whenever and wherever you feel like. This is another fantastic invention that keeps us challenged even when we are on the move. Handhelds are an acquired taste and are generally owned by children. The only real problems that handhelds have suffered from has been the lack of screen visibility due to the LCD screens. You generally had to have a light or it was pretty much useless; but this is changing and the latest GAME BOY/ADVANCE SP™ has a backlit screen and is much better. It also has a rechargeable battery, which means you don't have to keep running out and buying new batteries. The games are great and they can pass time when you're on a train or in the back of a car on a long boring journey. The games are usually twitch games, in that you can save at any time. Consequently, puzzle games are very popular with handhelds.

These machines constrain the designer, as the old 8-bit computers did, and will test your skills as a designer.

WORKSHEET | **Audience definition**

- Pick a selection from the current top 20 games and define their audience.

- Write down why you think the game is targeted at that particular audience. Do not try and guess what the designers were thinking and why they did it that way; pull specific elements from the game that tell you who the audience are and list them.

- If you target an obvious choice such as Formula 1, or some other licence, then it will generally speak for itself. Therefore, you might want to consider whether the interface, structure of the game and gameplay theme, were tailored for the audience, and indeed if it is suitable.

- Examine the same product on different platforms and study the differences, particularly between PC and console.

Norbot: audience definition

We have established the genre, and now we define the audience. Norbot will be targeted at the casual gamer, developed on console for the mass-market. It's easy enough to say that and type it into a document, but I need to explain why I am targeting that audience. My reasons are purely monetary. It also happens to be where most of my experience lies. I want my game to make lots of money so I can make more games. However, I want it to be fun, challenging and a creative masterpiece. It has to be something I can be proud of. Table 3.2 shows you the chart I created for Norbot.

TABLE 3.2	Norbot audience definition

Game: *Norbot*		**Platform:** *All Consoles*	
Age	Core audience	Other games played	Secondary audience
7+	Male and female. A casual gamer that typically enjoys playing action adventure games	Mario Crash Bandicoot Luigi's Mansion	Older fans of this genre

Market research:

Action adventure games are one of the best-selling genres of video games. However, in recent times, there is has been a tendency for these games to be repetitive in nature, offering nothing in terms of original design elements and gameplay. Norbot offers several original game features that would appeal to my target audience. Norbot is also a character-based game, and will stand out as an original and highly competitive contender in the popular character stakes. It offers potential for merchandise and spin-offs. To support this potential, cross-platform development will be pivotal in the development process.

Other activities my audience will typically participate in:

My audience might be found at family places like a bowling alley. My secondary audience will read teen magazines, listening to popular music, particularly chart music. They are most likely to own a PS2 and/or a Gamecube, but not an Xbox.

Developing Norbot for consoles will ensure I have a chance of exposing my game to the biggest audience.

Summary

Using all of the above information, you should be able to create a profile of the person who will play your game that will subsequently help you construct your design. It may attract a broad range of people, which is always good, but a designer must be certain of his target audience. Here is a checklist of things to consider when defining your audience.

CHECKLIST **Target audience**

- Male, female or both
- Age bracket
- Other games they are likely to play
- Other related hobbies, activities, likes and dislikes
- Hardcore gamer or casual gamer
- Hardware formats
- Product potential and scope

CHAPTER 4

Ideas and themes

Now you have your audience embedded firmly in your mind, you can begin to think about your game and the way your audience might interact with it. You need to mould your idea into a challenging, interactive experience. This chapter will discuss ideas and themes, where they might come from and how they are presented in computer and video games. It will also discuss how ideas are drawn from the theme to create gameplay.

Gameplay theme

In today's competitive industry, a game has to have a theme. By this I don't mean graphical theme, although that is important too. What I mean here is gameplay theme. A game without a theme is like food without any flavour, very bland – you just wouldn't eat it. A thematic strain will give your game focus and direction. It will also give any prospective player an idea of what your game is about and unify your setting. Gameplay theme is the topic, or subject matter of your gameplay that exists consistently throughout the game.

Take a theme park for example. What do you do when you go to a theme park? The park is generally divided up into sections. Each section is usually based on a popular story, myth or character. Maybe there is a pirate section or a Greek mythology area; are these themes? Yes they are, but they are themes for each ride, not the theme for the park as a whole and the things you do in the park. If visiting the park were a game, the gameplay theme in this example would be 'extreme rides' or 'thrill-seeking rides'. The reason for this is because 'extreme rides' describes what you do in a theme park.

The gameplay theme should be directly related to the gameplay. Pirates and Greek mythology might be the graphical theme of your setting, but it doesn't describe the theme of your gameplay. I know this might seem obvious, but I have read many designs that described the gameplay theme something like this:

Gameplay theme: 'It's an action fantasy game set in a world full of monsters and magic.'

You know where that design is going! That sentence could describe a million games. It loosely describes a setting, but it doesn't even attempt to describe the theme of the gameplay.

When you present your gameplay theme, you should give the reader a piece of the whole, place the reader or listener directly into your gaming world so they have a vivid image in their minds. Use colourful words like 'war', for example. It immediately conjures vivid imagery and the reader already has some idea of what is coming. War is a state of armed conflict; how much more vivid than that can you get? The reader will be intrigued and will want to read more.

As a simple exercise, try to guess what games relate to the themes below:

1 Strategic life simulator

2 Trained licensed killer

3 Heroic spider man

4 Comical ghost catcher

5 Extreme skateboarding

As you can tell from the above, your gameplay theme could also be based around the actions of your central character, like a secret agent with a licence to kill, or a superhero with spider-like abilities. If you are creating a design from a licence, then the theme for your gameplay will already have been decided for you.

For those of you who have not guessed the games above …

1 The Sims

2 James Bond

3 Spiderman

4 Luigi's Mansion

5 Tony Hawk's Pro Skate™

Your gameplay theme can often depict your setting. If the theme of your gameplay is something like 'pirate wars', then you can determine what the game might look like. I think in this example, the player would expect a pirate connection with everything in this game, but imagine if there were no pirates, just ordinary people; no pirate ships, just regular wooden boats; no skull and crossbones and no treasure. Your setting wouldn't be based around pirates and your gameplay theme wouldn't be pirate wars.

The art style, however, is something different again. For example, the art style for a pirate theme could be realistic, like a real pirate movie for example, or perhaps it could be set in a cartoon world. As mentioned before, your target audience will have a major influence on the style of your art. This is something the art director should be concerned with and although you can suggest ideas, it is best left to the art director to decide.

Command and Conquer/Luigi's Mansion

Let's look at two games that have very different gameplay themes. But before we begin, I would just like to make it clear that we are not comparing these two games to each other, merely pointing out elements within them.

The first game is a PC game, Command and Conquer – Red Alert, developed by Westwood Studios in Las Vegas. The gameplay theme here is obviously war. War immediately suggests battles, which necessitates the need for more than one player, be it computer versus player or player versus player. The second game can only be found on the Nintendo Gamecube, Luigi's Mansion. The gameplay theme for this game is ghost-catching.

Let's imagine for one moment that the art styles are swapped around, so Command and Conquer is set in a cartoon world and Luigi's Mansion is in a realistic world. Do you think it changes the theme of the gameplay at all? No it doesn't! It can work whichever way you do it. Whether they would be as appealing to the relevant audiences is another matter altogether.

The toybox in Command and Conquer consists of tanks, soldiers, guns etc. that are all controlled and manipulated by the player, and are all related to the gameplay theme (war). The toys are the catalyst for the players to manipulate in order to overcome the challenges presented to them. The challenge for the player is controlling the toys successfully towards his core objective and the victory state – destroying the opponent.

Your gameplay theme definition and the genre or sub-genre should convey a vivid picture of what your game is. These two pieces of the whole will depict imagery in the minds of the reader. For example:

- Strategy war game
- Ghost-catching action adventure
- Stunt car racing

From three or four key words, you should be able describe your game and plant an initial seed into the thoughts of the reader. Of course, the words won't tell the reader what the player does in the game or how he does it. We'll get to that a little later.

What are ideas?

An idea is initially only a thought or a suggestion as to a possible course of action. In the context of gameplay, if you can imagine the gameplay theme is a container, the ideas of your game are the objects that go inside that container. The word 'football' defines the gameplay theme of soccer perfectly. However, if you didn't know how to play football, the theme wouldn't tell you what ideas are used to define the challenges of the game. The idea of controlling the ball with your feet and not your hands presents a challenge for the player. The idea of kicking the ball into a net past a goalkeeper in order to reach the core objective (the victory state), presents a challenge for the goalkeeper and the player.

If football had not been invented, the two examples above would still only be ideas, or a mental impression that needs defining as a game mechanic with rules.

The core idea

The first thing you should consider is the main idea, which you probably already have. You may have a main idea bubbling away inside of you, but unless you know how to express that idea, it may never come to fruition. I will show you how to express that idea as you move through the book. Once you know what your core idea is, invent as many secondary ideas that are related to the core idea as you can. Too many ideas are never enough. You can pick the best ideas and save the others for another game. It doesn't matter how ridiculous it sounds, get it down on paper; if it gets dismissed the first time around, you may get to use it in a sequel or in a different game altogether.

I call it the core idea because that's exactly what it is. It is the one idea that defines the overall fundamental gameplay. Be sure to define what your core idea is in your game design documents. The core idea can be defined in a simple sentence that expands the gameplay theme with actions. For example:

> Command and Conquer is a *real-time strategy war* game using various *tanks, soldiers, ships and aircraft* to rage *war* on the opponent and defeat him.

The great thing about the games industry and being a designer is that you can invent your own ideas for a given theme. If your gameplay theme is war, for example, you don't have to use the traditional ideas that spring to mind; you can be imaginative and create your own ideas of how war should be presented and controlled in a game environment. This is an area of your game that you can work on, that will make it stand out from the crowd. In Luigi's Mansion, for example, he uses a vacuum cleaner to catch ghosts, which is strapped to his back. What a great idea! And … it's fun! The designer also took that idea and created additional sub-ideas. They are sub-ideas because they couldn't exist without the original core idea.

So what else can the vacuum do?

EXAMPLE	Core idea: A ghost-catching vacuum cleaner

- Primary function is to capture ghosts by sucking them up.
- Secondary function 1: The player can suck up large objects like giant beach balls, hold them on the nozzle to aim and fire it towards a target. You can also suck up material such as curtains, and pictures from walls, revealing hidden items and switches.
- Secondary function 2: Blower. The designer has now reversed the suction and is using the vacuum to blow obstacles around the scene, put out flames etc.
- Secondary function 3: Flamethrower. You can shoot flames from the vacuum, which enables you to light candles, melt ice etc.
- Secondary function 4: Water hose. You can squirt water from the vacuum and put out fires, water plants etc.

The flamethrower and water ideas are sub-ideas of the core idea. The designer wisely decided not to let the player use these functions perpetually as it would make the game far too easy. It may even get boring very quickly. So to combat that, the designers came up with the idea of re-sourcing the water and flames. This is not an original idea by any stretch of the imagination, but it's a tried and tested method that game players are familiar with. They used the core idea to retrieve and subsequently feed the secondary functions of the vacuum. This leads to additional tasks and challenges for the player because it now become a necessity to go around and collect water and flames to fuel the extra features. This creates another layer in the structure of the game and gives it more depth.

To define a great idea, and apply several secondary features to it, are great game design principles, but they will still need proving. This method also utilises assets that currently exist. Every idea that is created should have a secondary function that is embedded into the gameplay architecture. The flamethrower idea spawned many ideas like melting ice and lighting candles etc. Subsequently when the candles are lit, it illuminates the rooms so you can see your way around dark passageways and rooms. If you blow the candles out when they are lit, the player can reveal ghosts. Each idea leads to an additional function within the game.

Source of ideas and themes

Where do ideas and themes come from? Of course, ideas are only thoughts initially, but they are usually seeded by something. Perhaps it was an image, a movie, a conversation you had or a TV show. Whatever the source, the ideas need to be shaped and solidified and are often influenced by something that already exists.

Trends play a large part in the choices designers make. Since Harry Potter and Lord of the Rings became so popular with the mass-market, RPGs and fantasy-themed games have never been so prevalent. That's not to say designers are copying other products, but merely following a trend and capitalising on the wants of the audience.

If you have your gameplay theme already decided, go and research it, e.g. if it's a case of 'I want to do a war game', go and research war. What I mean by this is, study the mechanics and tactics of war. Do not assume that simply pitting two opponents with huge arsenals against each other is a war game – there is so much more to it than that. While doing your research, you will inevitably find a wealth of ideas that you can mould and shape to fit your game. You may even find something that nobody has ever thought of including in a game. Every town and city has a library – use it!

If you examine the video game charts at any one time, you can be sure they are peppered with licences, sequels and renditions of games that already exist. The designers are hopefully attempting to add something new to their version of the game, but the point is, having an original core idea and bringing it to fruition is extremely rare. Tetris and Lemmings™ are two original game ideas that made it through the developer's web of game production.

But even the game Lemmings is based on the rodent that lives in circumpolar countries. In Scandinavia, lemmings become restless in years when their populations are high. In the mountainous terrain of Norway, for example, when lemmings begin to move they tend to go downhill and get funnelled into valleys. The result is that large numbers eventually reach the sea or a large lake. They may proceed onto sea or lake ice or jump into the water, which has given rise to the popular conception that they are committing mass suicide to relieve a problem of overpopulation – although in the absence of an authentic account to back this up it remains controversial.

From this, you can see where the idea for the Lemmings game came from. The creatures' characteristics are evident in the game. The fact they move relentlessly in a straight line provides the designer with a powerful mechanic. The player is required to guide the rodents through various obstacles and get them to safety without killing them. This is the core, overriding idea of the Lemmings game. The challenges and obstacles are sub-ideas that bolt into the main idea of the game. The core objective is to save as many Lemmings as you can. The core *idea* is they move continuously without stopping. Those two elements form the nucleus of the game and exist for the remainder of the game to be built around.

USP or hook

Unique selling points (USP) have become, to some publishers, a necessity for a game to exist in their portfolio. If you hear this at any time, make sure you have your marketing-to-game-speech translator with you. Defining unique selling points for a game is such a pointless exercise, it makes my bones quake. It simply implies that you are creating a feature in the game for a marketing department to sell the product. To me that is complete madness. If they can't sell the game that you propose, it is lacking more than just a USP!

Today the USP is known as the hook, which is a much better term. When you present your game to a publisher, they will be looking for something different, something unique that will turn heads and cha-ching the tills. It will be an idea or a feature that marketing can grab hold of and get excited about, and possibly use to help push it into the market-place. It will not be in the game for that reason; it will be there because it is an integral part of the game structure.

Let me just stop there and explain that not all games *have* to have a hook; although it is preferable, games often get made without one, so don't let it jam the creative process. If it's there, great, if not, make up for it in quality.

So what exactly is the hook? It is an element of the game that has not existed in a game before. It could be the visual style that has never been seen before or tried before, in which case, you needn't worry about it too much. It could be a new gameplay mechanic that is fundamental to the game. Occasionally it is a technical breakthrough that has been applied to a tried and tested genre.

Let's look at our two previous examples. What does Luigi's Mansion have that's unique about it? When I first started to play it, I thought I was playing a cartoon, but visuals soon become transparent and the gameplay steps to the fore. The hook in LM is embedded within the game mechanics and is the core idea. It is the vacuum cleaner, and the way in which Luigi uses it to suck up ghosts is the hook in this game. I have never seen it in a game before. Of course I have not played every single game ever made, but the way in which it was presented provided unique challenges for me as a gamer.

Beyond jumping

A unique hook, like the vacuum cleaner, will have an immediate reaction from the player, but taking an old idea and improving it, which many games do can also be a good thing. A good example of this can be seen in Zelda, The Ocarina of Time™. This game is flooded with fantastic ideas, gameplay devices and structure, but one thing that I instantly noticed when I started playing was the jump feature. I know what you're thinking, 'jumping isn't original – they've been using that device forever' and jumping is not fun. How many times have you played a game only to hurl your controller across the room because you repeatedly missed the jump? Maybe your timing isn't perfect, maybe the gap is too wide to make it easily, or maybe the camera is in the wrong place for you to judge the distance accurately. Whatever the reason, it is infuriating for the player to keep missing. This is not gameplay and it's not fun.

In Zelda, the jump was different – it was automated, so when you ran around the scene, the computer controlled the jump, not the player and it took away the frustration of always missing and having to repeat the jump over and over again. This is one simple example of a traditional idea that has been enhanced to allow the player to see beyond jumping. It felt fresh and new, but Zelda certainly didn't rely on that for the core idea.

Presenting original ideas for your game that have never been tried before presents a potential problem and will be highlighted as a risk. You will need to demonstrate your unique feature during pre-production and prove that the idea can work. If you can do this, and it proves to be a huge hit and a great game mechanic, you will be well on your way to creating a noteworthy game.

Feature set

You may hear this expression in the games industry and it is fairly self-explanatory. It's a term that basically refers to your toy box within your game. The feature set is your ideas defined and established as gameplay mechanics, in other words, these are what your ideas become.

Norbot: ideas and theme

Let's continue with our 'Norbot' design. We have defined our genre and target audience and we have established a preference for the visual style of the game. The visual style may change because the art director will have his own ideas about it, which is great, because that's what he's been hired to do and will most likely do it much better than you. The point you've made by defining your art style preference is that you want the art like that, because of your target audience.

So what is the theme of our gameplay? Let's say that it's 'Robots capable of carrying out a series of automated actions through robotics'. This gives us plenty of scope to create interesting ideas for gameplay.

Our 'core idea' for the game is a friendly robot – Norbot. He is a service robot that is capable of attaching several gadgets to his person, consequently allowing for an interesting array of possible game mechanics. He also has a number of components of his personality missing that the player will need to find. I am going to use Norbot's robot abilities as my 'core idea' for the game. This in itself is not that exciting so we have to extend the idea and come up with features that will complement the core idea and contribute to the game architecture. I am also going to extract ideas from the unemotional qualities of robots, which will be explained in more detail in a later chapter.

Other things to think about are Norbot's navigational and combat abilities. What ways can we help Norbot get around Tobor, his home planet, for example? Of course he can walk, but keeping with the 'core idea', we can very easily give him additional bolt-on devices, such as a helicopter type device that pops out of his head. I might also equip him with a foot-boost pack that can lift him across ravines and gaps or reach great heights. Perhaps we could give him a winch device that will aid him to reach high places.

- Core idea: Robotic abilities
- Complementary idea 1 – Helicopter enhancement
- Complementary idea 2 – Foot-booster enhancement
- Complementary idea 3 – Winch device
- Complementary idea 4 – A torch/light attachment

These are still relatively simple ideas and are mainly navigational devices. The world in which Norbot exists is currently infested with evil Cybods, which are part organic and part robotic and we have to consider how they will challenge Norbot and how Norbot is going to dispose of them. A variation of weapons will be available to the player, starting with the standard laser eventually upgrading to bigger more powerful homing weapons, etc.

I also want to include an element of stealth and allow Norbot to sneak past guards or through Cybod-infested buildings, for example. Perhaps he has an inbuilt camouflage ability but it has limited timed use, which will add an element of tension for the player. He is programmable, therefore retrieving custom chips and downloading software from the terminals scattered across Tobor will give Norbot additional features and capabilities. The player could also adopt outriders that will travel with Norbot, but existing independently and functioning as a separate unit.

The list of ideas I have is endless and I could go on … and designers generally do. Once I have finished thinking about my ideas, I will need to ensure I have made an organised list that segregates them into function; for example, navigational, weapons, defence etc.

What I have described is still relatively simple in terms of a deep meaningful experience for the player, which is why I am going to fall back on my gameplay theme to add depth to the game. I will go into more detail on this later.

Summary

You can see that by defining these elements they will help shape and define the game and will give you focus when designing the gameplay itself. Try to define your game as clearly as possible. The more you do this, the easier it becomes to visualise the content.

WORKSHEET   **Definitions**

- **Gameplay theme:** Identify your gameplay theme. This is the subject of the gameplay, i.e. racing or war.

- **Core objective:** Identify your core objective. I realise it's not the subject of this chapter, but it is related to the core idea and, for clarity, I have included it here. The core objective is your overall goal of the game.

- **Core idea:** Define your core idea. The core idea is the vehicle for the actions in the game and is fundamental for completing your core objective.

- **Sub–ideas:** Outline the sub-ideas for further development later in the design process. These are usually subsidiaries of the core idea.

You now have a basic shell or a seed for your game, something to plant that will grow and blossom into a fully functional and entertaining piece of interactive entertainment. The next step is to determine *why* the defined audience is going to play your game. The craft of game design is used when you masterfully collate and shape the themes and ideas into a well-organised, beautifully structured, balanced game.

CHAPTER 5

Player motivation

Reason, incentive and purpose are all appropriate words that can be associated with the topic of this chapter. When you design your game, you have to ask yourself 'why will anybody play it?' and you need to have an answer. Some designers will say, 'because it's fun', and that is a good answer – well, in most cases! But it's not enough. The point is you have to know why it is fun and include lots of it all the way through your game. You also need to ask yourself, 'what will convince a player to continue playing my game to the end?'

Before we go into the motivational qualities in a game, I would like to point out some of the reasons why players never get through games and thus become demotivated. How many games have you played all the way through to the end? If you are an ardent games player, I will bet my bottom dollar that you have more unfinished games in your collection than games you have completed. Why is this? Well most likely for several reasons. Here are a possible few.

Reasons for not finishing games

- The developers put all of their efforts into the first quarter of the game and consequently, it became boring and very thin thereafter.
- It lacked content. There was no incentive for the player to pick up the controller and continue playing.
- It became repetitive. There is nothing worse than playing a game that is the same all the way through. In this scenario, the developers would have simply cut and paste due to time constraints.
- The game mechanics suddenly changed beyond all recognition.
- There was no time to balance the game.
- It was frustratingly inconsistent.
- You hit an ambiguous puzzle and froze.

Another big showstopper can be exposition. There is nothing more frustrating than exposition in a game. The longer it goes on the more you want to switch the game off. The reason people buy games is to play and interact with them, not to sit and watch some dull, drawn-out movie that attempts to justify why the player character is there. Scriptwriters and novelists strive to eliminate exposition from their work – because it's dull. So why do we see so much of it in games? Don't use it! There are better ways to deliver information than through exposition. In the book and movie world, you often hear the expression 'show, don't tell', this is also true for games.

What is motivation?

There have been much research and theorising of motivation over the years, in an attempt to understand why we do the things we do. I will discuss a few of these theories here, as they are pertinent to games.

Expectancy–value theories

The expectancy–value theories speculate that a person's motivation to perform a task is the result of two central elements: the expectancy of success in the given task and the value that the person places on the successful completion of the task. The greater each one of these factors is, the greater the person's motivation to perform the task. On the other hand, if a person does not perceive success to be likely or does not value the outcome of the task the person's motivation will be very low. So you can see from this how gameplay balance becomes a very important aspect of game design.

Researchers have presented various factors that they believe are part of the cognitive process of developing expectancy of success; the most important factors include 'the processing of past experiences (attribution theory), judging one's own ability and competence (self-efficacy theory), and attempting to maintain one's self esteem (self-worth theory)' (Zoltán Dörnyei, 1998).

Researchers Eccles and Wigfield (1995) developed a model to define the aspect of value. Value, as they define it, is composed of four related components: attainment value (significance of the outcome), intrinsic value (interest in or pleasure derived from the actual task), extrinsic utility value (usefulness for attaining other goals), and cost (effort, time, and risk involved). The first three values have a positive correlation with motivation and the last has a negative correlation. The combination of these components determines the value attributed to a task.

One of the reasons why multi-player games are so popular, particularly one on one, is because the attainment value, intrinsic value and cost are extremely high.

Goals and quests

One approach to motivation that particularly applies to games is a goal-directed approach. Goal-directed theories identify a goal as the main instigator and director of motivation. The goal-setting theory developed by Locke and Latham (1994) is a framework that has evolved from the goal-directed approach. The goal-setting theory maintains that goals, which are both defined and difficult, lead to higher performance than goals that are vague or easy to achieve. With the goal-setting theory, performance is enhanced when goal achievement is seen as possible and important (Zoltán Dörnyei, 2001). The intensity and commitment of the goals will determine the amount of effort expended and encourage persistence and strategic actions towards goal achievement.

Goals and quests, obtainable from completing challenges, are the primary motivations when playing games. In every game there is a core objective, an end goal that the player has to achieve. This goal could be to rescue a princess, save the world from Dr Evil, win a football match or come first in a series of races. Whatever your ultimate goal, it is the 'core objective' of the game. You can call it what you like in your design, but for the purposes of clarity, it will be referred to as the 'core objective' throughout this book. I use 'core' because the main purpose for playing runs through the heart of the game, and every goal, task and challenge is attached to it in some way. The terms 'goals' and 'quests' are to imply an objective or a target that has to be reached, after successfully overcoming a series of challenges.

| CASE STUDY | Luigi's Mansion/Dungeon Siege |

In 'Luigi's Mansion', Luigi has won a mansion in a competition. On hearing this news, he calls his brother Mario, and arranges to meet him at the mansion. Upon arriving, Luigi discovers it is haunted, and furthermore, the ghosts have abducted Mario. With the help of Professor E. Gadd, Luigi's core objective is to save Mario from the biggest and most evil ghost of all.

Some people could be confused when asked, 'what is the "core objective" in Luigi's Mansion?' It could be perceived that it is to clear the house of ghosts, but it's not, that is a sub-task that stems from the 'core objective'. Rescuing Mario is the core, and without it there would be no pot of gold, no reward and no climactic event at the end of the game. But more importantly there would be no motivation for the player to play the game.

In Dungeon Siege, the 'core objective' and motivation for the player is to save the eroding Kingdom of Ehb from evil infestations. But in order to do this, the player must battle and clear the infested kingdom in order to confront Gom and destroy him, thus saving Ehb.

Both Dungeon Siege and Luigi's Mansion are thematically very different, they are from different genres and targeted at different audiences, yet both games are structured in a similar fashion. Here are some similarities between the two games:

■ Both games have a tyrannical adversary causing problems and challenges for the player.

■ Both games are resource-based in that the player needs to collect items in order to progress through the game.

■ Both have a progressive environment in that it unfolds as the player overcomes successive challenges as he plays through the game.

▶

- Both are character-based games.
- Characters in both games grow and evolve as the game progresses.
- Both games have an element of mêlée to rid the world of its enemy.

You can see there are many things that are similar, so what defines them as being different? It is the very elements that define their genre that makes them different.

Core objective

Of course, not all games have a big monster to kill at the end. As I said before, all games do have a 'core objective'. In a rally game or a racing game, the motivation here is more likely to be the coveted first place and gold cup in place of the big monster, but the satisfaction is just as rewarding. This is particularly so if you are playing multi-player with a friend, as the contentment is amplified because the value of the reward is much higher.

Whatever your core objective, the player needs to know about it and be lured towards it from the outset. At the beginning of any game, the player should be fully aware that there is a problem to be solved or an objective to be met. Dungeon Siege does this particularly well. When you begin the game, you are introduced to the story through a quick, clean-cut scene, which informs the player that something evil is afoot in the Kingdom of Ehb. You are not entirely sure what it is, but the player is lured into finding out. This is great because you are immediately intrigued and pulled into the game from the moment it begins.

Most fighting games, for example, have a core objective. Defeat all the fighters and become the champion of champions. Each fighter is a sub-quest to the core objective and these games probably have the most basic of progression trees you could find in a game. However, fighting games are much more than this. They offer the thrill of combat, particularly in a player vs player situation. Special moves are built into the combat for the player to discover, and finding and perfecting these moves could be labelled as a sub-task or a mini quest.

 ## Norbot: Defining the core objective

Before we begin defining and clarifying other design elements in Norbot, we need to have a core objective. Many designers work differently, but I always like to know the core objective in my game before I begin the monumental task of building a design. I feel it makes the task easier if I know the ending to the game before I begin, but no two designers will work the same. Some designers will build a game around an idea, subsequently defining the core objective as they go along, which is fine.

We have already determined an outline for the game and we know that poor old Norbot only has one hand. Therefore, the core objective for Norbot is to find his missing hand so he can be *normal* again. The situations, challenges and problems involved in retrieving the hand will be defined later.

The other idea I will play on in the game and use as a theme for my story (not game) is that having his hand in place again will make him normal. The message will be that we are all different, which ironically makes us all normal.

Sub-quests

On the player's journey towards the core objective, there will be a host of smaller goals and quests the player will be challenged with. These are generally referred to as 'sub-quests'. They are usually related to the core objective and also need to be completed before you can complete the core objective. Most games have sub-quests or sub-goals, and you are challenged as a gamer to confront them. Some games do not appear to have any sub-quests, such as fighting games, but they are inherently built into the structure of the game.

Pulling the player along

Motivation is becoming very important in games, particularly as games get larger and more complex. Players need a reason for spending twenty hours in front of a monitor, something that will be worth their time and money. How do we draw players into a digital universe and keep them there? This is probably one of the biggest challenges a designer will confront and one that needs perfecting to be a successful designer.

The moment anybody begins to play your game, they will expect to be drawn in from the outset. Whether your game is an adventure, a racing game or a puzzler, your game needs the elements that hold the player's attention and pulls him or her through the game to the end. Ultimately, there must always be a reason why the player is playing your game.

Never leave the player with nothing to do; it is the worst thing that you could ever do in a game that is supposed to be interactive and progressive. The player must always be aware of the next goal, whether it is simply collecting some health, reaching the next checkpoint or obtaining an item. The player must be able to see it, or be informed of its whereabouts one way or another.

Previously I mentioned the beginning of Dungeon Siege. You're not sure what your core objective is, but it's made perfectly clear that you have to make your way to Stonebridge because something evil is sending Krug to destroy the people and the land. This is your first sub-quest as soon as you begin playing. Not only that, the direction you are to travel is made clear and visual. This type of introduction and carrot dangling, if done well, can lure the player into the game. However, the game has to sustain the curiosity and interest for the player by presenting obtainable challenges along the way. There is little point in dangling the carrot if it is unreachable or undesirable.

Longevity

Ok, so you have the player playing your game, and it's going well. What is going to make this player continue playing after ten or even fifteen hours? What makes a player come back to the same game the following day? It's not because he spent his hard-earned cash on it, although that is probably one of the initial motivations for playing. Perhaps it's just pure addiction, or does the player really want to know what is around the next corner, in the next level or what the boss is going to look like in a particular scene?

Intrigue and curiosity are just a couple of examples of how you can reel them in. Of course the gameplay has to be great, but intrigue and curiosity are part of the designer's toolbox.

CASE STUDY   **Dungeon Siege**

Dungeon Siege kept me fastened to my monitor from beginning to end. There are many reasons why it did this. You could say the game is a great piece of entertainment, but that would be too easy. You have to ask why it is so, and how it kept you playing.

FIGURE 5.1   Dungeon Siege

The game was never too difficult that I had to give up playing. The balance was perfect. You were always aware of where you were going, from the use of characters in the world talking to you and feeding you information, to the paths and signposts providing informative feedback. Between each objective, the combat was rarely too hard in relation to the player's position in the game, but just challenging enough to provoke a little thought, strategy and well-balanced action. You were always rewarded when you defeated the foe. The extrinsic utility value (usefulness for attaining other goals) for your tasks is always high in RPGs, because you collect items and money in order to accomplish other goals. For example, the ability to collect large sums of money is a good motivator, because the player is aware that when he gets to the next shop, he will be able to update his characters with better weapons, spells, clothes, mana and health – perhaps even pay another person to join his team. These are all great motivation devices.

Dungeon Siege's progression is perpetual in that it keeps you wanting to see the next location, see what the next creatures are, and discover what the next challenge is. It is always fun, intuitive and, at the end, it leaves you wanting more, which is exactly how a game should make you feel.

Perceptive boundaries

Do we have to have an excuse for a character or other objects to exist in a game and do we have to inform the player of that excuse? Or can a game exist simply as a box of toys to be played with? In today's climate, everything in your game must be there for a reason. If you have a door with a handle, it must function as a door should, either locked or unlocked, and the player be able to open it. If you have a parked car in your scene, make sure you can drive it, destroy it, jump on it, set the alarm off etc. If you can't drive it, be sure to tell the player the car is locked.

The genre, style and context of your game determine its perceptive boundaries. Within a realistic environment the player will expect to see and use things as though they were real. If you provide the player with a feature that allows him to pick up cars and smash through walls, you have to provide an excuse for that to maintain the suspension of disbelief. A good example of this is The Incredible Hulk. Through an experiment going badly wrong, the antagonist possesses a green alien skin condition combined with incredible superhuman strength.

The point is, you can put anything into a game that you want, but it will enrich the experience if there is a reason for it being there. Take the reasons for playing the game out, and the player's motivation will recede.

Hidden secrets

Hidden secrets, or cookies as they are sometimes known, can be a great motivator for the player, but they only work in this context if the player knows they exist. It's great to find them if you don't know they exist, but they can easily be missed if there are no clues. Finding the secrets should be the challenge, not discovering that they exist. Once a secret is found and it is part of a whole, the revelation that more hidden secrets exist can motivate a player even further. One important thing regarding secrets that you must keep in mind: they should never be relied upon for completion of the game. The player may simply miss it and get to the end and find he cannot finish the game.

So what are hidden secrets? They can be anything from a simple cookie/life pod or money stash. Or perhaps it's a shortcut through a level, which is very rare these days. Maybe it can be an object that temporarily enhances the player's abilities. It can also be a part of a whole object that, when collected in its entirety, will give the player something special that enhances his experience throughout the game. Whatever it is, it is usually a reward with a positive value. Occasionally the player might find a secret that's guarded by a monster of some kind. Be sure to balance the reward up against the monster. In other words, the larger the monster, the higher the value of the object should be. You want the player to feel positive when he defeats the monster and finds the object.

There are many ways you can inform the player of secrets without altering the fact that they are there to be found. Blatantly telling the player there are secrets to be found doesn't alter the fun aspect of finding them, so I would recommend you inform the player somehow at the start of the game that they do exist.

TIPS	Secrets

- Build the secrets into the story or game structure somehow. Don't let them exist for no reason.
- Never kill a player when retrieving or discovering a secret.
- Audio clues are great. A good example of this can be seen in Zelda, The Windwaker™. When the player sails past a chest that is sitting at the bottom of the ocean, a sound can be heard right where the chest lies.
- Visual clues are always good. A crack in a wall or a boulder that looks like it might be blocking a large hole. A door that looks different from all the rest, or a movement in the undergrowth that is out of the ordinary. Those are just some examples I have seen in games I've played.

You can hide secrets in all games and I would certainly encourage it. If it's a racing game add an extra car that is hidden. If it's a fighting game, hide an extra move that can only be revealed by pulling off a super-special combo of some kind. Use your imagination, but you should always make it fun and positive for the player. If it's a multi-player game, never tip the balance in favour of one of the players finding a secret. It wouldn't be fair on the player that hasn't found it, so be careful how you use secrets.

Teasing the player

Teasing can also be a great motivator for the player. For example, if you show the player a high value reward through a crack in a wall, or a tiny window, which is unreachable at that point, the player will want to find out how he can get to it. Again, it's all about balance and adding enough value to the object to motivate the player to want to retrieve it. If it's a few gold coins that will do very little for the player, he will most likely not bother. If it's a fundamental piece of the player's toy box that will make a significant impact on the game, he will want it badly. Never tease the player to the extent that he gives up trying to find an object. That is torture, not teasing.

Set pieces

A great set piece can help break the monotony of repetitive gameplay and punctuate the game with key moments. A specific set piece can also constitute word of mouth among gamers, which is always good. Other gamers will be encouraged to get to that set piece in order to experience the same rush.

Designers have to stay within the confines of the feature set, but will need to use them differently to create a break in the stream of normality. Boss characters can be perceived as set pieces because they are a departure from the norm. When designing set pieces you have to be careful not to scare the producer and project manager by introducing new elements that will require additional resources to create them.

EXAMPLE **Destructible scenery**

Imagine a game where the scenery is destructible, which plays a major part in the game's infrastructure. Here is an example of how we could use that technology in a different way, to create a set piece.

Scene: Late at night in a London back alley. Several unearthly creatures are chasing our hero, as he smashes his way through walls using his superhuman strength. Suddenly, as he ponders his next move, the ground begins to shake like an earthquake. Large red and orange glowing cracks appear in the ground when, all of a sudden, the ground begins falling away into a pit of fiery lava.

▶

The idea here is that the player has to run, and keep running, avoiding objects and negotiating scenery while the environment falls away into the fiery lava, which chases him down the alley, eating everything in its path. If the player stops or makes a mistake, he too would fall victim to the lava.

This is just one example of how existing features, like destructible environments, can be used to create a set piece with little additional work or asset creation. We have already decided the player can destroy the environments and we will use the fire assets later in the game. This is not so much motivation but pushing the player through the game, creating tension and panic in the process. It is also one of the oldest design tricks in the book.

We could also build in emotional feedback. Because the player knows he has to make it to the end of alley before being swallowed by the eroding earth, this creates panic and tension in the player – emotional feedback. Once the player reaches the end, there will be a pause to allow the player to save the game before proceeding with his core quest. He doesn't want to have to keep doing that every time he dies, particularly if it has taken more than one time already.

Sound

Sound can be a very powerful tool for grabbing the attention of the player, particularly speech. This is much more extrinsic motivation that's being driven by something external to the player's action. Sound should be part of the design process not just audio treats. If your characters can speak in your game, they can deliver important information in relation to your quests and goals. Sound can also be used to give clues to the player using both negative and positive sounds.

'Black and White' is a fine example of great sound design and extrinsic motivation. At the start of the game, there are many sub-tasks that the player has to solve. You are drawn to many of these by the use of sound and speech. The little people of the world call out to their god (you) asking for help. They will inform you of what has happened and what you need to do in order to help them. Often the speech is delivered with an emotional attachment, which the player can find irresistible. For example the boat builders are very funny and sing their needs to you, but the women who has lost her child is very upset for obvious reasons. These toy with the player's emotions and motivate the player to want to help them.

Once you begin building villages, your little people will continue to call out to you and request things like 'need more wood', for example, which encourages the player to do just that.

Punctuations in gameplay (sub-quests and goals), like boss scenarios for example, are used by designers as milestones and a tool to define a section of the gaming world. They also make great subjects of discussion for players.

Summary

You can see that motivation plays a large part of gameplay and is a tool that is misunderstood and under-used in the industry today. Without motivation, the player is bored and finds no reason to play the game. Here are a few tips and things to consider when including motivation in your game.

WORKSHEET	Motivation

- Each task in your game must have a victory condition with a reward of some kind. This will motivate the player to complete the task.
- The values of the task must be seen to be worth striving for.
- Always make the player feel like he can actually do the task.
- Include various types of motivational devices to lure the player into your game, such as hidden secrets.
- Always inform the player of his next goal and tell the player the value of the reward (i.e. what he will receive) for reaching the goal.
- Make the goals progressive and the rewards equally progressive.

CHAPTER 6

Feedback and fulfilment

In this chapter, I will be discussing two vital components of gameplay and game design – feedback and fulfilment. Feedback is the conduit between game and player. Fulfilment is the follow-up, the after-effect, the sense of achievement delivered to the player by the feedback. Another big challenge for you as designer, is to provide a sufficient balance of feedback and fulfilment for the player. Feedback should stimulate all the senses of the human body – except smell of course although I'm sure that's only a matter of time!

Feedback: The return of part of the output of an electronic circuit, device, or mechanical system to its input, so modifying its characteristics.

Fulfilment: To satisfy.

When designing video games, one of the most significant and important tasks is defining and implementing feedback. Imagine playing a game with no sound, no special effects, no clues, no hints, no directions or the lack of rewards. You might as well switch the monitor off and not play at all! Designers rarely talk about feedback and you rarely see it labelled in game design documents. Designers have to fully understand feedback (although it comes intuitively to some) in order to create a fulfilling, interactive experience. Designers also need to understand what makes humans react to things they see and hear.

When I play games and comply with the rules and boundaries, I want to feel good about my achievements. I want the game to tell me that I am great and it should reward me for my efforts.

Feedback

For me, as a designer *and* player, feedback is one of the most important elements of a game. If you have no feedback in your game, the player will simply get lost, bored and confused very quickly, and become demotivated. Feedback can be subtle and unobtrusive, but it can also be big and thrust at the player, but not always as a result of the player's input.

As I mentioned in Chapter 1, there are two categories of feedback we need to consider. The first is explicit feedback, which is a direct response to the player's input and makes things clear and without doubt. The second is implicit feedback, which is implied and not expressed directly, such as a signpost or a path through a forest, for example. Implied feedback is not always a direct response to the player's input, which contradicts the term 'feedback' to some extent. However, the player is moving through the game, interacting with the whole, and therefore the entire game should be feeding back information to the player. Ultimately the game *must* be telling the player how good or bad he or she is performing, subtly guiding the player through the game, feeding information from the world around him – at all times.

Visual feedback

Visual feedback is generally explicit, nourishing just one of the senses. Because games are a visual medium, visual feedback is very important for games. It is a delicate area for the designer, as it exists on the fringes of art and design. It is important for the designer to document where he wants feedback to occur; because more often than not, it is the result of an action the player has executed. The game that you design could potentially be anything, a racing game, platform game, role-playing game, a simple puzzle game etc. Whatever it is, it will require visual feedback. When the player picks up the control device and performs an action, he will want and need to see the results of that action. This could be a simple walk, or a jump, or maybe you are controlling a car hurtling around a racetrack.

EXAMPLE   **Knight versus monster**

The effect of an action, whether it is positive or negative, requires visual feedback to reveal the modified state. Imagine a scenario where you, the player, are controlling a knight in shining armour, wielding a large flaming sword, and you are about to confront a monster twice the knight's own size. The first thing you might feel is trepidation (emotional feedback), which is good, due to the physical size (visual feedback) of the creature. However, you are still going to do battle with it regardless because you know it's going to be fun.

Let's pause the scene for one moment and focus on what we are talking about – visual feedback in a one-on-one combat situation. This will not happen in a racing game for obvious reasons, but I cannot cover every genre and the principles used here can be applied to every genre. A combat situation may also involve the environment, but we are going to keep it simple and not include any props in this example. Neither am I going to go into detail as regards AI or the interface; this is discussed in later chapters.

Let's continue with the scene. As you move in close to the creature and strike an awesome blow, what can you see in your mind's eye? Hold the vision and now amplify it so it prompts a reaction and you are saying 'wow … how cool'. When a player surrenders to the game and becomes engrossed, they often unknowingly move about in the seat, which incidentally, happens a lot with racing games. Also,

▶

consider how you as the player would want to feel right now. With every blow of the sword, the player should receive feedback from three sources:

1 The first visual feedback is from the player's input directed towards the knight. Depict what the knight is visually doing on the screen once the action is executed. The animation of him swinging the sword has to be fast, look convincing and in context with the visual style of the game while maintaining the feel-good factor.

2 The second visual feedback is from the creature and how it's reacting to the player's input. The AI will mostly determine its movements and decisions, but the monster could also give the player a clue as to how weak or close to death it is for example. This needs to be shown visually, perhaps through animations or by using unobtrusive stats or health meters temporarily displayed on-screen during combat.

3 The third is the visual effect of the actual blow. Consider what you want to see when the sword makes contact with the monster. This needs particular thought if it's a 'special move' or the final blow, for example. Instead of the monster simply flopping onto the ground, it would be far more exciting to see the monster explode into pieces, combined with a big flame special effect, all executed in spectacular fashion. Remember, you want to provoke a reaction from the player as a result of his actions.

Every action needs a reaction and every cause has an effect. Even a single step will activate a sound effect and perhaps a cloud of dust under the characters feet, delivering feedback to the player. The smallest of actions and the tiniest detail is what makes the difference between a good game and a great game.

There is a fine line between what is art and what is design in this scenario. The way to separate them is for the designer to detail what actions he wants to happen, when he wants them to happen and what feedback is required. The artist's job is to make those actions look good based on the designer's instructions.

If you look at the table below, I've broken down and detailed all visual feedback required for the knight vs monster scenario.

Table 6.1 is a very simple example of how you could keep track of any visual feedback you want, and it will inform the person who is scripting the scene what visual feedback needs to be implemented when the player performs this particular action. It will also help the artists, who have to create the visual content for this particular scene, visualise the action and effect.

Many other aspects of a combat situation like this would need to be considered. You might want to consider extending the chart to show what happens when the monster attacks the player. This is usually done on a global scale, but it is worthwhile to occasionally surprise the player with a cookie. For example, in the knight scene, you might decide that if the monster is going to kill you, why not let him pick you up by the leg, and throw you across the environment. This would certainly cause a reaction from the player, because

TABLE 6.1	Knight versus monster – visual feedback

Name: *Knight hits monster type #01*		**Visual feedback:** *Scene 001*	
Input	*Action type*	*Visual feedback*	*Comments*
Player presses 'combat' button	Knight swings sword – #01	Convincing knight animation	Also include a flaming motion blur on the sword as it travels through the air *(visual speed indicator)*
	Sword hits monster – #01	Monster being hit animation. Special effect for hit type #01 *(include the name of the animation if you know it)*	Monster reacts to hit type #1 *(you could also give suggestions of imagery if you are feeling brave)*
	Sword hits monster – #02	Monster death sequence on final blow. Special effect for hit type #02 *(include the name of the animation if you know it)*	Creature dies – explodes into pieces and drops item #17

it's a departure from the normal death routine. These droplets of creativity are resource expensive and are spot effects that the player may never get to see, but it could make the difference between a good game and a fantastic game! Attention to detail will set your game apart.

On a side note, this type of information would probably end up in a database, but all developers work differently and may use various forms of database software.

CASE STUDY	**Dungeon Siege**

When I completed Dungeon Siege, I found it to be a fulfilling experience for many reasons. One of the most striking things about this game is the staggering amount of feedback and how it is presented, from the changing weather to character development and combat feedback.

One negative aspect found in most games but not in Dungeon Siege, is the need to 'load' sections of the game once an area has been completed. Dungeon Siege

▶

keeps playing without pause or delay and you are kept in the universe at all times. This is fantastic and sets precedence on rival products, offering a benchmark for future games. This continuous momentum grips the player's attention and holds him there, which is what all games try to achieve, whereas save-and-load options push the player out of the game, back into reality. Dungeon Siege, however, pulls the player along, transfixing him every step of the way, until something in the outside world pulls the player from the game, rather than the game pushing him out.

This feature is a benefit from developing the game on PC in that it has a hard-drive and the programmers can use it to stream data. The Xbox also has a hard-drive, so perhaps gamers will be seeing more of this in the future – I certainly hope so.

In the screenshot in Figure 6.1, you will instantly notice visual feedback in abundance. I'm not just talking about the special effects that are clearly evident here; there is much more in this scene that is informing the player than you might think:

■ The environment and characters coexist convincingly and look like they belong together. This maintains the suspension of disbelief. Occasionally a game will come along that has badly designed characters which seem to belong in a different world. This can instantly detach the player from the game. The player

FIGURE 6.1 Dungeon Siege visual feedback

may not consciously realise what is wrong, but subconsciously will know that something doesn't look right with the game. However, when it works, as in Dungeon Siege, it is a combination of great game design and art direction, working together to portray a convincing world, providing visual feedback and eliminating players' doubts.

■ All characters have shadows, which also provides the player with feedback. Shadows fix characters to the environment; without them, the characters appear to float around the scene.

■ It is patently obvious in the screenshot that the characters are in combat:
  – The character's posture is in full combat mode.
  – The bodies of the enemies are strewn all over the floor, also signifying successful combat.
  – The most obvious visual feedback is the special effects, which emphasise the action.

■ If you look at the floor, you will see a path leading into the woods. This will help the player with navigation and orientation once combat is complete.

This is all part of the global visual feedback within Dungeon Siege, and punctuates the effect of the action the player has input and the extrinsic feedback the world is presenting to the player. The point is, just by glancing at the image, you know what is going on in this particular scene by subconsciously identifying the features I have pointed out, even though it is a static image. A designer will need to be conscious of all explicit and implicit forms of feedback and not rely on artists to automatically build them in.

Exercise

For a simple exercise, you might want to consider creating a visual feedback chart, like Table 6.1, for the Dungeon Siege screenshot in Figure 6.1. Look at it closely and apply the same principles as before. Remember, there are multiple characters in this scene and you have to consider all of them, the various types of character, all of their animations, special effects and anything else that might be relevant to the scene.

More visual feedback

If your game requires the player to race a vehicle around a track, and the player can crash, don't allow the player to simply crash and spin off; it's not very exciting and it's what all past games have done. If you do this, eventually the player will get annoyed because he is not performing well, and if this happens often, he may even give up playing.

Alternatively, if your car smashes into a barrier, is then sent hurtling into the air, smashes through some scenery and then explodes on impact, this is far more spectacular, almost stuntman style, and the player may not mind crashing as much, because it is almost rewarding to do so. Of course, a lot more resources are required for the second example, but be creative and re-use resources like this where you can.

'Visual feedback' can also be small and unobtrusive, but still providing the player with feedback and information. A good example of this is shadows, of which we have seen one example in the Dungeon Siege screenshot above. 'How can shadows give a player feedback?' I hear you cry. Well, in many games where the designer requires the player to jump, the player may rely on the shadow as a way of locking his position to the ground. I always feel that this is a cheap cop-out, mainly because I want to control the character, not a shadow. I personally would much prefer the designer take time and position the camera effectively, allowing the player to see where he has to land. If you have jumping in your game, make sure the programmers give you plenty of control over the camera, allowing you to position it in the best possible location for the action. However, implementing the shadow to ground positioning, can be a good back-up device for the player.

Shadows can be used to create atmosphere. But if they are dynamically lit, they can be used as an effective, subliminal navigational device. If you are travelling through a sunlit or moonlit environment, the shadow being cast from the avatar can guide the player through the environment. If the player is informed of the position of the shadow in relation to the light source (providing it's not moving) he will know the direction he is travelling.

Simple effects can help solidify the character into the world and provide feedback to the player. Dust on the feet when a character is running and jumping. A small screen shake, if the character falls from a great height. The character reacting to the world around him. These are all useful subliminal types of visual feedback. You might want to attract the player to a particular place; in which case, ask the artists to include an animated object near where you want the player to go. It could be a flickering torch outside a cave, or a glowing health pool off the beaten track, or perhaps a subtle change in the brick texture to indicate a secret passage.

One aspect of games that many designers find difficult to balance is killing and punishing the player character. If your game has a central character that relies on a health reservoir to exist, the balancing of the depletion of this is tricky. This should be relayed to the player at all times; don't try and hide the status of your character's health. When the player's health is reduced to almost zero, send a signal to the player signalling the fact he is about to die! If he is engrossed in some action, he won't have time to glance around at stats, so a familiar audio warning combined with on-screen feedback will suffice for this particular scenario.

Use of colour

Using colour as a form of visual feedback is an excellent way of informing the player. We see it in our daily lives, particularly when out on the streets – traffic lights being the perfect example of colour-coded information. As a driver, you see the traffic light and you know red is stop and green is go. Red and green are the most common colours used in many aspects of life as they represent many things, particularly red. As well as stop, it can also mean danger. In the UK, the green and red man signify walk and don't walk, understandable even to a child. This method of feedback can be applied to games, particularly action games that require quick reflex action that leaves no time to read text. You can also use many more colours to relay information to the player; providing there are not too many to remember, the player will interpret them very quickly.

To summarise, visual feedback is a tool a designer can utilise to dispense information to the player, from awe-inspiring special effects, to passive subtleties that draw the player into the game.

Audio feedback

There was a time when audio was often neglected in the design process. Often it was forgotten about until the last moments in the development process, by which time any sound would do. Today however, it is just as important to consider sound at the start of your design, as it is to consider any other element of the game.

As an experiment, play a game with the sound turned off and you will soon realise how important sound can be. Developers often leave little time to design the sound, which can potentially spoil an otherwise great game. Sound can also be used as a gameplay device as well as the traditional playing music and sound effects. In Chapter 5, I discussed how sound can be used as a tool for motivation, but sound also gives the player important feedback, feeding another of the human senses.

There are many games around which totally rely on sound as the game's core feature set. In the arcades and on consoles, you will have seen the dancing games that require you to tread on a dance mat in time with the music, directed by on-screen instructions. Far too energetic for me! I think I'll stick with the thumb-pad and mouse!

Tetris uses audio feedback as a tension builder. As the blocks fall from the top of the screen and land on top of one another, the wall gradually gets higher, eventually touching the top of the arena, signifying game over. The player's task is to eliminate horizontal strips before the wall builds to the top of the screen. However, filling horizontal strips of blocks clears them from the wall. Unless you are successful in negotiating the blocks to fill the gaps across the screen, the music tempo quickens as the wall gets closer to the top, and injects a sense of panic into the player. This really works well – observing an anxious player as the music kicks in speaks for itself!

Atmosphere

The designer is the visionary of the design; therefore, it is important that the designer influence the atmosphere he wishes to convey in every section of the game. In Chapter 5, I described a scene where the player is being chased through a dark London alleyway. In this particular scene the music should reflect the action: it will need to have pace, inject fear, panic and urgency into the player, but it should also be in context with the game. Imagine a sound-track from a cute puzzle game – placing it in this scene just wouldn't work!

Perhaps the theme of your game is realistic horror, where the player is creeping around an ancient haunted temple, for example. The music should be creepy and build tension. It should be haunting and induce the sensation that something is about to happen. When it does … BAM! The sound hits you. Movies often do this and it can be good practice to study them. Many design-ers I know (including myself) collect movie soundtrack CDs for inspiration.

TIP

Look at a movie that is similarly themed to your game, and analyse how they convey the action, tension, sadness etc. using music and sound. Sound alone (with no visuals) conjures thoughts and emotions. Try playing different pieces of music, close your eyes and note down what thoughts come into your head whilst listen-ing. Many designers I know listen to music when writing, it stimulates the imagination and helps them visualise the content of their game.

CASE STUDY   Case study: Luigi's Mansion

Speech is an obvious choice to convey information quickly and easily to the player. When playing Luigi's Mansion, which is targeted at a young audience, pressing the 'A' button on the controller will tell Luigi to call out for his missing brother Mario. The 'A' button is primarily an action button and is context-sensitive depending on where Luigi is standing. He can open doors and examine things with the 'A' button, but when Luigi is not close to an object that he can interact with, he will call out for Mario. It sounds fairly simple, but when you first do this, you think it's great and each time you press the button, it sounds slightly different. Kids love it because it expresses the emotional attachment between Luigi and Mario and deliv-ers it to the player. Luigi's voice is quivering as he speaks which is also important, because it signifies that he is scared, which children can also relate to. This is a per-fect example of simple, effective audio feedback. With one simple press of a button, it reminds the player of the core objective, in a fun, interactive but trans-parent way that doesn't interfere with the gameplay … perfection!

In Zelda, The Windwaker, there is a section where the hero must creep past several guards under a barrel. Providing the guard doesn't see the barrel move, the hero is safe. If the guard detects the barrel moving, the player suddenly hears a drum roll and is warned that the guard suspects something is wrong. If the player remains still, the guard will forget he saw anything and continue guarding, giving the player a 'chance'. This is another simple example of how sound can be used as a gameplay device.

Remember, you can attach sound to anything you like. For example, perhaps your game has a huge scary-looking dragon in it, but the nature of the dragon is somewhat passive. Let's imagine, as a sub-plot to your game, that somebody has stolen the dragon's jewel from his pile of treasure and the dragon is very upset about it. If the player approaches the dragon and the dragon is weeping and sobbing, the player is less likely to be aggressive towards it. The weeping and sobbing would most likely induce curiosity and the player will want to know why it is upset even though it is a dragon, which is synonymous with danger.

Often in movies the music will change to portray characters in a particular way, or to convey danger. For example, when the protagonist appears on the screen, the music may become more uplifting and positive. This is just one device used by filmmakers to subliminally make the audience feel for the characters.

To summarise, sound is just as important to your design as any other element to the game. Use it as a tool, as a device to lure the player, to shock the player and induce atmosphere and tension. Study the way movies use it and make it interactive.

Action feedback

Another important type of feedback a game should deliver is the reaction from the player's action. On consoles, the player activates the action through a game-pad. I know what you're thinking now, 'the feedback is the vibrating pad'. No, that's not what I mean!

When you control Link in Zelda, for example, you feel like you are really moving him through the world. When you swing the sword and destroy something, you can feel it through the pad. The combination of the actions you perform and what you are seeing on the screen has to gel in order to feel the feedback. It's this type of feedback that is the hardest to master, even for seasoned designers. It is so crucial that the actions are tweakable and time should be embedded into the schedule for the designer to refine them. It could mean life or death for your game if this is neglected! Action feedback should be intrinsic and generally occurs in a system when something is fed into it. You feed in the actions and you get the feedback of those actions.

Good examples of this type of feedback can be seen in racing games. Have you ever played a racing game and your thumb has started hurting because you pressed the buttons too hard? This generally happens because you're not getting the correct feedback. Your car is not turning sharply enough and you tend to press the stick harder, thinking that it will turn more … but it doesn't! Often in racing games, the physical motion of the car is the reaction of the player's input, and you can feel if it's right or wrong through the controller. Sometimes the car can feel like a lump of lead, and sometimes it is as light as a feather. The physics of the car is the feedback and it is important to get the balance right. Allowing people who love racing games to play it at the 'first playable' phase will help you to decide if the balance is right or not.

Take a game of football from a spectator's point of view. Although it is implicit, you are constantly getting feedback from the game. This is particularly notable when either team scores a goal. This can be seen as positive or negative feedback, depending which team you support; both will provoke an emotion in the spectator and the players.

Going back to the combat scene with the knight and the monster. When the player attacks the monster and gets a direct hit, the player needs to feel that he has performed a mighty blow. How is this achieved? Firstly, you have to make sure your animation conveys the power of your action and then exaggerate it. When the sword hits the target make sure you explode the monster and you have a sound effect to match it. All of this combined, if done well, will make the action feel good. Also remember that unless you implement all types of feedback, you may not get the full effect of the action, so you need to make sure everything is implemented before making a final decision as to whether it works or not.

You may also want to consider what happens if the player misses the creature and hits a stone floor, for example. The sound effect will certainly be different as will the special effect, so the feedback you deliver to the player will be different. Perhaps sparks will fly instead of an exploding monster.

Non Player Character (NPC) feedback

You will need to ask yourself the following question when you begin designing the population of your world. How will the creatures of my world communicate to the player? How will the player know if they are friend or foe? This may seem obvious, but in a lot of games, it's not always clear. The AI should provide a vast amount of feedback for the player, but the player can't rely on this for affirmative feedback.

Let's go back to our knight and monster scenario. It's obvious the creature is no friend by the way he is leering and screeching at you. The huge sharp claws, drooling pointy teeth and the spiky cosh he's brandishing may also have something to do with it! Instantly you can 'see' that it is no friend of yours! Now, how does the player know when to attack the monster? Has the creature got a vulnerable state, a weakness where a window opens to allow the player to attack?

Games that present boss adversaries are a good example of creature feedback. The monsters generally have a pattern that can be studied and learnt. The pattern usually reveals an opening where the player can go in and inflict an amount of damage. This window of opportunity has to be reasonably obvious to the player, otherwise attempting to defeat it will become tiresome, and eventually the player will stop playing. Bosses, and other creatures, should pose a challenge and be valued in relation to their position in the game cycle, but they shouldn't be too difficult that the player gives up trying. The fulfilment is in the defeating and progression, not in the repetitive trying.

The player should be able to identify good and bad non-player characters visually, simply by looking at them. To achieve this, it is good practice for a designer to colour-code the characters, or adorn them in a particular fashion so the player can instantly identify them when he is playing. Friendly characters might look passive, while the foe might look aggressive, be animated aggressively and use harsh colours like red, for example.

Accumulative feedback

Accumulative feedback is an expression that I have invented – you can call it what you like. It's the depiction of progression the player achieves throughout the game's life cycle. If you simply drop a world in front of the player and tell him to play to the end, he will want to know how he is getting along in the whole scheme of things.

Accumulative feedback happens explicitly in RPGs and adventure games. When the player begins, he or she generally starts with the most basic avatar with limited weapons, objects and abilities. Accumulative feedback occurs when the player is rewarded for killing monsters and completing other challenges, and the monster drops items or the player is rewarded for the challenge. These items are usually cash, general game objects, weapons and clothes that the player can use or, as in most RPGs, sell for cash. This accumulative effect often provides the player with accumulative abilities when playing the game, and is food for character growth, thus providing feedback of progress.

Look at the screens in Figure 6.2 and 6.3 for a perfect example of accumulative feedback. Figure 6.2 is my avatar near the start of my game, and Figure 6.3 is the same avatar closer to the end of my game. The most obvious and striking aspect you notice initially is the visual build-up of the character. This is the ultimate garb this character could wear at this stage of the game, but the character accumulated and wore many garbs, each increasing in value, as the game progressed.

If you look at the stats, you will see a dramatic difference in the two screenshots. This is my reward for playing the game, which was accumulated over the duration of the entire game. I decided she was going to be a melee character and you will notice that her magic stats are very low. This is because I didn't practise using magic with this particular character and therefore there was no accumulation of magic skills.

Zelda also provides accumulative feedback in many aspects. One in particular is Link's health status. When you begin the game, Link's health capacity is at its lowest maximum level. As you play the game, you are occasionally

FIGURE 6.2 Dungeon Siege avatar at conception

FIGURE 6.3 Dungeon Siege avatar at completion

rewarded with, among other things, sections from big hearts, and once you have collected four of these sections you make a whole heart and your maximum health capacity increases by one blip on your health bar. This has been carefully managed and balanced to stop the player increasing the maximum too quickly.

Accumulative health capacity

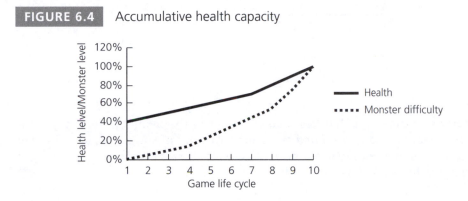

Figure 6.4 depicts a game that relies on a health system for the protagonist and the accumulation of the size of his health reservoir might look something like this. You can see the balance between maximum health capacity and the monster difficulty level over the life cycle of the game. When the player begins the game, according to the chart, the player will only start with 40 per cent of his maximum health capacity. Also, the monsters near the start of the game will be easy to defeat, but as the game ensues, the monsters get progressively harder to defeat. The player, however, will collect more health blips to increase his maximum health capacity to aid him defeat these more difficult beasts. Of course, the player won't simply be given extra life, he has to earn it one way or another.

Figure 6.5 shows you what can happen if the designer fails to give the player what he needs, when he needs it. If the monsters got progressively harder as depicted in the chart, but the player's health maximum remained at 45 per cent throughout the game, the player could not sustain his life to enable him to defeat the monsters towards the end. It would begin to get difficult at around 70 per cent the way through the game. It would simply get to hard, too quickly, which often happens in games. Sound familiar?

The same mechanism is used for Link's magic. As the game progresses, monsters and puzzles get larger and harder to defeat. By rewarding the player with extra magic blips for the tasks he has completed, the game provides the player with additional capabilities and power, which enables the player to defeat the larger, more difficult monsters. This is accumulative and has a steady rise from the beginning to the end of the game.

You can apply this methodology to any element within your design. For example, the maximum health capacity could be replaced with weapon func-

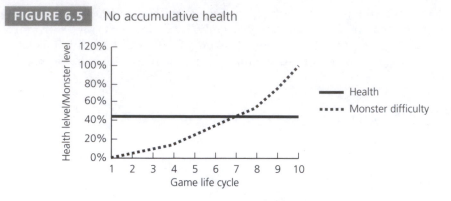

FIGURE 6.5 No accumulative health

tionality and the effect that the weapons have on the monsters. Therefore, the player's weapons do more damage towards the end of the game, allowing the player to defeat the monsters more effectively. He would accumulate bigger, more powerful weapons or upgrades to allow this to happen.

Emotional feedback

Emotional feedback is always a tough nut to crack. If you can trigger laughter, crying or gasps from the player's input, you have done exceptionally well.

There is a scene in Zelda, Ocarina of Time where Link leaves his village for the first time. He steps out of the village and onto the bridge that leads away from his homeland. Waiting for him on the bridge is a girl. The conversation is the classical 'I don't want you to go' scenario, but it is done exceptionally well for a computer game. You actually feel for the female character and the younger game-playing audience will relate to it completely.

Jak and Daxter offers a light-hearted comedy duo. One character is the serious hunter and explorer, while the other is the wisecracking comic. They work together as a team to defeat the villains, offering comical feedback as they venture through the world. This is great emotional feedback. However, unless you have somebody on your team who can write a great script and understands comedy, don't attempt to put it in your game. You are a game designer, not a comedian.

Fulfilment

Fulfilment is difficult to quantify in a video game, because it's the feeling you get when you have just solved a puzzle, beaten a big behemoth or completed a difficult section of the game. The challenge should be balanced sufficiently so the player feels challenged, but the solution is not out of reach, so when it is solved, the game rewards him and the player feels fulfilled.

Often when playing games a player will come across a puzzle he cannot solve, or a monster he cannot kill, and it takes him much longer than anticipated. This is not fulfilment, it's frustration, followed by relief once you are onto the next section. Fulfilment is when you confront the behemoth, fight him fair and square with all that you have earned and learnt, eventually killing it, sending it shattering into pieces after striking the final blow. Watching the visual feedback (special effects) as it dissipates into the digital world around it, consequently injecting a sense of fulfilment.

This sense of fulfilment is particularly notable at the end when the player has completed the entire game. The end is part of the game, which some developers spend least time on. The game is a whole, and therefore the ending should be as important as the beginning. After spending arduous hours playing a game, the last thing you want is a downbeat ending and to be cheated on the last hurdle. If anything, it should be balanced to allow the player to defeat the enemy using the skills he learnt through the game, but a sense of fulfilment and a longing for more is what you need to leave with the player. A player would sooner play a short satisfying game than a long thin game that is void of content and unfulfilling.

Summary

You should now understand now how important feedback is to a game and the designer's consciousness of it as he creates the design. Feedback is the language of games, the communication from player to game and back to player.

> **TIP**
>
> You can create a table like Table 6.2 to keep a track of *all* the feedback needs of your game. When typing your design, you may want to keep a blank copy by your computer and jot down any ideas that come into your head as you go along. This way, once you are onto your feedback, you can type it into a chart like this one.

 There are other elements to take into consideration when the player jumps. For example, what happens if Norbot jumps off a high platform and misses his target? Will he die completely on impact? Will he be injured, or will nothing happen? You may want to consider a life span for your character, in which case maybe a little health will be deducted from a long fall. The table below is purely for feedback purposes and shouldn't be confused with other aspects of the game.

TABLE 6.2 General feedback chart

Game-title: Norbot Action	Date: 30/06/2002 Reaction	Feedback: Visual	Audio
Press jump button	Character does a jump once	■ Jump animation of main character ■ Splintered particles for surface landing	■ Varied grunt for take off ■ Electronic movement ■ Thud for landing on different surfaces
Press action button ,	Context-sensitive to situation		
	■ Fire laser	Shooting red bolt out of the robot's right arm animation is played	Laser bolt – sound effect
	■ Activates switch	Norbot is aligned with switch and the 'push button' animation is played	Switch activated or switch deactivated sound played
	■ Etc.	Etc.	Etc.

The feedback worksheet below lists points and questions you may want to consider.

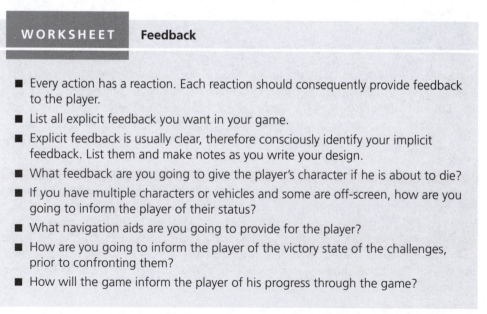

WORKSHEET **Feedback**

- Every action has a reaction. Each reaction should consequently provide feedback to the player.
- List all explicit feedback you want in your game.
- Explicit feedback is usually clear, therefore consciously identify your implicit feedback. List them and make notes as you write your design.
- What feedback are you going to give the player's character if he is about to die?
- If you have multiple characters or vehicles and some are off-screen, how are you going to inform the player of their status?
- What navigation aids are you going to provide for the player?
- How are you going to inform the player of the victory state of the challenges, prior to confronting them?
- How will the game inform the player of his progress through the game?

CHAPTER 7

Rules and boundaries

In Chapter 1 we discussed how rules and boundaries work in a game like draughts. The problem with board games and most other non-video games is that the rules are accessible. In other words, they can be altered, interpreted wrongly and you can even add your own if you wish. Apart from the fact they are not played inside a computer, this is one of the fundamental differences between non-video games and video games. Without hacking into the game code, which is a pastime of some hardcore gamers, or using a specific hardware device, the player can't generally change the rules in video games; they are embedded into the program and only accessible by the programmers during development.

In this chapter we are going to examine how rules and boundaries are applied to video games and how they can shape your game.

For any game to exist, digital or otherwise, there needs to be a pre-defined set of rules. One of the problems with video games is that, more often than not, the game fails to inform the player of the rules. Most games print the external rules in the manual but more often than not the player will never read the manual. Few designers actually think about how to inform the player of the rules of the game, and simply expect them to pick up the control device(s) and immediately know what to do. Often the rules are vague or don't work properly due to bugs or other technological and schedule-related ailments. The good news is, these sorts of problems are becoming less frequent as the industry formalises the process of game development.

You often hear that the simplest games are always the best, but the simplicity is often defined from the rules and how they are executed. If you delimit the rules before the programmer begins working on the game, the better your game will be. The programmer will code the rules exactly as it has been documented, which will be the foundation for your game. The documents will never be the final rules because they will need testing. However, I have seen programmers begin writing a game grasping only an idea, with no documentation whatsoever.

What is a rule?

We all know what rules are. For example, the rule of law is the restriction of power by well-defined and established laws. Some of the best rules are the tried and tested kind, the ones you know work and are hard to break because they have been around for so long. Some of these kinds of rules are beginning to appear in video games.

We've all heard the expression, to rule the roost, which means to be in complete control. A society without rules and regulations would be chaotic, to say the least. To maintain a balanced, disciplined society, we need rules for every human to follow and to be aware of. The same applies to video games, although not on such a grand scale as life itself!

There are rules for everything in video games, some of which the players take for granted. Players simply learn, for example, that if they open a treasure chest something nice is going to pop out. The rule here is that if the player does open a treasure chest, it should act the same way each time this action is executed. Of course you can have different types of chest that behave differently and you can change the reward that pops out, which usually increases in value the further you get into the game, but the delivery of the reward must always happen. To break this rule, you might have treasure in the chest for the first quarter of the game, and then suddenly slip a monster into it that can hurt the player. You might think this would be a surprise – no, it's not a surprise, it's breaking the rules and unfair to the player because the given rule was that the chest in question was always positive, not negative.

Once again, you must be consistent with your rules. Breaking the designer's rules is not encouraged. However, bending, stretching and modifying the rules are, particularly while prototyping. There are rules for different stages of game design which can be categorised into three sets:

1 The designer's rules
2 The player's rules
3 The player's invisible rules

The designer's rules

One of the biggest problems with video game development is that you can't test rules and boundaries until you can actually play the game, which for some can be very frustrating. You can theorise and test the design on paper etc. but it is never like the real thing. Therefore, in order for your team to move forward with prototyping as quickly as possible, it is necessary for the designer to create a basic set of rules. These are 'the designer's rules', as I like to call them.

What are the designer's rules? These rules will not just define how the game works internally, but will control what happens to your external design during the design process. I feel it is important to assign these rules to your design process because it clarifies the direction the game will take and defines boundaries, which nobody should move beyond.

When a designer begins the mountainous task of designing his game, he will generally define a basic set of rules that will help him shape and mould his gaming world. It doesn't matter what type of game you are designing, whether it be a racing game, an RPG or an action adventure game; you will need a set of rules to begin designing.

I have been in a situation where the team have been locked in a ridiculous Catch-22 situation. The artists insisted that they couldn't build the environments because they had no guidelines or rules, and if they did start, they would only have to do them again and they didn't want to keep building them over and over. I can see their point, although it is a little naïve to think you will never have to redo any art. However, the designer was arguing the fact that he had no environments to test his game design in. To me this was unprofessional and led to a ridiculous situation that was solved very quickly. This situation is less likely to happen today, but highlights the need for design rules. We calmed the situation by creating a design rule that stated we would always build what we call 'box maps' prior to building the artistic version of the environment. In Chapter 8, I discuss 'box maps' in detail. They are basically an environment constructed from primitive shapes, simply textured, and can be used for prototyping game design.

I have seen a team of artists build environments that have little or no relationship to the game design. This was a result of the designer *not* defining a basic set of 'designer' rules to begin with.

Another important reason to have designer rules is to keep the game consistent. You will hold the vision more so than anyone else and you will know the 'player rules' like no one else and therefore, it is important that nobody else has direct input without filtering it through the authorities, i.e. you!

Let's imagine for a moment that you are designing an action adventure game. You have your ideas burnt onto your brain cells and now you need to begin shaping them into a design. Let's assume that your hero can throw objects. Within your design you can't simply type 'The main character can pick up objects and throw them'; it doesn't work like that, the description is too vague. It will beg a mountain of questions. You need to apply rules to that statement.

The first thing you need to do is explain the interface – how the player will pick up the objects and what buttons he will press to perform the action. The text in your document might go something like this:

EXAMPLE   Designer rules

Using the context-sensitive control mechanism, the player can pick up objects within the environments and throw them, but only under these conditions:

- The object is not part of or attached to the environment, i.e. a lamp post, street sign etc.
- The hero is not superhuman and therefore cannot pick up anything out of context, i.e. a car.

▶

- Contextual items are things like tables, chairs, bins etc., something that a normal person could lift and throw. A list will be defined.
- Upon throwing a pick-up-able object, it is always destroyed and evaporates out of the gaming world (see feedback information for each object).
- When thrown, the objects can do damage to creatures and each item will have a damage value assigned to it (see object list).
- The cost to the player will be that he cannot run, only walk, while lifting an object.
- Etc.

These simple rules define what happens when the player picks up and throws an object in my imaginary game. I have assumed certain things here. For example, I have stated that the object the player picks up must be in context with the world, which is real-life in this example. However, your character may be superhuman and able to pick up large objects, in which case you must clarify that. Remember, you must be consistent with your rules. If in one level the player cannot rip up lamp posts and then in the next he can, this would be a major flaw in your design. The players will notice and the suspension of disbelief would come crashing down.

Let's change the controlling idea and say that our hero is superhuman. He can pick up cars and throw them; this is not the main gameplay theme, but a by-product of the design. This feature opens up a whole new bunch of issues. If you design a street lined with shops, what happens to the shop windows if the player throws a car into them? Do they smash? They do! Ok, that's great, and it would be great visual feedback too! But now you have another problem. Every time a player smashes a window, he will want to go into those shops. You have just quadrupled the workload for the artists. You might want to reconsider your design rules. If you try and fudge the problem by placing invisible barriers in front of every smashed window for example, you have just entered Lamesville. Maybe there are other ways you could fix it?

1 If you insist on having throwable cars and smashable windows, you could place metal barriers in front of all the windows – this might just work.

2 Avoid placing cars where there are windows close by.

3 Number two above, combined with rooting the player to the spot so he can't walk with the cars once he has lifted them. This rooting can also be the cost to the player for picking up the car.

4 Maybe the programmer could put in a piece of collision code that detects windows; that way the cars can veer away from the windows!

Do you see what is happening here? I am trying to accommodate a function while compromising other elements of the game. Not only that, it is so much extra work for the team. When you get into this situation, you know your idea is not working within your game world. The rules are simply too ridiculous to follow. Rethink your idea.

Let's turn it around and make the by-product the central feature of the design in that the player has to intentionally smash the windows and wander through the shops, in which case you will need to base your design and rules around that controlling idea. Looking at it from this perspective makes it far easier, in that you can design your environments with this in mind while also limiting your boundaries.

Can you imagine not having rules in place and going into pre-production? The wasted time would be enormous. You must always have a set of consistent rules when you begin designing. They will inevitably mature and grow as the game develops, provided there is vision, a starting point and an end.

For every feature of your game, you must apply these rules, eventually binding all rules together, making them work as a unit. Once you begin prototyping and balance your features, they will eventually become the player's rules and you will set them free into the wilds of gaming frenzy.

The player's rules

Ok, so you've set your rules free. They are out there ruling for themselves, defending against the best and the worst of them. So how did they become the player's rules?

When you're developing your game, it grows and matures. You sculpt it into a fun-packed, feature-filled interactive experience. The designer rules you used to create your world now govern your feature set, forming a complete game. Once this happens, the rules are set in stone. They cannot change even if you wanted them to. Your car will have a fixed top speed and the physics will be balanced to perfection. Your main hero will jump at a fixed distance and your magician will take X amount of hit points before he dies. These rules will remain intact until the end of time! Of course they can alter during the gameplay. The hit-points on your magician may increase and the speed on your car may also increase, but these changes will be controlled and sit within the rules and boundaries you have set.

Game players will play your game. They will learn the rules you have embedded into the design. They will become familiar with the distance the character can jump and the speed in which the tanks move across the play field. The player will learn them until he has perfected them and they work for him every time. They become his rules and he controls how he uses them.

Whatever happens, when designing your game, don't change the rules halfway through the game. You can enhance the rules, elevating the gameplay and player to a new level, but *never* change a rule so it is unrecognisable. Enhancing your rules is like putting fuel injection into a car or adding ketchup to your burger, it's the same, but better! In Zelda, Link can always jump and it is always consistent. The gaps that Link can jump never exceed a certain distance and it is always obtainable. The Tesla coils in Command and

Conquer always have the same range in every mission. The control mechanism for Luigi's Mansion remain the same throughout the game – it just gets better!

The point is the player should be able to learn to play your game. Each feature should be well defined and moulded so the player can remember what it does and how the player can use it in the gaming world you have defined. The player becomes masterful at the skills you have crafted using the rules and boundaries.

Invisible rules

There are many rules that the player simply never sees. These are 'invisible player rules'. The player will unwittingly abide by them but he will not consciously be aware of them unless they become a problem for him.

More often than not, games are set out on a grid system. Programmers and designers use this grid to calculate where things can and cannot move to. To emphasise my point I'm going to go back to the designer's rules. In our imaginary game, our hero can push objects around that would subsequently allow the play to reach higher places. The designer will create a rule that says, when these objects are pushed around, they must move around on a grid system, stopping at predefined boundaries with each push. Zelda, Tomb Raider™ and Soul Reaver™ all do it, as do many others. Once the rule has become fixed and the animations have been created, it becomes the player' rule. But this rule is invisible. The player never sees the grid in the game, but when he pushes those objects around, the animation and timing is composed to work within the grid system.

The reason why designers do this is to make it easier to define where entities need to be placed and programmers use it for navigational purposes, among other things. It also makes life easier for the player in that he will always push his object to the correct place. Games that allow the player to push a little at a time often become frustrating because he has to line the object up with a target and it gets fiddly. So the grid system works to simplify the process, but is invisible to the player.

Other invisible systems that are used throughout most games are waypoints and find-paths, which are mostly used for navigational purposes. Points are plotted throughout the worlds and NPCs use them to move around. Of course, the player never sees these points; they are invisible. The designer, however, may apply some rules to these points. For example, if your game has doors that the player can open and shut, the designer may well place a point in front and behind the door to provide instructions for NPCs. When the NPCs are instructed to go to the door, the designer can tell the NPC to carry out a series of instructions that will tell it to open the door, walk through the opening and close the door using a script. We'll cover scripts in more detail in a later chapter.

You will invariably have objects peppered throughout your world. Find-paths and waypoints can help the NPCs avoid these objects and make them appear intelligent, when in fact they are simply following an invisible curved line and performing some basic instructions governed by the rules.

Trigger boxes are another common element to games. These are invisible boxes placed strategically in the environments of your game, which, when entered by the player, will trigger an event. This event could be anything and is usually controlled via a script.

Breaking the rules

Unless you build it into your design, the player shouldn't be able to break the rules of your game. They are hidden and the player is forced to accept them as they are. In external games, such as chess and draughts, you can cheat or modify the rules, but this generally breaks the game altogether.

When implementing your rules, implicit rules will emerge due to a combination of other explicit rules you have created. Imagine a character-based game where the main character can collect power-ups that allow him to travel double speed, for example. Now, unless you have thought it through thoroughly, you will not have realised that this adds an extra rule to your game. Not only can the character travel at twice the speed, but this subsequently allows him to move twice the distance, which may well have been the intention. However, a good example of how it can break the rules here is this. If your environments are designed for him to travel around at normal speed, once he gets double speed he will have the ability to get to places you may not have wanted him to. I've seen this happen.

In this situation, the designer will end up fudging the game by placing invisible walls, pulling the environment around or placing the power-up thinly to stop the player from using them in certain locations. This is another reason to define your rules and test them in a simplified version of your game world.

You can find cheats on the Internet that will allow access to the game code, and there is hardware that will plug into your system and break the rules for you. These devices usually give you unlimited health or access all areas etc.

Rules govern your feature set

This is fairly straightforward … or is it? You can get very particular with this and start writing rules for everything. However, I believe the more defined your world is, the better the game will be. In Norbot, the robot can fly. In the design you will find the rules that define his flying ability. For example:

- Forward speed Norbot travels when flying
- Negotiating speed, when moving sideways or up and down
- Maximum distance travelled based on energy consumption
- Maximum height allowed
- Etc.

I think you get the idea, but to be sure the rules work as you expect, they need to be implemented and put into practice. It would be very important that the programmers have a good idea of what is supposed to happen before they start coding the 'Heli' feature for Norbot. It is more than likely that the database will change throughout development, but you must have the initial rules as a starting point.

Boundaries

Just like rules, boundaries exist all around us in our daily lives. Our homes, our places of work, our cars, all occupy a finite measurement of space, defined by boundaries. In the context of games, a boundary defines a perimeter of an entity to which it relates. The entities can be anything from the whole environment, to a small object within that environment. Whatever it is, it has boundaries. These boundaries provide the player with spatial limitations.

World boundaries

When you design and build an environment for your game, there will be a place where it will stop, a boundary or perimeter. Developers often discuss non-linearity in games, but I have yet to play a game that isn't linear or restrictive one way or another. Movies are linear, books are linear and so are

FIGURE 7.1 Maze environment

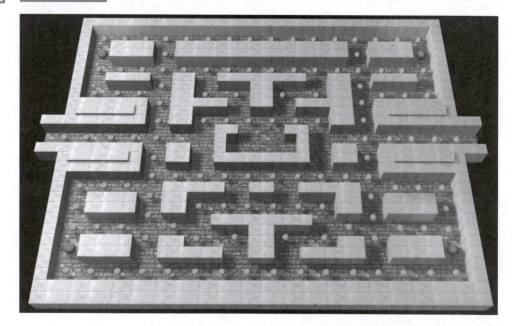

games. You can make a game appear non-linear using a few little tricks and by providing the player with options, but ultimately they are all linear. Environment boundaries prevent the player from venturing into no-man's-land, outside of the game world, which is no bad thing.

All of your world objects, characters and vehicles etc. will have boundaries. In other words they will have collision data that solidifies them and gives them presence in the world. Just like the draughts example in Chapter 1, deliberate arena-based boundaries can define your playing space, or the stage for your game, and this type of boundary is an important part of the structure and mechanics of a game that requires a defined arena or maze. Many games throughout video game history have used this type of boundary. Space Invaders® used the screen as its playing field. Galaxians did the same and Pac-Man defines it even further. The essence of Pac-Man relied on visible boundaries. They formed a maze of pathways for the player to travel along in order to avoid ghosts.

Linearity in games

What has linearity got to do with rules and boundaries? A linear game has the most obvious of all environment boundaries in any game. A linear game will go from start to finish forcing the player along between two points,

FIGURE 7.2   Donkey Kong

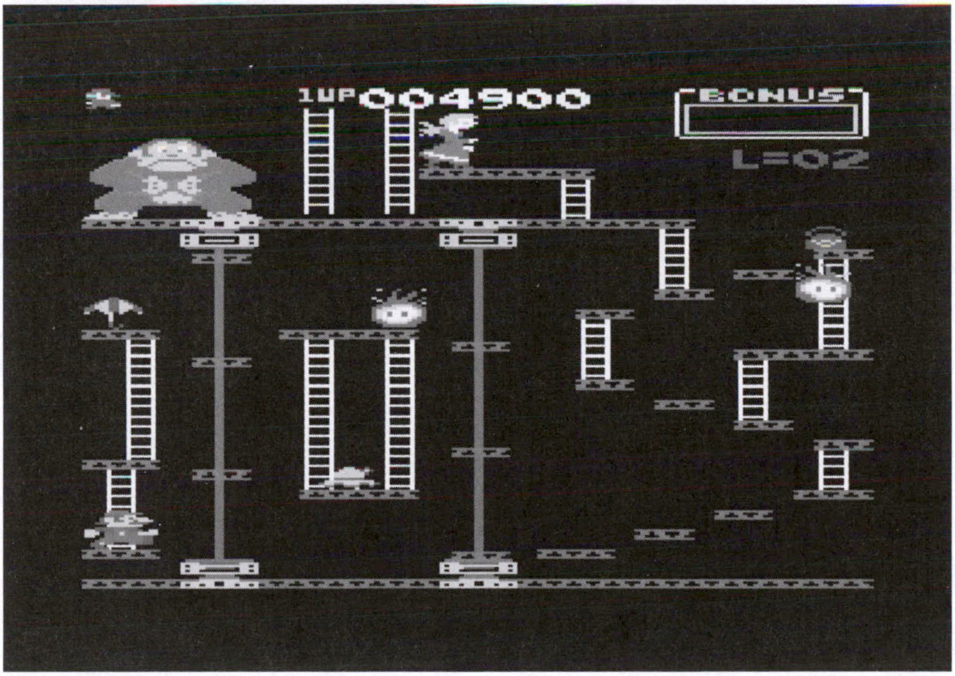

challenging the player with obstacles along the way. The boundaries force the player along this path with no other route, except doubling back down the path he came, available to the player. Although I believe all games are linear in one form or another, some are very obvious, while other games disguise it very well and can appear non-linear to the player.

Traditionally most platform games of old were linear in the truest sense. An example would be the 8-bit version of Donkey Kong. The player would start at the bottom of the screen and make his way to the top; that's about as linear as it gets! There are, however, several routes the player can take on his way to the top, but the start, the end and the boundaries force the player along in a linear fashion.

Games of today have a similar structure, although grander in scale, technical capability and visual content, but they too, generally speaking, have a starting position, an objective and challenges, which the player has to overcome following the rules and boundaries defined in the game. The player cannot pass through the defined boundaries except through a connection point, or 'portal'.

To understand linearity, a good analogy would be this. The structure of game environments is like a string of bubbles as shown in Figure 7.3. Each

FIGURE 7.3   Linear environments

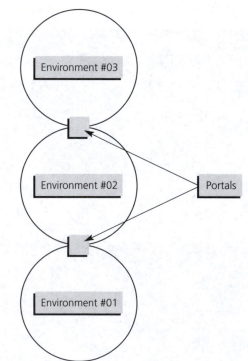

bubble represents a different environment and/or areas of gameplay. Also, each bubble is attached to other bubbles at predetermined points (the portal) around the perimeter of the bubble. The player can roam around inside each bubble, sometimes in a straight line but at other times freely, but to pass into another bubble the player must pass through a portal. It is within each bubble that the game will feel non-linear to the player, offering different routes from portal to portal, all governed by rules and boundaries. Such a multiple-route scenario does require more resources when it comes to creating this perceived 'extra' world, and producers and the like would rather not pay for it unless it enhances the game. Figure 7.4 depicts the bubble scenario that offers different routes for the player to follow.

FIGURE 7.4   Multiple paths

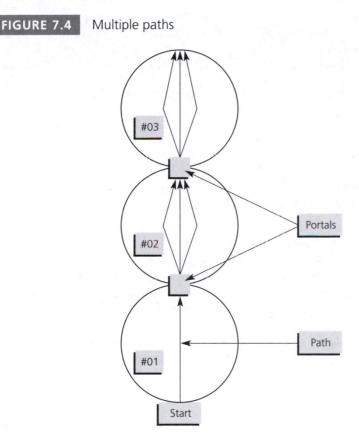

A game like Command and Conquer also has portals, but they are presented as a reward and not a physical exit. When the player has completed one scenario, another scenario becomes available. A game like Tetris exists within just one bubble and the boundaries of the playing area are defined very clearly.

So how do we recognise a portal? A portal is not always a physical entity within a game. However, many types of game entity can represent a portal. For example, adventure games often use bosses to guard a portal. This is probably one of the biggest clichés in game design, but once the boss is defeated the portal to the next environment opens.

Invisible boundaries

Every entity within your game will have a boundary – usually referred to as collision. Sometimes invisible boundaries can appear for no reason. I gave a good example of this in the smashed shop window scene above. Invisible boundaries, without a visual presence, are one of the worst things you can put into a game. At some time or another you must have been playing a game when you walked into nothing! Why do they do that? The illusion of disbelief is once again shattered.

There are many reasons why this happens, including:

■ The designer has deleted a chunk of the environment and didn't have time to patch it up.

■ The environment is destructible, but the designer doesn't want the player roaming everywhere.

■ Level designers became complacent.

■ They couldn't think of a better way to define the end of their worlds – you know, the ones they say are perpetual and non-linear!

Expanded collision can have a similar 'throw down the controller' effect. This is characterised by a collision boundary being larger than the object itself. In a platform game you must have experienced walking up to an object or standing over a ledge when there was nothing beneath your feet. Why don't they just make the object bigger? One theory, as regards the wider ledge collision, is that the designers believe that by making the collision bigger the jumping will be made easier, because the player will always try and jump before they reach the edge to avoid falling off. Therefore, they compensate late jumpers by making the collision bigger. Just make the ledge bigger … jumping is not fun.

The hub system

This system is very popular in adventure games such as Mario and Zelda and has been reproduced by many designers around the globe. The hub system is similar to the bubble approach described above, except the areas of gameplay are laid out organically to give the impression of an open, free-roaming world.

If you take our bubbles and arrange them as I have done in Figure 7.5, you can clearly see the connections. A central environment, called the hub, allows the player potentially to access any environment he wants, when he wants. However, to maintain a good structure, good progression and balanced gameplay, all environments cannot be open to the player at the start of the game.

FIGURE 7.5   Hub system

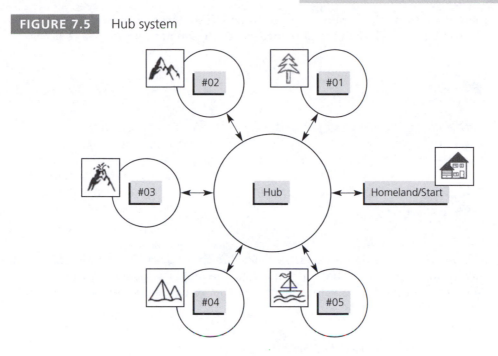

This is especially so if your game is being targeted at the mass market. A hub-based game generally requires that the player find an object of some kind, which usually represents a key, to open each environment leading from the hub. There is generally a lobby of some kind to allow the player access to the level for an introduction or perhaps to discover what is required to enter.

The environments themselves are often laid out in a similar organic fashion as the world hub system. The player enters the environment, performs all the tasks until he comes out at the beginning brandishing an important object. At the start of each environment there is usually a locked door, and behind it, a big bad boss character that holds the key to the next world. But to unlock that door, the player must traverse the environment to retrieve the key to open the door and confront the boss. The boss door is deliberately placed at the beginning of the world to allow the player to get to it easily should he die trying to defeat the boss, or wish to save and return at a later time. This way, the player doesn't have to travel through the environment each time he wishes to confront the boss. Of course this very much depends on the type of save system you put into your game, which should be decided early on in the design process to avoid potential problems such as this.

So, even a hub-based environment is linear. Once the game is complete the player can roam anywhere he likes, but he is still limited by the boundaries of each environment and the portals that lead from the hub.

One thing you need to be wary of is travelling across the world of a hub system. If you are in one area and you need to get to the other side of the world, make sure you offer a teleport system of some kind. The teleport system must be an integral part of the world also. Zelda, The Windwaker uses tornadoes to pick the player up and move him across the hub quickly, and place the player close to the entrance of the chosen area he wishes to access.

> **TIP**
>
> When designing your game, be sure not to drain your brain trying to think of ways of making your game non-linear. You'll be wasting your time! The whole point of 'game' is making it fun, focused and challenging as the player is pushed and pulled towards a core objective. Giving the player freedom with no rules or boundaries provides no conflict, no focus and the player is left wandering aimlessly. Rules and boundaries force challenge and conflict; use rules and boundaries as a tool.

Somebody said to me recently that The Sims games are non-linear. No they're not! They have their confines and the player is pushed towards a core objective; coupled with mini-objectives, the structure is very familiar, only presented differently.

Problem solving and puzzles

Puzzles often provide the game with temporary boundaries that can be pushed down by the player by solving the puzzle. Most puzzles are a correlation for a key and locked door. These types of boundaries can help define the space, balance and rhythm of your game. However, making your puzzles too difficult and ambiguous can upset the balance and rhythm, making the game feel bloated by jarring the flow of gameplay. Any ambiguity that may arise through the design of your puzzles, if not too problematic, can be corrected when balancing and testing your game.

If your game does have puzzles, make sure they are defined clearly for the player. I always say to designers that the player should know how to solve a puzzle and the fun should come from doing it, rather than figuring out how to do it. In an interactive environment, there is no fun in figuring out how to solve puzzles. You don't want the player sitting, staring blankly at the screen doing nothing while he thinks about how to solve it. Tell the player how to solve it, but make it challenging and fun!

Let's imagine we are playing an action adventure game set in a fantastical setting and the player's next challenge is to retrieve a golden amulet from inside a stone chamber. Here is an example of puzzle ambiguity and how not to present your clue:

To retrieve the Golden Amulet, you must first unlock the sacred chamber and free the inhabitants.

Uh … right, ok! At first you think, ok, that makes sense. But suddenly you are hit with a massive blockage. You wander aimlessly for hours trying to find the chamber and then you have to figure out how to unlock it. This inevitably ends in frustration. The clue should have read something like this:

To retrieve the Golden Amulet, you must first unlock the sacred chamber in the lost valley. King Takutta of the Trinky Tribe holds the stone key to the chamber and sits through each day waiting for a worthy challenger. Defeating King Takutta will allow the challenger to open the chamber, and free the inhabitants. The inhabitants will then give you the Golden Amulet as a reward for their freedom.

TIP

Avoid any unnecessary, out-of-context, frustrating puzzles. If your clues are too ambiguous, you will create a permanent boundary called a wall, and the player will simply walk away. I can remember traditional adventure games used to suffer from this a great deal. You often had to retrieve many items and fashion them together in some way, to form another unrelated object. This newly fashioned item would then be used later in the game, but it would never be clear what it actually did or how you were supposed to use it. Most of the time was spent trying different combinations until it worked. That's not gameplay!

Summary

Rules police your gaming world by enforcing laws onto the player and capping them with boundaries, while giving the player choices. When you write the design document, you must clearly define the rules and boundaries for every action in your game. Here are some things you may want to consider at the design stages:

WORKSHEET   **Rules and boundaries**

- Define the designer rules that govern your challenges.
- Modify the rules until they work in the game.
- Track and manage implicit rules.
- Hand over the rules to the player.
- Define your boundaries.
- Ensure your boundaries are part of the gaming world, i.e. not invisible.
- Ensure the player can't get an easy victory by cheating the rules.

CHAPTER 8

Rewards and structure

Back in the days of gun-toting bounty hunters, the reward for bringing in the villains was cash – pure and simple. But it was never easy and the stakes were always high, often fatal! The motivation of cash drove them to the edge of life and death.

So what are rewards in the context of games? Rewards are items, treats or Easter eggs given to the player for successfully performing tasks and completing challenges throughout the game. They come in various forms, and are awarded in many different ways. For some, a reward can be a beautifully edited cut-sequence after killing a boss monster, for example. Or perhaps a reward is receiving a power-up to a weapon. In a racing game it could be receiving the gold cup after winning a championship, or the keys to another, more powerful car. There are small rewards also, like packets of energy, ammo collectables, or in the case of Dungeon Siege, armour, gold, weapons, magic spells, health, mana potions etc. Designers call them different things, such as power-ups or pick-ups. I simply call them rewards because that's what they are.

Whatever the reward, I always feel the player has to earn them; you should never give them away. There was a time when rewards were simply left lying around in the environments for the player to run over and collect, but that's simply too easy and it doesn't make sense. I feel that in order to acquire a reward, the player has to successfully complete a challenge or an action of some kind, no matter how big or small. Once the player has performed the action successfully, he is then rewarded, but the reward should be commensurate with the action or challenge performed.

You can use rewards for motivational purposes, to lure players into areas of your game, but the reward must ultimately have a purpose. You might think I'm being too critical and that it's only a game, but the truth of it is, to be successful everything must work, bind together and blend into the architecture of the game. Rewards and other elements in a game are not simply put there for a player to collect or interact with; they have a place and a purpose in the gaming world. This effort will make your game more absorbing and plausible.

We have discussed motivation in Chapter 5, and rewards go some way towards motivating the player. If you were to never get rewarded for your efforts, why would you bother playing? Because it's fun, that's why. But without the structure and balance of rewards, the game would soon become dull and disjointed, there's no doubting that. Can you imagine confronting a boss monster? You step forward, your palms are sweating and your heart is racing, then battle commences. *Several* battles later, you finally kill it … but then nothing. The game simply moves on and drops you into the next section without so much as a wink or a nod. Is killing the creature reward enough? I don't think so. I would feel deflated. I want a juicy fat reward for killing that thing. After all, it killed me several times! Give me my just deserts!

There are many ways you can deliver rewards to the player. Do not just blindly place them for the player to stumble across. You can hide rewards on NPCs (non-player characters) for example, and the only way to retrieve that reward is by disposing of the NPC, tricking him into giving it to you, or earning it. All are potentially very worthy challenges. This forces the player to use the skills you have designed into the game. Always remember, the bigger the risk, and more difficult the challenge, the larger the reward should be. Boss characters traditionally carry important game items like keys and weapons, whereas smaller NPCs carry health pods, or magic pods, all of varying value but all equally important to the game structure.

There are many examples of rewards, from collectable items to visual treats, but they all need to be embedded within the structure of the game. It also depends on what type of game you are designing and the context of your world. A game is open to your imagination and you can do anything you like within the rules of the world you create, providing you are consistent.

Reward types

As I said before, there are many different types of reward that can be given to the player and for many different reasons. Some are integral to the existence of the character and what the character does within the game world, while other type of reward push and pull the character through the game, and some are purely visual and develop a story. Whatever your game genre, you will have rewards and they will need serious consideration and placement within your universe.

Gameplay rewards

Gameplay rewards are the most important of all. These are rewards given to the player for completing challenges, performing actions successfully and achieving goals, such as killing baddies, winning battles, winning races, claiming your opponent's base and defeating bosses etc. The actual reward can be many things, depending on the type of game you are playing, but they should always assist the player to further his movements through the game. If it was a big challenge the player completed, such as defeating a boss for example, the player is usually rewarded with something that elevates the gameplay, like a new weapon, a new class of vehicle or a new magical power. Using rewards, the game can progressively climb the structure it is built around and advance the player to higher levels.

Hidden rewards and secrets

Personally, I like these kinds of rewards. I find that it adds hidden depth to a game. When the player discovers a secret room behind a mirror, or he smashes down a wall to reveal a hidden chamber, or simply shakes a piece of furniture, often there is a reward waiting for the player to collect, or it may drop out and fall in front of the player. The reward could be anything, but it is always nice to give the player something that moves him up a notch. It is good to give the player something that he's not expecting, or something that he regards as 'cool' but has limited use or a limited life-span perhaps. However, the rule still remains that it has to be part of the world and work within the structure of the game. You should never make up a reward just for the sake of it; it will look and feel out of place.

The reward doesn't have to be a physical object either; it could be a secret passage or a shortcut to a later part of the level. These types of treats are great because they arouse conflict within the player. On the one hand he has an opportunity to jump ahead of the game and advance more quickly, but on the other, he may miss some great gameplay in the section he's bypassing. If you have this in your game, and the player chooses the latter, you must ensure the player is not evading an important item that is crucial for progression. That wouldn't be fair and the shortcut would have a negative effect, not positive. Remember, rewards should always benefit the player.

Racing games often hide cars and tracks within the game. If the player does something out of the ordinary, like drive around the track backwards for example, the game will often reveal new routes, tracks and cars. Players like this, and it also provides longevity. This type of reward was very common in 8-bit games, but today they are few and far between.

Zelda has an abundance of hidden secrets and chambers that are full of wealth and treasures for the player to discover. One notable feature was the fairy pools, which when found would completely replenish Link's health. These fairy pools were peppered all over the game, hidden away for the player to find, but not essential to completing the game. If the player had an empty bottle in his inventory, he could collect a small fairy and carry it with him. This would then be used automatically to completely replenish Link's health when drained away after a combat session or two. It is a perfect example of a hidden reward that if found, could enhance the gameplay, but is not essential for completing the game.

Impetus rewards

Some rewards pull the player through the game, driving him to seek the next reward and luring him deeper into the game. When you play a game and see an object that is out of reach, or locked behind a door, this motivates you to solve the puzzle and retrieve the item, particularly if the item is of value, which of course it always should be. The reward doesn't have to be something made up just for this purpose, it can be an existing reward type, but you must remember the structure rule and the world rules.

If, for example, the reward you place is normally found inside an NPC, then it has to be the NPC you place, not the reward. You can invent a different type of NPC that carries a different reward, providing the new NPC fits within the social structure of current NPCs. Abide by the rules of your world and be consistent. Impetus rewards, however, are often visible and can be seen by the player, but are often out of reach. They are placed like this deliberately and a challenge is usually placed between the reward and the player. The player, driven by the potential reward, must overcome the challenge in order to retrieve it.

Impetus rewards can also be used to guide the player, by pulling him in a certain direction like a moth to a light. Adventure games use this device; Luigi's Mansion has a good example at the beginning of the game. After completing several mini-tasks, a line of gold coins appears on the floor at the top of the stairs. They lead to a locked door. The player is led to believe that he must be able to open the door; he just needs to figure out how.

Impetus rewards serve two purposes:

1 They pull the player towards a goal.
2 When the player reaches it, he is rewarded.

When a player plays a game, he will hopefully be drawn in, mesmerised and give little thought as to the reasons why the designers put objects and rewards in the places they have, which of course, is the intention.

Visual rewards

Visual treats, particularly full motion video (FMV), have caused many a debate within the development community. Some say they should be banished because they are not what games are all about, while others believe they should be kept and welcome them because they offer a deeper experience for the player.

I personally believe that visual treats are a must. However, a long boring movie at the start of a game that attempts to justify why the protagonist exists in the gaming world is simply ludicrous. A short sweet visual burst is a refreshing break and can serve to drive the player further into the game.

Let's begin by looking at FMV. It makes my spine quiver just thinking about the money and time spent creating this stuff. I am as guilty as the next man, but you learn from your mistakes. If you can avoid it, do so; if it isn't part of the game and only serves exposition, then lose it. One of the reasons why FMV rarely works effectively in games is because we don't know how to make it. Game developers on the whole know little about camera placement, visual storytelling or dramatic effect, or the many techniques used by cameramen and storytellers to feed information subliminally.

Combine this lack of knowledge with poor animation and poor lighting and you have a flat, meaningless series of images that the player will become frustrated with. Also, taking the player out of the game into this higher resolution FMV breaks the golden rule – hold the player's attention. FMV instantly pushes the player out of the game and the hook is lost. This doesn't mean FMV shouldn't appear in games, but it has its own place, which we shall discuss later.

Let's move onto real-time cut-sequences. These are far better and more acceptable than FMV. They're usually rendered using the game engine and intended to look like the game, therefore the risk of losing the player's attention is reduced. It does not, however, reduce the quality of camera placement, scene construction and lighting etc. Somehow, these things have traversed from FMV, and we still know little about this medium. However, things have improved recently and occasionally you will find a game that uses it well and for the right reasons.

The original Tomb Raider used cut-sequences to reasonable effect. Once the player activated a switch, the camera would cut away and show you the results of the action. The problem was, the player had no idea where it was in relation to his character; there was no establishing shot. So unless you knew where the object was that the camera was pointing at, it was pointless. However, a good cut-scene done well can be rewarding and informative for the player.

Great visual rewards, like big explosions, special effects, giant monsters and things a player has never seen in a game before, can all add to the 'cool' factor of a game, and potentially reward the player for completing challenges. However, from a gameplay perspective, these are peripheral and implicit and you should never dwell on them for too long.

Structure and placement

The delivery of your rewards should run parallel with the key events in your game and at the correct altitude of difficulty. Look at Figure 8.1. I have used just a couple of reward examples that you might find in a game – energy and weapons. These may not be relevant to your game, but you can apply the same principle to most object-based rewards.

Every reward/item in your game has a value. The value of the item is determined by the effect it has on the characters and the game world at the moment in the game's life span at which the player collects it. For example, if it is a weapon, the value of that weapon is attributed to its power, or capabilities. If you look at Figure 8.1 you can see that each time a new weapon appears in the game, it subsequently decreases in value as the game progresses, so a new weapon or an upgrade is required. If the player is halfway through a game and you reward the player with a weapon that has the same power and function as something from the start of the game, it is already use-

FIGURE 8.1   Reward balance

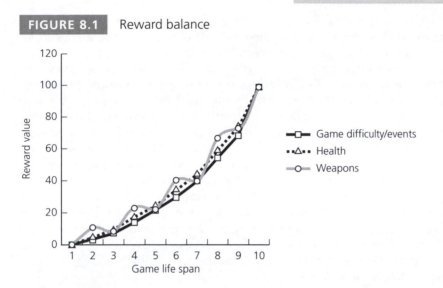

less and has no value whatsoever. This is because the bad guys in your game have progressed, the difficulty level has increased, and therefore the player needs better, more powerful items.

By the time the player reaches the end of your game, he should have collected all or most weapons, ultimately ending up with one that does maximum destruction, thus reaching maximum power. It's all about balance, which we'll go into more detail about later.

So, your reward/item must have a value. If it has no value then take it out of your game, it shouldn't be in there. The level of difficulty and the placement of the reward within the game's life cycle will reveal its value to the player. Therefore, when designing your items, you must consider item longevity versus item value. If the player collects a weapon, you have to be sure it can do its job up to the point the player collects the next item. If an item goes beyond the point in which it has no value, your game will become difficult and frustrating for the player. You must upgrade or change the item before its value turns negative.

Let's assume the player must collect life pods of some kind in order to sustain his existence within the gaming world. If he doesn't retrieve any life pods, he will keep dying because he would have no life to sustain any damage. So what do you do? You balance the game so that when the player needs a life pod, he receives it. Perhaps you will want to extend the maximum life the player can receive too. Zelda does this extremely well and is built into the architecture of the game. Zelda even rewards you for collecting rewards. When Link receives an extra life container, the game makes a big deal of it that essentially says 'you're great' to the player. This is good, but the game would have made sure the player had earned that container. Subsequently this reveals to the player that his character is growing, progressing through the game. Link gets stronger and more powerful and is able to do more things with more items. The designer has embedded all of this into the structure of the design, and has delivered it using rewards.

One of the reasons why games get hard too quickly is because the designer hasn't taken reward progression into account. Platform/adventure games are often guilty of this. The energy reward at the start of the game most likely serves its purpose, but the designer fails to build on that. He'll make his creatures or tanks do more damage to the player, but will often keep the energy reward at a consistent level, so therefore the player dies much more easily. This lack of reward progression is often the case with ammunition resources also. The player will get a box at the start of the game, and the same box will keep appearing at the same frequency, which is expected to take him all the way through the game. This is not good because the player will use so much more in the latter stages of the game. As you can imagine, this only leads to frustration.

Most of these issues are corrected when balancing the game, but if you don't accommodate the ability to increase the reward value, then the balancing becomes much more difficult.

Reward growth

As I said before, all of your rewards should be part of the game structure and if you take any one of them away, your game will eventually fall apart, which is how you know that your rewards are working and part of the game structure.

We've discussed giving your rewards a value, but you also need to understand how important your rewards are to the player, and how and when you need to deliver your rewards. If you look at Figure 8.1 again, you will notice I have included an energy value curve. I am using energy as an example because it is universally understood, but in your game it could represent fuel for your cars, fruit, gold or ammunition. Whatever it is, the principles are the same.

I am going to use the hit-point system and lay some very simple ground rules to emphasise the point I want to make here. Let's set up an imaginary game and everything in it can be valued between 1 and 100 as depicted in Table 8.1. In a real game, the numbers would probably be in the tens of thousands to give the designer the flexibility to fluctuate, but I want to keep it simple here. Now, in our imaginary game, we will give the very first level a gameplay difficulty rating ranging from 1 through to 10 to keep it nice and simple. Small sections of my level will be assigned a number between 1 at the start, and 10 at the end. Foe number one in this location has a minimum hit-point value of 5 scaling up to 10. But in the first section of the first level, they will start with a value of 5 and by the time the player reaches the end of the level, they will increase to 10. We will also use, just for fun, hard dried peas as our ammunition that can be shot from our weapon, the peashooter. Each pea has a damage value of 1 and the peashooter has a value of 5. Simple!

So you get a table that looks something like Table 8.1.

| TABLE 8.1 | Hit-point system |

Level	Level value		Foe #01 hit-point value		Foe #02 hit-point value		Pea damage value	Peashooter value
	Min	Max	Min	Max	Min	Max		
1	1	10	5	10	10	15	1	5
2	11	20						5
3	21	30						5
4	31	40						5
5	41	50						5
6	51	60						5
7	61	70						5

You might be asking yourself, 'why did he give the peashooter a value?' There are two reasons I did this. The first is so that I know whereabouts in the game I can place it based on the difficulty level. If you observe Table 8.1 you will notice my first level of difficulty ranges from 1 to 10. Therefore I know I can place my peashooter somewhere at the start of that level, with basic ammunition and it will work fine. Beyond that point it may not be as effective or even completely useless in subsequent levels. You will notice I never upgrade the peashooter all the way through the game. However, there is no reason why you can't upgrade it as a reward, but for argument's sake and to reveal a point, it is going to remain the same throughout. The second reason I didn't increase it is that I will use the peashooter value combined with the ammunition value to determine a damage total.

That was the set-up, now we come to the action. With these simple values applied, you can determine that if the player hits a foe successfully with a hard dried pea, just once, he will kill it. How? Taking the damage value of the pea (1), and multiplying it with the peashooter value (5) will determine the damage caused to the foe. In this case you will notice it will be killed with one pea at the start of the first level, but towards the end it will require two hits. Of course this is visually represented in a game and you don't actually see the numbers. The foe that has increased to a hit-point value of 10 may also have a slight graphical change to represent his greater resistance to peas.

At this stage, it's the next bit that interests us most – the dying of the foe. Now, at this point in our imaginary game, when the foe dies, the designer can, if he wants to, look at what the player has in his inventory, i.e. energy, dried peas etc., and decide what to give the player. If the player has almost run out of peas when trying to kill the foe and got hit himself just once, the foe could drop a stack of 5 peas that individually has a hit value of 1. This would be a good decision because not only does the player need to replenish his stock of peas, it would also make the player feel good about what he received and would encourage him to continue. On the other hand, the player may have found it incredibly easy to kill the foe with his first hit. In this situation, the designer might decide to give the player something else other than an inventory item, like a visual treat perhaps. For example, the foe could die in a number of amusing or spectacular ways, and pulling out a particular funny one at this point in time, that the player hasn't seen before, will reward the player and provoke an emotional response. However, this type of cookie reward can only be used sparingly. During development little time will be given to 'extra' asset creation because of the time and money spent to create them. They also take up space in the game and can only be used a few times before losing value, so they are often deemed unworthy. As the game progresses you will find yourself using less of these treats because you will gather more rewards and have more room to move among your reward pool.

Now let's fast-forward towards the end of the first level of our imaginary game. We are now in an area that has a difficulty value of 10. The peashooter is starting to feel a little feeble and the dried peas are becoming somewhat pathetic. As suspected, your foe has smartened up and they now have a hit point value of around 10. They may have also learnt how to defend themselves perhaps with an additional shield, and therefore, the skill required to kill them has increased. The additional armour or shield is a good addition as it provides visual feedback of a difficulty level increase in the enemy, and to take them out with hard dried peas that only do 1 damage, requires more effort from the player. Not only that, your energy is decreasing faster because they hit harder too, although I have not shown that on this chart for simplicity's sake.

Now is a good time to increase the value of our rewards (Table 8.2). At the end of the level, I would hide an energy container that increases the player's maximum energy limit. Once the player collects it, it also fills the energy reservoir to its maximum. I would also upgrade the peas to something like

TABLE 8.2 Hit-point system extended

Level	Level value		Foe #01 hit-point value		Foe #02 hit-point value		Walnut damage value	Peashooter value
	Min	Max	Min	Max	Min	Max		
1	1	10	5	10	10	15	2	5
2	11	20	5	10	15	20	2	5
3	21	30						5
4	31	40						5
5	41	50						5
6	51	60						5
7	61	70						5

walnuts that does perhaps damage 2 per hit but can still only be fired from the peashooter. This gives me a single-shot minimum damage value of 10. Now, foe #1 has become easy and it feels satisfying to take them out with my walnuts. I drop a bunch of these guys in the level to add a flurry of action, providing the players with an adrenalin rush. Then I would up the ante with foe #2 soon thereafter. These guys are a little tougher, requiring between one (damage 1–10) and two (damage 11–20) walnut hits to take them out in level 1 and 2.

When it comes to balancing the game, these numbers can easily be modified to alter the game's difficulty level. Increasing the number of baddies and hit-points, and decreasing the damage value of the peas, walnuts and peashooter, will make the game much harder. Doing the opposite will make the game much easier.

You may also want to think about what would happen if you ran out of peas and walnuts. Well if that does happen, and the possibility is clearly there, then you would need to think about how you would resource the ammunition so the player can replenish his ammo reservoir without frustration and unfairness seeping into the gameplay.

The scenario I have just described is very basic and only touches on how and when you should deliver rewards to the player. It also gives you some insight into how complicated balancing a game can become. Most games, like Dungeon Siege for example, have attributes bestowed to a reward that are complex and add diversity to a number of character-attributes and subsequently their abilities. The reward attribute might well affect the character's strength if the reward was a melee weapon, for example, or armour rating if it was a piece of clothing.

Rewards in current games

I am going to look at other games and see how they reward the player and the type of rewards they award. We will also look at the situations in which these games deliver their rewards in order to clarify the structure of a good reward system.

Dungeon Siege

The reward system in Dungeon Siege is complex, as it is in most RPGs. The reason for this complexity is inherent in RPGs' core game structure, and often based around character progression, combat and the increasing value of rewards. However, Dungeon Siege has been designed to be accessible to non-hardcore gamers, more so than most RPGs, which I believe has made this type of game more enjoyable.

Before I go into detail with the reward system in Dungeon Siege, I will give you a brief but necessary overview of the character types and attributes that will make understanding the rewards a little easier.

The player is given the opportunity to control a party of diverse characters such as mages, sorcerers, sharpshooters and champions etc., all with the ability to hone their own skills and attributes. The type of character they are reflects their combat expertise, although any character can train in any skill by using the associated weapons. A combat mage, for example, will be much better at combat magic than a sharpshooter, while a sharpshooter will be particularly good at ranged and **melee** combat.

As well as their combat characteristics, the designers have also given them additional attributes such as strength (physical power), dexterity (agility and accuracy) and intelligence (mental aptitude). Each of these attributes often determines whether a character can use a given weapon, wear armour, use shields and cast magic. Incrementing the strength, by combat, also allows the characters to wear bigger and better armour and carry heavier and more powerful weapons as the strength increases. The character's strength value will also inform the player if he can use a weapon that he has bought or collected that requires strength, simply by looking at the weapon's strength value.

All characters have a health and mana attribute. Mana is the fuel reservoir for magic power and allows characters to perform magic, providing the character has high enough magic and intelligence attributes. Health is the reservoir of life for characters and when depleted, will see the demise of your character.

So what has all this got to do with rewards? Let's look at one type of character in particular like a champion for example. A champion that is good at melee combat requires great strength to be successful at it. Using the character's melee combat will rid the evil from Ehb, and the character's strength will consequentially increase. As each creature dies, they often drop rewards, in the form of weapons, armour etc. that the player can collect, use, or put into his inventory.

The player will most likely be using a weapon of some kind. Each weapon has a 'damage value' and if it's a ranged weapon, it will also have a 'range (distance) value'. As the player progresses through Ehb, he will be rewarded with better weapons that will have a greater damage value than the one the player is currently using. In Dungeon Siege, they are delivered in abundance, which is great because if one character can't use it, another can. If it has little gameplay value at your current stage you can sell it for gold at the next trade post, which can be contributed towards a better weapon later in the game. All rewards, including clothes, weapons, shields and magic spells etc., hold a monetary value that can be exchanged for cash. But the value of the reward's functionality within the game structure is what's most important for the gameplay.

Here are a couple of examples of the different weapons I used when playing the game, one from the beginning of the game and the other from about three quarters into it. Figure 8.2 shows you the weapon I was using early in my game. As you can see it was a mace and it had a random damage value of between 10 and 13. The damage value of the mace doesn't change, but the creatures do get tougher. You can also see there are no conditions attached to the mace because it is an early weapon.

FIGURE 8.2 Dungeon Siege weapon value

Figure 8.3 shows you the bow I was using later in the game. It had a damage value between 41 and 55. So you can see an obvious progression there. Because it is a bow, it also has a range limit of 12 metres. The range limit can improve with better bows. However, this bow does require my character to have two other attributes progressed to a certain level – strength at 13 and dexterity at 18. As you can see, looking at the attributes of my character, I fulfil those requirements, which allows me to use it.

The monetary system in Dungeon Siege backs up the reward drops nicely, in that you can stop at shops at regular intervals, and buy health, mana potions and additional equipment with the gold you yield. This is actually a crucial feature in Dungeon Siege because if you don't find and collect that all-important weapon, for whatever reason, and you couldn't buy items, it might well topple the balance of gameplay into the realms of negativity.

Dungeon Siege also places containers, like chests and crates, throughout the world, and these too hold rewards. You will often find these chests sitting behind a swarming mob of creatures and they can only be opened once the creatures are dead. Again, this is rewarding the player.

This process of defeating monsters, increasing character attributes, and delivering rewards applies to all characters in Dungeon Siege and is an ongo-

FIGURE 8.3 Dungeon Siege weapon value

ing process from beginning to end. As a player, managing all of this is complex and demanding, but very rewarding and absorbing.

Those of you who have played Dungeon Siege will know that it is far more complex than I have described here. For example, the player can control seven characters at once as well as a donkey, all of which can carry hordes of juicy gifts that the game awards to the player in abundance. Some rewards can have what we call a modifier that can positively or negatively modify characters' attributes. All of this is handled in such a manner that the player will learn each element as he progresses, and is drawn into the game without being overwhelmed by stats and other complexities at the start.

Luigi's Mansion

You couldn't have two games that are as different in game style as Dungeon Siege and Luigi's Mansion. The reward system in Luigi's Mansion is not as complex as Dungeon Siege, for various reasons. One obvious reason is that Luigi's Mansion is targeted at a much younger audience than Dungeon Siege and therefore deliberately avoids such complexities. Dungeon Siege is also an RPG developed on the PC and very few RPGs of this nature successfully traverse the void between PCs and console. This is often due to the intricate interface designed around RPGs that is difficult to emulate on a games console.

Dungeon Siege allows you to carry a vast quantity of rewards for seven characters and a donkey or even two donkeys. This on a console could become a technical nightmare due to the limited space when saving to a cartridge. Luigi's Mansion requires the player to carry very little and stores a fraction of the information required for Dungeon Siege.

All of these issues, and more, need to be considered at the design stage, not halfway through development or near the end, which has been the case before now. The game is then constructed to take advantage of the limitations of each platform and genre, which can generate creativity. So let's look at the rewards in Luigi's Mansion and the effect they have on the game structure.

There are very few types of rewards in Luigi's Mansion, but the rewards it does have are there for a reason and have been carefully built into the architecture of the game, just like the rewards in Dungeon Siege. Luigi's Mansion has the traditional health pod rewards in the shape of a heart and is awarded for various actions. The heart shape of the reward is also visual feedback because it informs the player, particularly a younger player, what that reward does as soon as it appears – there is no question. If you study when and where these rewards are delivered, it becomes apparent that they're not always in the same place, and I suspect the designers are delivering them when the player needs them most.

Another reward appears in Luigi's Mansion when the player clears a room, or defeats a portrait ghost. It appears in the form of a little chest. Inside the chest is a small gold key that will open the next room and encourage progression. This is 'the key effect', as I like to call it. The player has not actually been rewarded with a chest or a key as such, but a section of gameplay or a new piece of the gaming world.

Periodically the player will encounter a boss ghost which when defeated will reward him with a large gold key. This key will open a large section of the house for the player to explore. This pattern of small key and big key is rhythmic throughout the entire game.

The coolest reward the player receives in Luigi's Mansion is the vacuum cleaner that lets Luigi suck up ghosts and other items around the house. When the player first discovers how to use it, it is reward in itself and lots of fun! This device is the centrepiece of the entire game and every challenge involves the vacuum cleaner one way or another. Without the vacuum, the whole game falls down.

Further into the game the player is rewarded with fire, water and ice elementals that can be expelled from the vacuum. If the player isn't expelling or sucking up ghosts he can be vacuuming the furniture. Most things are interactive and react to the vacuum and if the player is adventurous and explores the furniture, he will be rewarded with cash. The amount of cash, although not vital to the progression of the game, does determine the reward at the end of the game.

The cash comes in various denominations – coins, notes and gold bars. The gold bars are few and far between and are only awarded in rooms populated with portrait ghosts. When capturing a portrait ghost, it will also drop pearls, which can be very valuable. The pearls modify the total amount of cash you collect by multiplying it by X amount, depending how many pearls you have.

Norbot: rewards

This is another instalment of Norbot. We have established a few ideas and the theme for our game, and we know our target audience. We are now going to define a reward system based around the elements of the game we have already established. However, I am going to leave some blanks to enable you to devise your own reward ideas.

The rewards for Norbot will not be as complex as an RPG for obvious reasons, but it has an element of action and therefore Norbot's life will need maintaining. The first question is – do we give Norbot collectable energy/ health, or does he receive it in some other form? Whatever delivery method we choose, one of the challenges for the player will be to keep Norbot alive, and therefore he will require a life support mechanism in the game.

One of my pet hates are games that give you a health bar, but offer no way of restoring lost health if the player should get hurt. Games that adopt this type of energy system are usually very short and attempt to extend the game's life-span by killing the player often, sending him back a few stages or to the start of the level. Bad designer!

Anyway, we have to remember that Norbot is a robot and therefore he wouldn't have health in the same respect as an RPG or first-person shooter; it wouldn't feel right for Norb to travel around collecting hearts or medi-kits – he's a robot! Therefore we have to think of something that has the same mechanic as a health system, but is related to the theme of the game, in context to the world, and is recognisable by our defined audience. So I started to think about what a child might recognise as energy or power. The obvious is an electric bolt, but I felt it didn't really give me much freedom to expand upon. Then it hit me – children's toys! Children always get toys for Christmas that require batteries, and batteries are always associated with energy/power. Therefore, it makes sense to use the idea of batteries in Norbot as the main source of power/energy. We will name them 'power cells'. I can also build the power cells into the structure of the game and have all other things in the game powered by the cells. I also have to make one power cell a denomination or percentage, of the maximum power I can collect. Therefore I am going to have several types of power cells to ensure I can reward Norb adequately and segmentally as he propels himself through the game.

Note: When I create the design documents, I will include a comment in this part of the design to remind the artist that it is important that he creates an image that symbolises a battery, with a positive sign at one end and a nega-

FIGURE 8.4   Norbot power cell

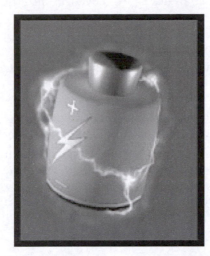

tive at the other. This will be recognised universally. You could, if you're feeling brave, attempt to model it like the one I have done in Figure 8.4. It's big,
chunky and bold and it suits the style of the game. However, a lead artist may
have other ideas, which is cool, but I'm sure he wouldn't mind you putting
your ideas forward.

So what are the other types of power cell I want in Norbot? I am going to
use 'cell banks' for my power cells to live in while Norb is carrying them
around. Each cell bank will have ten slots, to accommodate ten power cells. At
the start of the game, the player will have one full cell bank and he will be
able to find three other cell banks throughout the game. There is one more
source of energy I am going to include, and that is a 'power pack'. What the
power pack will do is fill Norb's cell banks to the maximum no matter how
many cell banks he has. This may be too much power, but we can modify this
once we begin fleshing out the design in more detail.

So the basic reward structure of my energy source throughout the game is
as shown in Figure 8.5.

FIGURE 8.5   Norbot energy reward structure

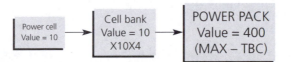

You can see that I've put in a little reminder in the power pack box to tell
anybody who reads this that the power pack maximum will be confirmed
during pre-production. It's also a reminder to myself.

There are still many things to confirm regarding the power cells, which will be covered in different chapters as we move through the book:

- How are we going to present the cells to the player?
- Where are we going to place them in the game?
- When are we going to award the player? The cell banks and power packs are regarded as important objects in the game, and placement will be very important.
- How will Norbot collect them once they are available to him? Do they come to him? Or do we invent a device like a magnet so he can collect them?
- How does each cell affect the player's energy status upon collection? This may seem obvious because I have already defined their strengths and we have already defined what we want to happen, but are we sure? Not really, because we have already put a question mark over the power pack and the proof is in the implementation.

Additional rewards

What other rewards do we want to give the player? Remember, the core objective is to find Norb's missing components, but we have to keep in mind that this is only the pay-off for you, not the big pay-off for Norb as a character. The big reward for Norb as a character is freedom. Freedom is one of my story themes and having his components will allow Norb to live a free fulfilling existence, just as he used to before the wars came.

Because we are going to inject a lot of character into Norb, we can use the missing components of Norb as rewards and a vehicle for feedback to remind the player of the core objective throughout the game. We will go into this in more detail later.

The other rewards I want to build into the game must slot into the architecture and have their own place and functionality in the game, or, like I said before, it's pointless having them there at all. I also want to apply the robotic theme to all rewards and build the gameplay around them too. In Chapter 4 we discussed ideas; all the features mentioned there may also appear as rewards for the player to discover throughout the game.

WORKSHEET   **Rewards**

Here is a simple experiment you can do. Pick a game that you've already completed, play through it again and make sure it has a pause function. The reason for this is for study purposes. The game is less likely to lure you into its grasp if you know what's coming. When playing it, make a note of all the rewards that you find in the game and document the following details.

- Where in the game you collected it.
- Its value in relation to the difficulty level. This you will have to gauge for yourself, but it shouldn't be too difficult if you know what is up ahead.
- Its value in relationship to its purpose. If it's an energy pod, for example, how much energy is it and was it worth collecting?
- Was it easy to see and visually obvious what it was?
- Did you miss any rewards?
- What type of reward it was.
- Make a note of what you had to do to get it.

Doing this will illuminate the reward structure of that particular game and highlight potential weaknesses that may not have been identified in the testing phase.

Summary

I hope I've given you an insight into rewards and you now understand how important they are to a game. You should study different games and genres – they all have a reward system and they're all similarly structured. Command and Conquer has many rewards. For example, you can capture your opponents' pieces and buildings and convert them into your own. How excellent is that for a reward! Soccer games often give you cool camera angles, neat player animations and pats-on-the-back cut-sequences when scoring goals.

When you start to design your reward system for your game, make sure you consider the whole of your game. The worst thing is inconsistency, creating rewards that have no real place in your world. Don't simply have health because you want something to collect. Give it another reason for being in your world – for example my batteries in Norbot are going to power the bad guys; that is until I blast 'em and collect the batteries for Norb's purposes.

Questions and answers

Here are some questions I've been asked in the past:

Q. How many rewards do I have to give the player?

A. That all depends on your game. Give the player as many as it takes to keep him interested, happy, and more importantly keeps the momentum of gameplay moving forward. Give him rewards when he needs them. Playing a game only to be cheated by bad design rather than skill is disastrous and should never happen.

Q. I can't think of any rewards, what do I do?

A. If you can't think of any, then it's probably a bad idea in the first place.

CHAPTER 9

Environment design

Let me begin by making it clear that this chapter is about 'environment design' from a game designer's perspective. It is not meant for artists, although an artist may benefit from the information contained herein. An environment artist will apply his creative wisdom once the game designer has defined the gameplay. They are two separate parts of game development united by a common goal.

Every game has environments in one form or another, from the two-dimensional Tetris to the three-dimensional ever-expanding perpetual world of Everquest. The quantity and variation of worlds created from the imaginations of games designers is simply staggering. They vary in size, shape, depth and meaning, but they all serve the same purpose. Environments are the catalyst for the game, hiding unobtrusively behind the gameplay.

In today's world of games, the majority of them are created in a three-dimensional world, and if they're not, they soon will be. The biggest dictator of this is the market-place. Sad as it may seem, if it's not 3D, it's not cool and it will lose points for this. This doesn't necessarily mean that three-dimensional games are any better, because often they're not. The inclusion of an extra dimension can make the interface to the world very complex indeed. Therefore, this chapter will focus on the three-dimensional world.

Every environment should be planned in detail and created to stage the gameplay. Take the houses in The Sims, for example. I never question the environments because the gameplay draws you in and carries you along without hindrance from the environment. After the initial 'nice graphics' fix, a well-designed environment will only be noticed when it gets in the way of the gameplay.

Environment design is an art form in its own right. The moment you have your feature set and your toy box defined is the moment you begin creating your worlds. To become a master of environment design is one of the most valuable assets a designer could have. However, it takes many games, many years and sheer hard work to perfect. You need to possess good spatial understanding, creativity and the ability to concede when your design is not working.

One big mistake development studios often make is to give environment design to junior designers. Why do they do this? It defies logic completely. I don't want to go into the politics of it all, but this role is really important. It's up there with programmers and AI specialists. It's not a junior job!

The designer needs to look beneath the polygons and textures, strip them away and concentrate on the space as an arena in which the player can perform his role using the toys the designer has created for him. Leave the aesthetics to the people that know how to make your design 'look' great after you have designed it to perfection. However, if you have strong ideas about the final visual content, there is no reason why you can't put them forward. I know I keep saying this throughout the book, but it is a team effort and more ideas are better than few. This doesn't guarantee that the lead artist will use your ideas, and more often than not, they probably won't. But that doesn't matter because you've designed a great level and it's going to play like no other!

Defining the environment

What is an environment? In The Sims it is the houses the Sims live in. The house is a toy box. The player has no control or interaction with the houses; he can only influence the Sims that lives in them. In Tetris it is the clearly defined arena enclosed by the boundaries that define its environment. In Everquest, it is one of the expansive environments, which the player can roam and fight mystical creatures, and are joined by portals to other environments.

In Dungeon Siege, the way in which the environments were designed was what initially grabbed my attention. Dungeon Siege doesn't have levels as such. It's a continuous streaming world, spanning numerous themed locations. From a gamer's point of view this is fantastic and I believe we're going to see much more of this in the future. However, even though the world is perpetual, Ehb can be broken down into a progressive structure. It has milestones and punctuation that can be segmented and book-ended, otherwise it would become too repetitive.

A segment of game is often defined as a level, which in today's world of video games is not entirely accurate. We strive to make our worlds seamless and consistent, desperately attempting to cover the seams with FMV or some other misplaced doodle resembling an animation sequence. Every designer of every genre fractionates their environments, some more obviously than others. Racing games are obvious and easy to define. It's usually technical limitations that delimit the size of tracks or racing environments. RPGs and adventure games are better described as environments, but puzzle games are more likely to have traditional level-based arenas.

So to answer the first question, I believe an environment is a segment of game space that has a beginning and an end. It is carefully balanced with challenges, culminating in an event that rewards the player and increases the player's abilities and presence in the game.

The worst kind of environment is big and sprawling, void of any actions. It is an environment in which the player simply passes through in order to reach the other side with no challenge, no puzzle, and no value. This type of environment should not exist in a game. Why waste time creating something simply to look at in what is supposed to be an interactive world? They only serve to boost an artist's ego, nothing more.

How big should my environment be?

There is no given size. No set rule on how big your environment should or should not be. There is a myth that dictates we should have small environments at the start of the game and larger ones towards the end. They can be as big or as small as you need them to be to achieve your design goals.

WORKSHEET	Environment

- Do not create blank space for the sake of it; always make sure it's there for a reason. If you do have blank space where nothing happens, get rid of it, it's pointless. There is a difference between blank space and space that is placed to build tension. If you are building tension, then the space is there for a reason, but make sure the player is aware of this tension building.

- Step back from your environment design and look at it as a whole unit with all of its elements in place. Does it have rhythm? Does it have a consistent pace? And more importantly, does it have increasing value? If there are holes and gaps that do nothing more than bore the player, delete them or tighten them up. There are ways of doing this without losing hours or days of precious artwork, which we will cover shortly.

- One question you should always ask yourself is, have I seen my design in another game? If the answer is yes, think about how you can make it different while maintaining the challenge and the value of your environment.

- Designers are often guilty of creating big sprawling environments, simply because they can. At the initial design stage, too much can be better than too little, but it can also be difficult to manage and edit, particularly if the designer is emotionally attached to it. In my opinion, quality is better than quantity.

- It can be useful to design and plan your puzzles and challenges prior to building them inside a computer. This way, once you do get to the computer, you can create them individually and piece them together as you progress. This way you know you have consistent pace and there is no waste of space.

- Study other games and their environments and choose games that are of the same genre as your game. Make a note of what is good and bad about a particular scene. Another way to study environments is to look at maps in strategy guides. These can be purchased in all high street games stores. This, however, is not a licence for plagiarism.

- Some games are bundled with a world editor, like Quake and Command and Conquer, for example. If you have a computer at home that has the capacity to allow you to build maps, this is a good stepping-stone towards learning the different types of world editors a designer could use to build game worlds.

As I said previously, there is no set size. Tetris has one screen, one arena, while Everquest has a sprawling world that traverses many continents. What you should remember is that you should be wrapping your world around the gameplay, not vice versa.

Environment structure

Environment structure is very important for the pace and rhythm of your game. Each subsequent scene you construct doesn't have to be physically larger than the previous one, but the value of your scenes must be incremental. The player is always striving for more, bigger and faster rewards. They want to see something new and exciting around each corner that will keep them interested and motivated. You as a designer have to feed that hunger and the structure of your world will be important for this.

Many designers place a location at the beginning of their game that teaches the player how to interact with the interface and mechanics within their game. This is generally a good starting point, but there are mixed feelings rattling around the games industry as to whether this is a good idea or not. I go into this in more detail later, but one way or another, I personally feel it is a vital component of any game. However, I feel it has to be part of the game structure and not just exposition. It should be subtle yet accessible and functional. Each environment you build will be part of a whole and should be designed as such. Look at the balance of each environment within your game and make sure it's in the right place.

All of your environments should grow as the player moves through them, revealing more and more of the world as he does so. It is good practice to break down your environments and label the sections. Table 9.1 depicts how this could be done as an overview or a game design storyboard in the first instance.

The letters in the row across the top can be replaced with names of the places in your first environment. The second row can be a description of what happens in each section. Here I have merely called them challenges, but you can be more specific than this if you know what your challenges are. These could be anything from solving a puzzle, to a one-on-one combat situation, or the building of your facilities.

You can also include other information, as I have done in the additional rows below. This is a good way to initially structure your environments, events and challenges in your game and it will give you an overall picture of the world you are creating. It will also give you some idea of how you can begin to edit them and move elements of your game around should you need to do so. If you print them out, you can stick them up on a wall and stand back to see if your game has rhythm and pace. Adding colour to the boxes, as I have done here, illuminating bosses, rewards and other important elements, will also stand out when up on a wall, giving you first-glance insight into the overall structure, rhythm and pace of your game.

TABLE 9.1 Game world blue-print

Environment#01	A	B	C	D	E	F	G	-	-	A
Start game – front end, introduction	Teach the player	First single real challenge (a taste – no harm to player)	Challenge 1: Crossing the threshold. First confrontation with adversary	Challenge 2: Increase difficulty	Challenges 3–9: Increase and maintain difficulty	Tension builder – prepare for action – give rewards	First major challenge (boss, massed army battle etc.)	Enter portal/safe haven	Story progression	Enter Environment #2
Value	0	2	3	4	5–8	0	9–10	0	0	
Level of difficulty	0%	0%–2%	3%	4%	5%	–	6%		–	
Player: positive physical change/ item reward/ motivation	X	–	–	–	–	–	X		–	
Small rewards/ motivation (dependent on needs)		X	X	X	X	X	–		X	

By adding elements and taking elements away, you can see the affect it will have on the rest of the game. This is often done whilst in production and the balance is upset. If this is the case, there is rarely time for the designer to modify and rebalance the game and the player generally comes up against a wall.

Realism versus fantasy

Realistic games are becoming all too common. When I play a game, I want to be propelled into a universe I have never seen before. I want to explore the deepest darkest corners and fight saliva-drooling monsters I would never otherwise see.

What I don't want to do is explore the same depressing dark streets that exist in the corners of our real towns and cities. If I am forced to do this, I want to do things that I can't do in real life. I would like to drive my car into a brick wall, jump off tall buildings and basically create mayhem. If I can't do these things I might as well go for a real walk in the park!

Think carefully when designing your game whether you want to place it in a real-life setting or some other alternative realm. The theme or subject matter may determine this, so you may not have a choice. If your setting is real, it needs something to contrast the normality of realism otherwise you will be playing a life simulation of some kind. Stuntman™ by Atari is a good example of a real setting combined with arcade action and driving stunts that you would never normally do in a real life situation.

Designing an environment

Here I want to take you through the process of actually designing an environment from scratch. We will begin with the initial idea to a fully realised, graphical representation of a 3D environment that you might find in a game.

So where does a designer begin? Once you have created your design storyboard similar to the one above, and you are happy with the structure, you can begin mapping out the space of your world.

Designers will visualise the game in their mind's eye. They can see their character traversing the hilltops and trees, or imagine their car hurtling around a track at breakneck speeds. Having a vivid, perhaps overactive imagination is a great asset for a game designer. You will already have broken down your environments into playable sections, which have a start and an end with defined challenges and goals.

I have chosen to illustrate the process with a simple design, depicting a boss scenario, for an imaginary action-based, third-person adventure. The reason I have chosen this is primarily for simplicity and the time factor. The amount of work involved in creating virtual worlds is astounding and therefore to create more than this would add to my schedule substantially. The principles are the same and you can apply this process to almost any genre of game. I'm not claiming it's the only way, but it's one way that I have seen a lot of designers use successfully. It will give you insight into the preparation required when designing environments of any kind.

TIP

Do your research and be prepared! When you begin to design your environments, be sure to have all the information available to you relating to the part of the

▶

game that you are designing. Have *all* the documents, concept sketches and information in front of you. This might include, for example, the documents that describe the challenges at this point in the game, a list of abilities, features and rules the player will have available. Having this information will utilise the maximum potential for your environment. If you are a level designer, be sure the lead designer has given you all the design documents and information you need.

The sketch

It is important to have an idea of the visual theme of the environment you are designing. The concept artists may have already visualised the style of the world during pre-production, long before you begin your environment design, so there should be no problem in that respect.

This is where you as a level designer begin, by sketching and noting your ideas onto paper. At this stage, it doesn't matter if you can't draw, the point is you are sketching and laying down your ideas based on the proposed design. If you have a particular contraption in your design, sketch it so you can visualise and explain the workings of it. Sketch the basic layout of your environment, particularly highlighting key points such as creatures, props, entrances, exits and traps etc. If you have a particular puzzle in the design documents, draw that too. Keep sketching and making notes until you come up with a set of scribbles that satisfy you, and represents the details and ideas in the game design documents. Now go through it with the lead designer and/or other designers on your team, and take notes on their suggestions that you feel would enhance your sketch design. The lead designer may simply tell you to come up with more ideas from scratch, in which case you simply do just that. The lead designer will be conversing with the other leads on the project and therefore will have a good understanding of the graphical and technical limitations involved.

Once you have a sketch that you and your team are happy with, draw a fair and final representation of your environment, noting every important game feature.

Figure 9.1 is my final sketch for a boss arena that I have designed for our imaginary game. Let's go through it a little at a time. We shouldn't care for the visual aspects at this stage, provided it works for the game. The sketch typifies an area of game, and identifies key elements for the person who will build the design.

You can see the environment has boundaries and no matter what anybody might say to you … all environments have them! There is no such thing as a free-roaming perpetual environment – if you go far enough, it ends … it has to.

At the bottom of my sketch you can see the entrance to the arena and at the top is the exit. Once the player has completed the main objective, the exit will open and he can leave. Here are the imaginary rules I had in front of me when designing this section.

FIGURE 9.1 Boss arena sketch

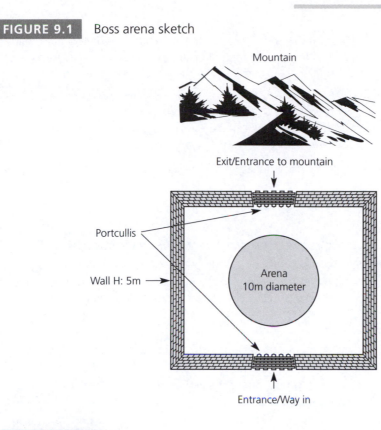

Mountain

Exit/Entrance to mountain

Portcullis

Wall H: 5m

Arena
10m diameter

Entrance/Way in

EXAMPLE **Boss arena: Instructions/design**

Core objective: 'Defeat the scorpion demon and retrieve the "seeing stone" embedded in her chest'.

Scene description:
■ On entering the scorpion's domain, the metal portcullis at the entrance will crash to the ground, trapping the player inside the boundaries. There is only one way out!

■ The boss is half scorpion, half human. The tail end is scorpion and has one particular move called a 'tail slam'. When performing the 'tail slam', the scorpion brings its sting over its head and thrusts it into the ground. Fatal if the player is standing in the way! This is the move I particularly focused on. The attack has a *two-second (exact timing to be modified during production)* wind up – a window of opportunity long enough for the player to rush in, strike a blow, and get out.

■ The scorpion will take four killer blows (player must use sword which will reduce hit points by 25 per cent) to diminish her life to zero.

▶

- The action takes place in the area defined as the 'arena' on the sketch. Once the player steps inside the arena (forced through a cut-scene), a magic fiery force field will activate, encircling the arena and trapping the player inside the ring.

Note: The player will have a particular weapon, and special move, that he will use to destroy the Scorpion demon. We don't have to define them here, except that in a real design it would have been described prior to designing this environment. In this case, let's imagine our hero is armed with a large sword.

- If the player touches the flaming barrier, the player is hurt and is deducted 10 units of health.

- The sequence for killing the boss is as follows.

Play sequence:

1 The scorpion demon comes crawling out of her hole in the mountain wall.

2 Play begins once the short cut-scene is complete. The cut-scene ends on the scorpion performing the 'tail slam' – smashing its tail into the ground, causing the screen to shake and debris to fall around the player. This depicts the scorpion's power and strength. It also provides important informative feedback to the player!

3 The scorpion is in the middle of the arena. It rotates to focus on the player. If the scorpion can't focus on the player, it scuttles and turns until it can.

4 When the scorpion fixes on the player, it will fire poison from its tail, directly at the player. The player must avoid it.

5 If the poison hits the player, it will hurt him by reducing 10 units of health from the player and the player will become stunned for two seconds.

6 Regardless whether the scorpion has hit or missed with the poison (a hit will make it easier for her), she will scuttle over, wind-up and perform the 'tail slam'. If the scorpion hits the player with the 'tail slam', the scorpion will do 'X' damage (TBD) to the player. However, the player has enough time to avoid being hit.

7 The scorpion will rear up her front legs when winding up for the tail slam, at this point she will expose her weakness – the red glowing belly. If the player is not stunned, he has a timed two-second chance to run over and slash the scorpion in the belly while it's in this state. A successful hit will anger the scorpion, reduce her hits points by 25 per cent and then she will begin chasing the player (the player will be informed of a successful hit with visual and audio feedback).

8 Repeat the sequence three more times to kill the scorpion and reach the victory condition.

9 Once the scorpion is dead, the fiery seal around the arena will dissipate and she will drop the seeing stone.

10 The player must pick up the stone before he leaves.

11 The exit will open.

You can see my illustration portrays the arena for the fight. Nevertheless, the action needs putting into practice. Now we have a clear idea of what is going to happen, it needs to be approved by the lead designer and possibly the producer. Once that has happened, you can move on to the next stage.

The box map

This part of environment design is called many things in the industry. I call it the box map because it's a simple three-dimensional representation of your sketch. There are few textures used, no complex geometry and no special effects, just bare geometry, the required basic props and gameplay mechanics. This is an important stage in the design process, for both you and your environments. It should never be skipped. If your team skip this part of the design, it could cost hundreds of thousands of dollars in wasted art. Not only are the box maps good for defining the game world before mistakes can happen, they also provide a good template for the artists to follow. They can provide a sense of composition, and camera placement can be planned which will inform the artist where he can use most of the polygons and textures.

The idea of the box map is that it allows the designer to build his environment to scale with placement props in all the right places, which can then be implemented into the game engine. Once implemented, you can test it for playability prior to the artists getting their eager mittens on it. This method gives you the option to change things if you need to. Perhaps something isn't working as you expected, or the arena is too small and you need to scale it up. You can easily go in and make your changes to the box map without the worry of breaking any art.

Imagine making changes to the environment after the artists have modelled the detail, textured it and lit the scene. You won't be very popular, believe me!

It's one of those unwritten rules – art never changes. I'm not sure why this is, but I think it's mostly due to the mentality of the industry and the lack of formal procedures. The most important thing to remember is that gameplay is king. It has priority over anything else, therefore you have to test it, modify it and get it right before the artists do their thing. If the artists can see what the designers are planning, they will produce art that works for the design.

The box map is where designing environments become a little tricky for beginners. You have to have a basic ability with a 3D application to do this, and understand how to create simple shapes in 3D. Figure 9.2 is a render I created using 3DS Max 3.1. It's a box map representing my sketch. Each developer will do this differently. Some developers will have their own proprietary world editor while others will use a 3D package such as 3DS Max or Maya, for example. The position of the camera in Figure 9.2 is located at

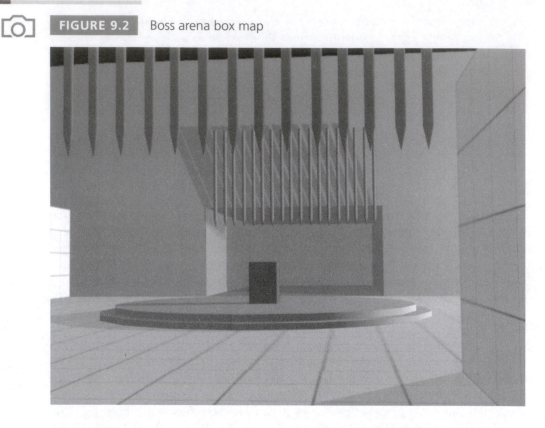

FIGURE 9.2 Boss arena box map

the entrance looking into the arena. If you refer back to Figure 9.1, you will see where the entrance is.

You will notice I have included all the props I proposed in my initial sketch, like the portcullis and the arena, and I have also used a block, approximately the same size as my character would be, as a reference point. It does look crude and it is simple, but you can pull and push this around until the space is perfect.

You can see in the box map that I have focused primarily on the core of the environment, which is where the focus of the gameplay is centred. It's not my concern what goes on around the perimeter, as it doesn't affect the gameplay. Therefore, as the designer, I will leave that part of the scene entirely to the artists' creative discretion.

This scene can now be given to the programmers to code and script, and the testing of the gameplay mechanics can begin in earnest. You must ensure it plays as you expected. If you require any additional props, you can drop them in or ask the programmers to include some primitive shapes, or whatever shapes you want, providing it serves its purpose.

Many people within the industry find it difficult to understand this part of development primarily because of the way it looks. Gameplay is not about how things look, it's about how they feel and this process will save so much time in the long run. You should never show marketing people this part of the design phase – it will scare them! They want to see great graphics and a saleable product, not a character leaping around a bunch of boxes.

If you look at the process for creating animated movies, they use a similar process. Before the animators and background artists draw the final artwork, they will go through several iterations and concept drawings before they decide on the final look or style. They create a story reel, with the sound included so they can get a feel for the sequence to determine whether it is going to work or not. The box map, or 'blue box' as it's also called, serves the same purpose as the story reel. It confirms, within a small time frame and at low cost, that the interactive content validates the game design.

Colours and markers can be placed within the box map to ensure important elements remain intact. If you've placed things in strategic positions and you need things to be exact sizes, the artists need to know about this. If they are not informed, they may alter elements of your scene that are crucial for the game to work. This can be avoided by planning the format of your box maps before you begin. You can have specific objects and colours that represent different things. You can see in my box map that I've painted the floor red, indicating that this must not be changed in size. I'm sure the artists will make them look great with detail and textures, but everything must remain in the same place and be the same size as I have depicted in my box map.

Once your scene is boxed up, tested and working as expected, it will get signed off and the artists can begin to model the final scene. There may very well be small tweaks once it is complete, but this will most likely consist of balancing and fine-tuning. The artists will use your box map as a template, combined with the art style guide, and have a clear visual depiction of what they are going to do with the final scene.

This technique doesn't have to stop with your environments either. Your characters can also be boxed for prototyping particular animations and game mechanics. Once your box character is created you can send it into your world to sniff out any design flaws and test animations, again before expensive animation is created.

Another thing you might want to consider at this stage is feedback. Now you can see your scene, even in its basic form, you can visualise it much more clearly. You may want to revisit your feedback for this section in your documents.

Space

No … not the final frontier. I want to talk about the use of space within your environments. The way you use space and construct your environments can have an enormous impact on the gameplay. Tight compact spaces with contrasting open spaces will give your game rhythm and make it look and feel more interesting.

One of the first things I did when I learnt to use a 3D application was model my house. Yes, I know it is very sad. But I measured it and built it to scale, and the first thing I noticed was how small everything was inside the computer. Of course when I passed a camera through it, it was perfect, but often, and I have done this myself, designers tend to build large – not just in terms of open space but scale can also be a big problem. One of the reasons for this is that within a 3D virtual world, land is free. You can build as much real estate as you want and as big as you want, there are no virtual boundaries. Your only limitation is the target platform.

When building an interactive environment, too much space can be as bad as having too little space. Think about the dimensional space in the context of the avatar, and the challenges he will confront. Of course, an RTS point and click will require a smaller amount of physical space than that of a high-speed racing game like Wipeout, for example. Marching a military outfit across the expanse of ground covered in Wipeout would take a monotonous amount of time and the player would simply get bored!

Rapid technological developments have allowed us to become complacent and greedy with our environments, without any thought to the game and the player. You must make sure you have utilised all the space you have created for your game and that you have not included dead space. If it doesn't lead anywhere and doesn't do anything then it probably shouldn't be in your game.

You also need to think about your boundaries as discussed in Chapter 7, 'Rules and boundaries'. Some gaming environments will have a natural boundary like a cliff face, while a football stadium will define its own boundaries, for example. If you have none of these and your world is outdoors, you need to think about the boundaries of your world; it can't simply end. The suspension of disbelief will be broken. The setting can often help with this. If you are in an apocalyptic city, fallen buildings could block the players' path. Or if you are trekking through jungles, the ocean can be a good edge to your world. Whatever the case may be, make it believable and keep it consistent.

What does the camera see?

I can remember vividly when the PlayStation arrived and the three-dimensional worlds hit the mass-market like a blow to the head. Suddenly the game designer had to become a movie director. We had no idea what effect a camera in a gaming environment would have on games. Needless to say we were tried and tested in every which way and it was never easy. However, like most things, we learnt from our mistakes, but we still don't seem to have mastered it completely. This is another very good reason for creating box maps. Cameras can be a hit and miss affair in games. Unlike movies, you can never truly predict where the player is going to be and the cameras are rarely in the right place at the right time. I believe there are several reasons for this. One major reason for this is that we don't know how to use them. We are not cameramen or movie directors – we are games designers! What do we know about placing cameras?

Another reason for this is the inability to experiment with cameras while developing games, within the gaming environment. Where camera placement is important for a game, the ideal situation for camera placement is this. You should be able to play the game in box mode, and if the cameras aren't working, freeze the game and move it to where you, as the designer, think it works best for the situation. A camera editor would be great, or a world editor that has that function. But for it to work, you need to see the action actually taking place, to be able to place the camera in the best position. Why? Because the game is interactive and players do things that even the developers don't anticipate. More often than not, a camera will be fudged into the game at the beginning of development and it will stay like that throughout production. When the end of development comes to pass, there is no time to fix it or change it, and the player ends up with a half-hearted attempt at a camera. One of the great things about computer games is that we can do things with cameras that movie people can't do in reality, unless of course they use computers, which is ironic when you think about it! I believe we have a long way to go with the game camera and we'll eventually see games mastering the art form.

Further reading

Two books that you can study that will enlighten you as far as space and cameras are concerned (although you will need to add the interactive element) are: ***Shot by Shot*** by Steve D. Katz, a good beginners' guide as it takes you through visualisation, design and storyboarding right up to the moving camera.

For more advanced reading, particularly for the cut-scenes in your game: ***Cinematic Motion*** by Steve D. Katz, which focuses on the camera and where to place it in a particular scene. It goes from a single subject, car interiors and confined spaces to outside the car, large open spaces, choreography, and multiple subjects.

Saving mechanism

Why place saving games in a chapter about environment design? More often than not, the progression through the gaming world determines whether the player should save or not. However, some games like Tetris, for example, don't have saves, so why do we need them at all?

The save mechanism is often another element of game design that gets left behind or left until the last minute. The designer will often drive into the heart of the game and stay there, until one day he steps out and looks back at the world he has created and realises the player can never turn his computer off! So where and how do you implement a save game mechanism?

Of course there are several factors that will determine the type of save you have. Your first restriction will be the platform the game is developed on. If it's a PC, for example, you can save much larger files than you can on a console. Dungeon Siege for example allows the player to save anywhere at anytime and you can build a huge library of save files as you play through the game. This is great if you want to go back and start playing from a particular point in the game. You could not do this on a console; the memory cards simply don't have enough space for this type of sequential save. The Xbox does now have a hard drive and, I suspect, future consoles will have the same or similar mass storage device as this.

Another defining factor is the type of game you are designing. If it's simply a level-based game, perhaps you only want the player to save after the completion of each level. If it's a racing game, perhaps the player can only save after each race, which is often the case with those games.

The designer has to build in a failsafe save function also because the player will not always remember to save. Auto-save has become a prerequisite, particularly in PC games. Your game should also ask the player if he wishes to save, especially when the player decides to quit from the game. If the player has played for hours and switches off without saving, it can be devastating.

The save anywhere function can work for PCs and the save after every level is fine for level-based games. So what other types of save mechanisms are there? Many console games, like Zelda for example, do let you save anywhere, but when you load the game back up, it places you at the start of the section you were in. This is fine because the game saves the state of all puzzles. Therefore, the player does not have to repeat gameplay. If he did, you would be effectively punishing the player for no reason!

One of the worst types of save, I feel, is when you have to search for an object or get to a specific location before you can save. It could take a player several hours before they get to their destination or find the object. This type of save is often found in small games that try and extend the gameplay by placing you back to the start of level when you die, forcing the player to do it all over again.

Whatever type of saves you choose, make sure the player can't cheat with them, which can happen sometimes particularly if you have random events in your game that the player could avoid by saving and restarting. Never force a player into a situation where he has to reload to be able to continue playing the game. If this is in your game you have a major flaw that needs to be addressed.

Maps

I get disorientated at the best of times. My sense of direction is almost non-existent. When I'm driving, walking around a hotel or out with the family at a safari park, I simply get lost. I'm not the only one; lots of people get lost all the time.

If your game has complicated mazes or tunnels that require lots of exploration, design a map function into your game; the player will really appreciate it. Getting lost in repetitive featureless mazes, tunnels and forests is a bit like jumping – it's not fun. Even racing games can benefit from a track map in that it informs the player of approaching corners etc. You might be thinking that giving the player a map will make your game too easy. If that is the case, this may be because your game is lacking in challenges, the challenges are too easy, not because the player is informed of his location in the world!

Maps that reveal themselves as the player progresses are great maps, because nothing is revealed until you have been there, which is ideal.

Summary

As we trawl through the workload of the designer, it becomes more apparent that game design is a crucial part of development, and environment design makes up a significant part of that workload and an important feature of your game. When you begin to design your environments, you should have a checklist in front of you to remind you of the elements you need to think about.

WORKSHEET	Environment

Ask yourself the following questions:

- Have I defined my boundaries clearly?
- Are my boundaries in context with the world?
- What type of 'save' should I have?
- Do I need to give the player a map for my world? Would it help him navigate around my environments?
- Do I have dead space in my game – will the player ever see it or use it?
- Does my environment have rhythm?

CHAPTER 10

Educating the player

Educating the player? 'These are games we're playing, we're not at school now,' I hear you cry. Yes you're right, they are games, but non-hardcore, mass-market players wish to be taught how to use the product they have just purchased. After all, they have just spent their hard-earned money on your game; give them what they paid for. Let's face it, how many game manuals have you read? Well, I rarely read any of them and the sad fact is, very few people do.

It is the duty of the designer to inform the player how to interact with the product. This is a tricky job and not to be taken lightly. The first thing you need to consider, as with most things in game design, is your audience. If your game is targeted at the mass-market, you need to be gentle with the player. You need to be able to lure him into your game, without the wall of frustration popping up before the player has even begun.

On the other hand, you also need to consider the hardcore gamers. They don't want their hands/held throughout the game, they just want to get on with it and get stuck in. Every genre has its conventions, and hardcore gamers know what those conventions are. When a hardcore gamer buys a game, he already knows what to expect from it and therefore simply wants to get on with playing it.

Stand back and look at your game and ask yourself, 'has my target audience ever seen anything like my game before'? If the answer to this question is no, you will certainly need to teach them and you will need to hold their hands when doing so.

The mass-market

I once sat through a large meeting in which most of the people represented various departments of the publisher of the game we were developing; the rest were the heads of the team who were going to make the game. It lasted four – long – hours. For the duration of the meeting we, or rather they, discussed the definition of mass-market. Eighty per cent of the time the publishing team were arguing among themselves as to who the mass-market actually were, and if they actually existed at all. I was speechless!

The idea of mass-market gaming seems burdened with ambiguity. The mass-market truly does exist and the future of gaming belongs to it. I apologise to all those hardcore gamers for saying this, but – get used to it – that's where the money is. You, the designer, need to be fully aware of who they are and what they want, before you put ink to paper or pixel to screen.

Mass-market is a blanket term for every gamer who is not a hardcore gamer – a person who plays games, perhaps not very often, maybe only buying two or three games a year. They are often termed casual gamers; they can take it or leave it, they know what they want and they don't play games unless the games provide what they want.

Mass-market gamer

A typical mass-market gamer can be defined by identifying characteristics and habitual tendencies:

- **Non-technical:** this is generally the case. The masses do own PCs, but they won't be the fastest, cutting-edge piece of hardware money can buy. And if it was to go wrong, they probably couldn't fix it, although some might try.

- **Gaming session:** a casual gamer will not sit in front of a game for very long and will easily be pulled from it, unlike a hardcore gamer. A typical gaming session might last between thirty minutes to an hour.

- **Plug and play:** he will want to switch on and start playing immediately. Downloading patches, updates and expansions is not what the mass-market does. It's not that they couldn't, they just don't want to spend their time doing that. If they buy something, they want it to work, first time and without a technical nightmare.

- **Learning curve:** make it very small, almost non-existent. They're not fervent gamers and will not endure a steep learning curve. You should make it quick and easy, taking into account that a typical play session is only approximately thirty minutes. They need to be in, have got over any learning curve and having fun in this short space of time.

- **Interface and rules:** your interface needs to be transparent. The casual gamer does not want to struggle with the controls or be confused by a complex screen display. If they look at the screen and there is too much information, they will switch off. You must also make sure the rules are plain and simple and there is no room for ambiguity. The rules are the rules and they cannot be miss-interpreted in any way.

- **Censors:** lose the blood and gore and have little or no gratuitous sex or violence, or anything that could be construed as such. There is already too much of this smeared across the media and they see it in their real lives. They want to escape from that and have some fun. The game has to appeal to the family and there should be nothing in your game that stops any member of the family playing it.

▶

- **Themes:** avoid all religious, satanic or cult themes and deliver a positive family message with positive feedback.
- **Feedback:** this has to be plentiful. Informative, positive, visual – the works. The game has to speak to the player and provide feedback as soon as the player enters the world.
- **Information:** don't overload the player. Spoonfeed it gently and make sure the information is clear and precise.

As you can see from this defining list, the mass-market is not made up of game-crazed adolescents; more likely to be part of a family with a games console in the living room and a PC in the study. They eat fast food, and spend their time doing many other things besides playing video games. The mass-market is one reason why designing games is becoming more difficult – you have to attract that audience to make the financial aspects viable.

Mass-market games are also in serious competition with the cinema, the video stores, music, fashion trends, magazines, the Internet, eating out and many other things besides, because this is what the mass-market likes to do and they only have so much surplus cash to spend. So we have to reel 'em in with great designs and the sort of cool gameplay that they want and can play without any blockages and frustrations.

A great example of a mass-market game is The Sims on PlayStation2. It has everything a mass-market game should have. You could walk away from it and let it play itself for a while without any intervention, although I wouldn't recommend that as a design aspect. It can be picked up and put down at any time and most people can relate to the themes. It is also fun to watch, which should also be a consideration when designing your game. The game is not a technical masterpiece or innovative, but pushes the daily grind of real life to one side nicely.

Another, more obvious mass-market game is Tetris. It is timeless and has spawned more clones than any other game I know. At the time I write this, there is yet another version of Tetris being released for the Xbox, which is testament to its perfection. It also means that it has survived and surpassed the multi-million dollar developments and the high-tech extravaganzas for twenty years. Countless versions of this game can be found all over the Internet, created by enthusiasts. The simplicity of Tetris is brilliant, and coupled with its exasperating challenge makes it unspeakably addictive. So many games have tried to copy the format, but few have succeeded. Standing on the podium, tall and proud with its head held high is Tetris, where it remains to this very day. It's the greatest video game ever, the mass-market game, a game that anyone can pick up and play, with a genuine chance of success.

Hardcore gamers

What is a hardcore gamer? He is a complete contrast to the above. However, this doesn't mean that hardcore gamers don't enjoy the same games as the mass-market; they just do things on a different scale.

A good example of hardcore gaming would be Quake. It is one of those games you can drop into and it will absorb hours of your time, particularly in on-line multi-player arenas. The kill thrill, action and pace of Quake is so absorbing that a hardcore gamer would sit through an earthquake and not even notice it! I have played this game myself, with a group of friends, and have lost hours of time immersed in the Quake arenas. If you're playing with a team over a local area network (LAN), your awareness of time becomes distorted and your alertness and senses are devoted to the game completely. That is until you are pulled back into reality by the phone, or some other external distraction.

Hardcore gamer

A typical hardcore gamer can be defined by identifying characteristics and habitual tendencies:

- **Gaming session:** a hardcore gamer will tolerate playing a game for hours at a time, sometimes through the night until they can't stay awake anymore. He will often complete a game within days of purchase, ready for the next. I'm not suggesting they are computer game addicts, but playing games is something they are particularly good at, and they enjoy doing it more than most things. In the same respect a tennis player might play tennis endlessly, or a football supporter will watch football, because they enjoy it.

- **Forgiving:** hardcore gamers are also more forgiving than the mass-market and will persevere if a game crashes or they get stuck at a particular section of the game. If they can't get past it, for whatever reason, they may even look on the Internet and find a cheat or download a patch that will help them get past it.

- **Technical:** you often find with hardcore gamers that they know everything there is to know about games – from the games that are available, consoles and peripherals, to cheat modes and hacks. They will most likely own a PC and possess the ability to take it apart, upgrade it and put it back together again, without too much problem. They are most likely to be hooked up to the Internet and will tolerate lag and downtime, unlike the mass-market gamer.

- **Censors:** if a game has blood and gore, it doesn't bother the hardcore gamer. But the game has to have serious action and credible gameplay, which allows them to be completely immersed for hours at a time. There is a myth that games make people do bad things, but there is no real evidence of this. A screen full of game-related computer pixels is as detached from reality as you could get.

▶

- **Game mechanics:** the hardcore gamer likes a real challenge. Providing it is not beyond the realms of possibility, they will stick at it. The learning curve can be steep and the interface complex, but the interface has to be functional and not clunky or impossible. Hardcore gamers do not like to be cheated by bad design, nor does anybody else for that matter. The goals must be achievable and logical, but at the same time challenging.

- **On-line gaming:** playing MMORG (massive multi-player on-line role-playing games) is currently a hardcore gamer's activity. Contrary to popular belief, the mass-market just isn't ready for this yet. These are discussed in more detail later as they are likely to play a significant role in the fast-paced evolution of games. These games are attracting the hardcore gamer like nothing before. They are perpetual in that they never end and the worlds that you play in are enormous. Days, even weeks can be sopped up playing these games. However, they can be a technical nightmare for your mass-market gamer, waiting for patches to upload and not fully understanding why there is lag and downtime. Why should the mass-market gamer pay for a service that doesn't work? It doesn't make sense to them. But the hardcore gamer will put up with this and continue playing relentlessly.

Teaching the player

So where does this leave you, the designer? You have the mass-market on one hand and you have the hardcore gamer's market on the other. Who do you design for? Only you can decide that for your game, but if you decide to make your game easy and accessible for the masses, it doesn't mean the hardcore gamer won't play it. I would consider myself a patriot of hardcore gaming, but I do enjoy a simpler game that can be played for a short time, without the commitment of stupidly long hours and a steep learning curve. This is purely down to the fact that I don't have that sort of time to commit to a game these days, which I believe applies to most people in today's world.

CASE STUDY   **Black and White**

A good example of mass-market versus hardcore gaming is Black and White, developed by Lionhead Studios and published by Electronic Arts™. I eagerly waited for this game to arrive and I was justly rewarded when it came. It was, and still is, a great game and it had everything I had hoped for. However, I don't feel it sits comfortably in the mass-market pool of games, for several reasons.

Typical of a mass-market game is a mentor type character and Black and White does have character mentors that teach the player how to play and interact with the game, and delivers it exceptionally well. However, the game does have a steep learning curve and it requires several hours of continuous play to get to know the game confidently, which is not a trait for mass-market gaming.

Another element of the game that doesn't sit with the mass-market is the allocation of time one needs to commit to the game. Playing beyond the initial introduction, where the core of the game begins, requires a lot of commitment and a lot of time. If you're prepared to allocate a substantial amount of your time to playing games, then this might possibly be for you. It's not a bad design fault; it's more of a design choice.

I recently saw a design for a racing game which had a very complex front-end. It allowed you to choose a vehicle, set up its characteristics and then go and do the same for a character. There were settings and sliders for game options and it all seemed endless. But this is ok, because some people like this. The one thing that I loved about the design was that it had a button on the front menu that basically said 'set me up and get me in'. This launched the player straight into the action, letting the game choose options for the player. This too is great. The designers thought about the market and catered for all tastes.

The mentor

This is a popular way of guiding and teaching the player, and many games use it successfully, Black and White being a perfect example. There are however, different types of mentor you could use to introduce the game mechanics of your game.

The character mentor

A good example of this can be seen in Black and White, which presents it in a humorous way. The mentor is actually represented by two characters, one good, the other bad. It is their goal to lure the player down their respective paths as they introduce the game. They also introduce the tasks to be completed by the player and teach the player how to interact with the world in order to complete those tasks. The character mentor is an excellent way of teaching the player, but it has to be in context with the world you create. If it has no relevance to the game or the world in which the game is played, the mentor will appear misplaced. The two characters in Black and White anchor the gameplay, but can change the direction of the gameplay depending on which path the player decides to take.

The narrator

This is usually a voice, representing a god-like character that often can't be seen, just heard. There is usually no physical rendition of the narrator in a game, unless it's the main character speaking, but the rule that states he has to be related to the game still holds. One effective method for doing this, which was done well in Soul Reaver, is to use the protagonist's voice, as if the player is hearing the character's thoughts. This tool can also be used to add depth to your main character, by revealing your character's emotions and informing the player how the character is feeling about the situation. There is a problem with this method in that it could detach the player from the character. The player may feel that he's in control of another person, instead of feeling that he is, or wants to be, that character.

Instructional signposts

Personally I don't mind these. Many people frown upon them, but there is no real reason for not including them. What are signposts in a game? You must have played a game where graphics flash on the screen as you play, instructing you to press certain buttons at a particular moment. The arguments against these are that they're not part of the world in which the player is immersed. Therefore, seeing the graphics appear on the screen detaches the player from the game. They may also be considered a visual obscenity, which does not suit the style of art or genre of game. There is no evidence to suggest that it affects a game like this and I don't feel they are good enough reasons not have them. If they are designed and placed within your game and they enhance it, then that should be paramount.

The ideal solution is to build it into the game like Dungeon Siege, for example. Take a look at Figure 10.1 and you will notice a signpost on the path. There are many of these in the game and they provide the player with directions and other navigational information.

Forced gameplay

Personally I feel this is probably the worst kind of teaching you can put into a game. This method forces the player to perform certain actions to ensure he knows how to use a particular function. It sounds fine when you say it, but when it's implemented, it feels wrong. Why? Because you have forced the player into a situation that he has no control over, and he is being denied the right to explore. Whatever happens, never take away what the player has already learnt. A designer once suggested to me that it would be a good idea to deactivate all buttons and abilities, except those that the player is learning to use at any given time. This is ludicrous. This will confuse the player and you should never do this.

FIGURE 10.1 Dungeon Siege navigational device

One of the best ways to do this is to create challenges in the game world that allows the player to use the new functions. The first time the player uses it, it should be easy and if he gets it wrong, he should not be punished, but simply told how to correct his mistake by some other means.

Training ground

Often games will include a specific area or environment for the player to practice in prior to playing the actual game. It does avoid the player becoming frustrated with being pulled from the game, by keeping the training separate. Tomb Raider did this. You could explore Lara's house and practise all the moves before the adventure began. Because it was Lara's house, it was still part of the game and part of the Tomb Raider world.

This is a good way to introduce the player to the interface and game mechanics, providing it is kept in context with the world and is the beginning for the game rather than a bolt-on afterthought!

Progression difficulty

Progression difficulty is an aspect of balancing your game, but I feel that when it comes to balancing your game, you need to look at every aspect of your design and adjust it accordingly. Balancing can only truly be done once the game has all its features and is playable. But you need to have a starting point and you need to define what mechanics and challenges make your game easy or difficult to play. You must also consider what elements of the design you need to modify that will change the difficulty threshold.

Picture the very beginning of your game for one moment. There it is, on the screen, ready for the onslaught of feedback and digital interaction. Now cast your mind to the very end of your game, the last boss, the ultimate battle or the fastest track and car. At this point in the game, the player should have every weapon, vehicle, ability that the game has to offer, at his disposal. The enemy also is as large and mean as it is ever going to get. This, you may be thinking, is obvious and I would agree with you. But for some reason, developers insist on dropping brick walls along the way that are just simply too hard to get over. If this happens, which invariably it does, it needs to be calibrated to make it work for the player.

The beginning of your game should allow for the player to learn how to play it, particularly the mass-market. You must keep it in your mind that the player has never seen or played your game before, until the moment it appears on their screen. Therefore, it makes sense to assume the player will not know how to play your game. When I look at designs or design myself, I always look at the start as a playground. It is a place where the player can play with the toys and abilities that exist in the game, without the threat of being killed or banished from the world in which he has just invested. However, you must not leave them on the doorstep for too long or the interest will fade and the player will get bored. Ensure you give the player plenty of things to do. If he has weapons, put things in the playground that he can shoot and blow up but cause no threat. If your game is a racing game, include a test centre where the player can experience different cars until he is satisfied and can comfortably handle the cars on offer. The game can measure this by setting up a simple challenge that the player could easily overcome.

The main thing to remember is, do not punish your player too soon. Make it as easy as you can at the beginning. Give the player the option to leave this relaxed zone/playground whenever he wants to. Doing this will also appease the hardcore gamer and allow them to jump into the action.

Take a look at Zelda on the N64, for example. The very first time you play you are in your home village. There is no threat but there are many things the player can do and is required to do before he can venture on his quest.

Norbot: learning curve

We've already established which genre Norbot is going to slip into and we also know our target audience and that the game will appeal to the mass-market. This will give us insight into how difficult to make the game from the start to the last scene.

Due to Norbot's unusual characteristics, I am going to allow the player to get used to the control method before dropping him into something a little more challenging. Therefore, the first section of Norbot will be designed purely for informative reasons. It will not kill the player in any way, but will impose a simple challenge that encompasses the mechanics we designed previously. The aim is to allow the player to become familiar with all the basic mechanics and features for when he eventually leaves this cosy environment.

The setting for the first environment will be located within a scrapheap full of other lost and lonely robots. To keep it in context, it will be located at the factory where Norbot was dumped after being caught by the Cy-bods. The first big challenge for Norbot will be to escape from the factory, but before that happens, he will require several simple mini-tasks to ease the player into the game. We will define this later in Part 2 of the book.

Summary

Teaching the player how to play games is becoming a prerequisite of game design and is completely necessary. In most things we do we require some form of training or teaching and games are no different. At the initial stages of the game, be forgiving and don't cheat the player.

CHAPTER 11

Stories and movies

Stories and movies – why have I combined these in one chapter? Although they do exist to some degree in games, neither are what makes a game. I am certainly not fully qualified to teach you how to make movies, but I do know something about stories. One thing I have learnt from my research into stories is that the majority of video games do not truly have them. When a game claims to have a story in it, they are not true stories. It usually consists of the idea that flooded the designer's mind at the start of the design process, and never really progresses beyond that in terms of story elements.

Stories and full motion video (FMV) in games have been a controversial topic since the days of the Amiga and Atari ST. These two computers were the dawn of game FMV, allowing developers to indulge in such alien concepts within their video games. Game movies in particular are perceived to be trespassers from another medium and they're not what games are about. However, not *all* gamers think so. Some players buy games for the story elements alone. A good well-constructed 'game' story can have immense pulling power if done effectively.

I began to ask myself why stories in games were poor in comparison to other mediums. I initially came to the conclusion that it was simply because games are all about gameplay and not about story telling. But that was a very naive conclusion. Games like Zelda and Half Life® have what appear to be excellent stories coupled with unparalleled gameplay.

So this got me thinking and I began to study the form and structure of stories. From knowing nothing about 'real' stories when I began, I was astonished at what I learnt. After years of studying and even writing stories myself, I now realise that the majority of game designers generally know nothing about story telling, in the same way they know nothing about movie camera placement. Stories have a structure and substance, and there are certain principles that one can learn in order to tell a good story. Believe it or not, but every movie you see from The Sound of Music to Terminator all use a similar structure and set of principles which have been honed and polished since the days of Aristotle.

If the games industry insists on competing with Hollywood, which I feel it will do even more so in the future, and intends to survive, then designers need to learn the craft of story. There is no way you can simply turn up for work one day and say 'I am going to put a story into my game'. It really doesn't work like that.

Not so long ago there were games tagged as interactive movies. There are no such things as interactive movies. It couldn't happen. They are two different mediums, with different objectives and will remain as such.

When I buy a game, the worst thing for me is sitting through a long movie that attempts to justify why you are playing the game, when all I want to do is play. There are several ways of introducing the player into the gaming world and storyline, without the need for expensive, lingering computer-generated epics tagged to the front end.

A game designer must always remember, first and foremost, that he is creating a game, an interactive experience, not a movie or a story. This is paramount.

When you are designing games, you are a designer. You are not an author. You can certainly be both but not when you are designing games.

Designer: A person who designs things.
Author: The writer of fiction and/or non-fiction.

Story definition

To explain why I believe real stories do not truly exist in games, you need to understand what a story is. I couldn't possibly discuss every element that contributes to a real story in just one chapter. The topic is vast and complex, possibly more so than video games. I can, however, explain some of the basic principles used in story design. To discover why these components exist in a story, and for a deeper understanding of the structure and principles, one must study it in greater detail. This book is primarily about game design, not story. However, I will define what type of story works in a gaming environment, which I am going to tag 'interactive stories'.

One example of how different stories are to games is as follows. A movie will often show you, the audience, something that the protagonist cannot see. It could be a murderer lurking behind a door holding a knife that glints in the moonlight. Or perhaps it's a speeding car a few blocks away from the protagonist, being driven by a lunatic. In the first instance the protagonist could be approaching the door and in the second, a mother and child could be crossing a road, but in both cases, you the audience, have foresight and you know what is about to happen to them. Or at least you think you know. The director has given you insight and heaped expectation to the point where you almost want to cry out at the screen. But you can't. Even if you did cry out, it wouldn't change a thing. It's a linear, never changing, *non-interactive* movie. That is the fundamental difference between video games and movies. Next time you see the movie, it will be identical. The cameras will be in the same place, the characters will do and say the same things and the ending will always be the same.

Let's imagine for a minute that the audience could change the two examples above, so the protagonists could be warned of the impending danger; what effect would it have? It would be a very boring movie because movies are made of this type of substance. They are a roller-coaster ride of tension and expectations pulling on the cords of your emotions. If you could stop it from doing that, it would kill movies … and we don't want that.

That is just one example of the tools moviemakers use to build tension and make you believe that what you are seeing is really happening. Imagine giving the player foresight in a video game? It wouldn't work! The player would simply avoid the situation! What a boring game!

The basic elements

'Story' is a name given to a skilled process, using a set of techniques that creates a specific form of entertainment, in the same way we use the word 'game'. A story must have a beginning, middle and end, as do most games except massive multi-player on-line games. They generally have a protagonist and antagonist, but not necessarily in human form. The antagonist, for example, could be a volcano, a meteor, a deadly bug or some other opposing force. The protagonist must have a problem, or some kind of conflict, often caused by the antagonist, which needs to be solved throughout the course of the story. From the start to the end of the story, the protagonist will go through some sort of change – not necessarily physical; it could be a change in beliefs or values. The decisions made by the protagonist throughout the story reveal his character and drive the story forward.

To construct and mould an entire story requires knowledge, skill and the manipulation of a set of complex rules, just like game design. A story is made out of a series of acts, sequences, scenes and beats, all contributing to the whole. These elements are bound by a series of events and plot points that twist and turn the story, elevating it to a climactic event pushing the story towards a resolution.

Figure 11.1 depicts a common act structure for movies: three acts punctuated by plot points. The protagonist must have a call to adventure, something that motivates him to go on the journey he is facing. This journey may not be geographical like Lord of The Rings, but it could be an emotional journey like Kramer vs Kramer or Ghost, for example. There will be various plot points in the movie that twists the story and send it off in a different direction, usually catching the audience unawares. You could go into the structure of movies with a magnifying glass and break it down into tiny pieces, but they ultimately end with a climactic event that resolves the story.

FIGURE 11.1 Movie act structure

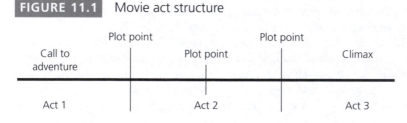

To add to the substance, a story usually has a theme running through it. We discussed themes in games earlier, but the theme of a story is somewhat different. The theme of a story generally opens the minds of the audience to some aspect of human nature like love and hate, for example.

There are also significant differences between stories in books and stories in movies. One of the biggest and most obvious differences is that a movie is a visual medium. Moviemakers can use the visual aspects to communicate to the audience, using no dialogue. Novels can't do this. They have to rely on the written word as the outlet to their audience, and words can be plentiful!

We also have to consider characters in stories; after all, isn't that what stories are made of? Characters are the linchpins of stories. Take your favourite story and remove all the characters, what do you have left? Story characters have a life, which is defined by the author with a back-story and revealed by the events that unfold as the character travels on his journey. Story characters have many attributes, such as values, beliefs, a job, a birthday, political views, a family, an education, and quirks; they also belong to a social structure. They always want something and do everything for a reason. They have emotions, which are often displayed to the extreme. All or some of these attributes can change throughout the course of the story.

Now do you think game designers consider all of this when designing their characters? In twenty years of working in the games industry, I have never witnessed that sort of character and story development.

So you see, there is a great deal to consider when constructing 'real' stories, and there is so much more I haven't mentioned here. Those are just some elements and tools that storytellers use when writing stories. I believe game designers could learn from a storyteller's principles and techniques and use them within games to provide a deeper experience for the player, but perhaps in a different format.

If we insist on putting more cut-scenes, interactive stories and full motion video within our games, then we need to learn and be prepared to do it properly to fully utilise that feature of the game.

Interactive stories

Now is the time we have to blend story and games and create interactive stories, not interactive movies. They do exist in games and some of them are done very well. However, as I write this, I feel like I'm probing the untouched, exploring a new frontier, yet it feels familiar. Interactive stories will grow to be a major contributor to games in the future. But if we are to be even more successful at this and compete with Hollywood, we need to learn the art of storytelling, dissect that art form, and apply elements of it to video games. Only then we will have true interactive stories that can be clearly defined and identified as a new type of storytelling. So what can we use from the art of story to enhance the experience of games, without affecting gameplay?

Of course games already have some of the building blocks of stories, such as conflict, characters, genre and many more things besides. Placing the word 'interactive' in front of stories implies that the player can interact with them and change them. To some extent he can, but not entirely. He has no control over the outcome of the core objective or the story resolution; it's always the same and this is the case for both mediums.

Two of the strongest elements of both mediums are the ability to grip the viewer and to hold him in place until the end has gone. The skill will come from designers using the principles of storytelling in short bursts, luring the player into the game, revealing the story as he moves through the world. If both aspects of storytelling and game are compelling enough, without exposition, then there is no reason why it can't blend together. You will often find that movie-goers play video games and vice versa, and there will come a time when someone acquires that special skill of blending the two together to create a new medium, particularly as games become more realistic.

Characters

Characters play a pivotal role in the creation of a story, but game characters still have a long way to go. Chapter 17 discusses video game characters, and goes into detail about traditional game characters. In this chapter I want to discuss the characterisation of a video game character. As I mentioned above, future video game heroes will need depth and growth in personality akin to animated cartoons and actors to appease future audiences.

Game characters will need to combine all the elements mentioned above, but how do we build that level of character detail into a game? I believe, the closer a computer character gets to portray emotion and life experience, the deeper the experience for the player. Doing this will add another dimension to video games in that the player will care so much more for his hero. Portraying real emotional feedback from player-characters, which sparks a connection with the player, is a feature yet to be fully utilised in video games. I can't think of one character in a game that I would seriously care about if it were to die. Is this because I know it will come back and it will be ok? But movies can make you care. Remember the movie Ghost. You must have wept in the cinema at some point in that movie – yes, the guys too! Is this the level of detail we want for our game characters? Yes is the answer, provided we can deliver the gameplay in unison; in fact the mass-market will come to expect it, especially after they experience it for the first time.

However, there are various reasons why we don't develop game characters further. The first reason is that game developers have traditionally created game characters that serve as a vehicle for gameplay. Designers generally have no experience of creating deep, emotional characters. Another reason is when a character dies, the player knows he is going to come back from death and the player simply needs to defeat the challenge that killed him in the first place. We also have to consider the cost and time involved. To create deep story characters means you have to give them a life. To do this can require enormous amounts of dialogue and specific animations etc. and the character will need to grow as the game progresses. Therefore the character itself becomes an ongoing project throughout development to reveal the growth and change both visually and emotionally. The technology required to essentially make a character 'act' in real-time is high risk for the programming team to adopt, and therefore would require careful management and monitoring throughout production.

Abe in Abe's Odyssey™ is a good example of good characterisation, although the game itself doesn't sit in my all time top ten. When I saw this game, the character was doing things I had never seen before in a video game, including breaking wind! Abe has his own language; he looks cute; he cares about his own people and the player is empathetic towards his plight.

Let's discuss how we can build this level of character development into a game. Of course, the same considerations apply: it depends on your audience, and it depends on the sort of game you are creating. If you are designing a RTS or a racing game, it is very unlikely you will need great depth of character. If you are designing an adventure game featuring a central character, then he could be given a personality.

The question is, what elements of character creation in traditional story-telling can we use in video games? I believe we will eventually use them all. Characters can be a great source of feedback that we just have not utilised in games as yet. Imagine guiding your character into a dark creepy forest; your character begins talking to you as you venture deeper. His emotions get the better of him and he begins to show his fear of the forest. This can be informative feedback, warning the player of impending danger coupled with a character trait leak. Or perhaps your hero is crossing a ravine while balancing on a log, and you soon discover your character hates heights! This could also be used as a game device, but it would only work if the player genuinely felt the character could not cross the ravine because of his fear. Using traits like these in a gaming environment is a relatively new concept, but will become the norm for future games. It is the usual scenario in that once we see somebody do it well and move the benchmark, everybody will move towards it.

Taking your avatar on a journey should also be about discovering your character through the challenges he faces. To do this, put him into situations that will reveal his character traits as described above, just like the movies. If the story is one of the central features of your game, it shouldn't be just about achieving your core objective. We can put our characters into *any* situation we like that's within the context of the game and the constraints of the market place, and the potential is enormous. We already put characters into some amazing worlds and settings, yet we fail to portray real character.

There is also the relationship between the player and the character. If the player performs particularly badly, let the character tell him so, which can be contextually performed in a number of emotional states. The game character can also be an authority figure, steering the game through dialogue and feed-back. The possibilities are endless.

Some well-established games are slowly beginning to create depth to their characters, and I believe we can do this without any cost to gameplay. Good examples of this can be seen in Tomb Raider, Mario, Zelda, Escape From Monkey Island®, to name but a few. But I feel there is still a long way to go for games in the character department.

What about the story itself? Can we adapt the principles of 'real' stories to a game without interfering with the gameplay? Lets look at some of the basic elements of stories.

Structure

While researching 'story', the first thing that struck me was the structure. We've already discussed the structure briefly and I believe the same structure can be adapted to games quite easily. A game can be defined, just as a story can, in acts, sequences, scenes and beats, but you must understand what effect each of those elements has on a story to enable you to use them in your game design.

Stories are segmented down to the second. Of course, every second must count in a movie, or it's dead time and will be edited out. Games are also structured, but if you study a lot of games and look at their structure, many of them appear knotted and unplanned, with each environment simply attached to the next, one after the other. The segmentation of stories can be applied to games, with the only difference being that the player forces the events along from one beat to the next in search of the next objective.

Movies are generally divided into acts, mostly three, but some have five. Each act is punctuated with a major event that forces the story in a new direction and each act supersedes the last. The first act is generally ten to twenty minutes long, the second act is the longest, sixty to eighty minutes and the final act is again, approximately ten to twenty minutes. The final scene of the last act climbs to *the* highest climactic moment in the movie, releasing the audience from the suspense and tension, concluding the movie and answering all questions posed in the story.

The first act of a movie generally introduces everything and everyone to the audience, including the setting, characters, the problem etc. However, within the first ten minutes, the first act will grab the audience's attention with a major event. Too much introduction can bore audiences, therefore something of great consequence to the protagonist must happen fairly quickly. Games are the same, but we need to introduce the 'major event' much more quickly than that, even if you have a story in your game. Your audience will want to play, so you must make your first act interactive, fun and short. Draw the player through the game and, at the end, set up a challenge that, when complete, reveals the core objective or a major revelation that makes the player sit up and take note, but more importantly encourages him to play more. I would equate the first act with the first environment in a game. It should introduce the player to all aspects of the game including, setting, characters, interface mechanism, the core objective etc.

Within each act you have a chain of sequences, each ending with a decisive moment for the protagonist. A sequence begins with perhaps a small problem or objective for the main character, like getting to work or visiting a neighbour, for example, and ends with it being resolved or revealed, but heightening the tension and expectation of the audience. It will also change the character in some way and the audience will see the character grow. A sequence can span many scenes.

EXAMPLE   **Visiting the neighbour**

Take 1: It's late at night and the protagonist's neighbour is playing music loudly. The protagonist's objective is to get his neighbour to turn the music down because it's disturbing the protagonist and he can't sleep. It might go something like this. The sequence would begin in his home (scene 01), which would reveal that the protagonist is annoyed at the noise (revealing a characteristic). He irritably walks outside (scene 02), across the garden, jumping over the fence into the neighbour's yard and up to the front door. He knocks on his neighbour's front door and his neighbour answers and invites our hero inside (scene 03). The neighbour is asked to turn the music down as it is disturbing our protagonist. The neighbour agrees and the task is accomplished.

But isn't that 'real-life' stuff? It's boring, that's what that is! In the movies (and in a game) it needs to be far more interesting and exciting than that. Let's run through it again, but this time, make it more interesting for the audience.

Take 2: Again it begins inside (scene 01). Our hero *angrily* stomps outside (scene 02) and leaps over the picket fence, but this time, his clothes are caught on the fence sending our hero crashing to the ground causing him to smash his face on the concrete. This physically hurts him, perhaps with a bloody nose (for a serious subject), or maybe you could give this scene some comedic value. Our hero picks himself up, walks up to the front door, but now he's really mad. He bangs on the front door with his fist, but this time the neighbour doesn't answer. The protagonist decides to venture around the back of the house, knowing his neighbour is in there probably laughing at him. Our hero notices that his neighbour is obviously listening to his music upstairs. In order to grab his attention, our hero picks up a stone and throws it at the first floor window. But the stone smashes the window. The neighbour switches the music off, appears at the window and is also really angry at the smashed window. They start hollering at each other. The neighbour decides to call the police who subsequently come and arrest our hero and take him away.

That's far more interesting and not only was it mission accomplished, but now our hero is in another predicament. The second scene in sequence two also reveals a lot about the kind of person the protagonist is.

The same structure can be applied to games. Each gaming environment can be broken down into sequences with an objective for each one giving the player choices as he plays. If your game is a story-based game, you need to consider how you will reveal your character's true personality as each sequence is performed. Both stories and games are linear, and you as the designer should know where the player will be at certain points in the game, so this aspect of character design can easily be incorporated into your game.

Within each sequence we have scenes that can equate to a particular task or puzzle and set in a specific area of game. The beats are the actions of the player. Every click, every button press and every movement is a beat in your game. Each of these segments has a beginning and an end, acts, sequences, scenes and beats. They all contribute to a section of game and they all help develop your story and your character. By using a technique like this, your game will have no dead space and will be consistently event-packed.

Setting

Stories generally have a setting, as do games. A couple of aspects of your story usually define the setting – the moment the story takes place, the place where it happens and the duration of the story. These elements also define what can happen in your story as they put everything into context, which essentially marks your boundaries. All of these things are possible in video games. One of the great things about video games is that you can set your game anywhere, real or fantasy. It really doesn't matter because the development team will create your world to spec and it's virtual.

Audience expectation

A key element to consider is audience expectation. Good storytelling will build the expectation of the audience to the point where they think they know what is going to happen, but the author will deliver something different, something bigger and more powerful than the expectation. How many movies have you sat through till the end, but it wasn't the real end; something else happened that shocked or surprised you? This technique is used time and time again in stories and it's this that keeps us watching to see what is going to happen next.

We can do this in games very easily, particularly in adventure games, which are mostly story driven. We can build the player's expectation, which can ultimately change and become something far more powerful. The structure of games will allow us to do this, and you will need to learn how to use this if you want to incorporate a great story into your game.

There are two technical aspects to consider very carefully when designing your 'game with a story'. The first is the save mechanism. The second is the length of your game. Imagine for a moment that a player has been playing your game, but has put it down for a week, or longer. You must consider how you are going to get him back on track, remind him what has happened so far in the game *and* the story. TV shows do this on a weekly basis by showing key clips of previous episodes. This is not impossible, particularly in a story-based game. The technology is there now to record key moments as the player performs them, or perhaps a pre-recorded video diary could play clips relating to the progress you have made to date. Whatever you decide, inform the player of his achievements.

The length of your game is a complicated issue and mostly depends on your design and the story. You should never add content to a story to fill time and the same can be said of a game. Be sure to include enough content to almost satisfy the player – you must fulfil the story, but leave the player wanting more. Less is certainly more in games.

Do we need stories in games?

We certainly *don't* need stories in games. Games can exist perfectly well without them and have done so since games began. After all, we want to interact with games, whereas traditional stories are not interactive; there are, however, some story-books that can give you the option to take alternative paths through the story but that's not true interactivity – there is no challenge, it's simply multiple choice! One could even class it as luck. But there is certainly a place for stories in games and some people want a story in a game.

When a development studio acquires a movie or book licence, they don't generally use the story as a vehicle for the game. They will pull out the elements that make up the action and create a series of goal-orientated environments, string them together, place the occasional boss character and call it a game. Some licensed games are dreadful and rely solely on the licence to sell it to the masses.

One product in particular that had more story than game was a game called Heart of Darkness™. The characters were superbly defined, the story was great and the visuals were to die for. I can remember it vividly. It attracted so much attention at the E3 convention in LA, there were long queues to get into the tiny purpose-built cinema. The game was so advanced in its rendering and visual storytelling techniques, even for animated movies, that the word spread to some *big* movie directors who came to the stand to view it for themselves. The problem was, it took so long for the game to hatch, when it did come out, it was passé. This is one thing you need to be wary of; you need to take into account whether your game will be outdated before it hits the shelf.

Rendered movies

That leads me nicely into rendered cut scenes, intros and outros. In games, full motion video (FMV) truly began in the 16-bit era on the Amiga and Atari

ST. Psygnosis, an innovative company that is now a distant memory, often put an awe-inspiring, beautifully rendered movie at the front of their games. They were doing something different, ground-breaking, then everybody began to follow suit, but it was costly.

There is nothing worse than playing a game and being pulled out of it by a rendered movie in the middle of the action. Often they are included to justify the cost of making them, whether they were good or bad. It pains me to think that a producer somewhere might be saying 'I don't care what it does to the game, I paid three hundred thousand dollars to create that movie, IT'S GOING IN'. Thankfully this doesn't happen so much these days, but it did in the past. If you are thinking of including rendered movies in your game, think again. There are better ways of doing it today. Technology has moved on and we don't need to use it.

FMV does cost large sums of money to create and we should leave it to those who know how to make it, and those who do it for a living. We are not movie directors! We are game designers! If you, or your producer insists on having movies in your game, get somebody else to make them. There are companies out there who know how to do it better than you! There are also companies who know how to write great dialogue and know how to edit it together, and they do it well.

Now let's assume for one crazy moment that you do have FMV in your game. Please ensure it can be bypassed at the press of a button. There is nothing worse than playing a game when suddenly the game is paused and FMV is loaded and played. This completely detaches the player from the game and the player can lose interest. Give the player the option to watch it or lose it, regardless of the cost.

You have to remember, you are making an interactive game, so therefore everything must be interactive to keep your audience fixated. Rendered movies are not interactive. I'm not saying they are wrong and shouldn't be done, but they have to be orchestrated and presented at the right time and for the right reason. You will often find there is a better way of saying what you need to say in an interactive way or a cut sequence using the game engine. Rule number one is to make your game fun, but rule number two is keep hold of your audience. Some gamers like rendered movies and view them as a treat or a reward, which is fine, but they should be built into the game as such.

Info dump – exposition

Often a game will use a movie for exposition, to dump a ton of information onto the player all at once. There are many ways in which to intrigue the player and pull them into a game, without dumping hundreds of thousands of dollars worth of movie onto them!

The intro movie should not be an excuse to lay down the rules of the game. In fact, no movie in your game should do this, particularly FMV. Sequences can be used to deliver objectives if a visual connection is required. If no visual connection is required, audio feedback can be just as effective and can be delivered while the game is in motion.

A designer needs to think carefully how he should present his objectives to the player, which should preferably be creative, coherent and interactive. In Dungeon Siege the player learns of his objectives by talking to the natives, which is perfect because the method is under direct control of the player and the player has choices.

Real-time cut sequence

One of the great things about today's technology is that 99 per cent of all games developed are rendered in real-time. If you are new to the industry, you can be certain that any game that you work on will almost certainly be 3D. Using this technology is a much better way of portraying game information. It can be done quickly and seamlessly and as part of the game structure. It also has a technical advantage in that it uses the game-rendering engine, therefore the sequence can remain seamless and not detach the player from the game the way a FMV sequence can.

All sequences in your game should have a purpose, a reason for existing – to aid the player and inform, for example. They should have a beginning, a middle and an end and deliver the necessary information as quickly and as dynamically as possible. If possible, make them interactive so the player feels in control. Long sweeping camera movements are not necessary unless you are establishing an environment, so try not to use them because you think it looks great! It will actually make your game weaker.

If you use a cut sequence with interactive elements, you can do things that can't be done with FMV. You can change the sequence based on decisions made by the player. If your game has an option to choose different characters for example, you can replace the models and animation without the need to render thousands of different images and store them on a CD.

Good examples of good real-time cut sequences can be seen in Half Life. You actually feel like you are part of the events taking place, you can control your character while the sequence is happening and it toys with your imagination, luring you deeper into the game.

Norbot: premise

As I mentioned before, there are no 'real' stories in games, not in the true sense of the word. To follow is my premise for 'Norbot'. It sets the scene, informs the player of the core objective and the antagonist in the world.

Norbot
Quest for Freedom

Norbot is a lonely robot, sitting glumly amongst a robot scrap heap destined to become a cube of mangled metal. He once lived a fulfilling existence serving his master, until one day the robot wars came. A race of evil Cy-bods, created by Dr Mega-bite, invaded his homeland of Tobor.

In the midst of battle, enemy fire blew Norbot's left hand clean off. It could so easily have been more, perhaps even fatal. In the chaos that ensued, he was eventually scooped by the Cy-bod-tec disposal-squad, stripped of all his vital components and dumped in the recycling factory.

While Norbot mourns his beloved kingdom, another more dishevelled robot is dumped on the heap next to him. The heavy crashing triggers a message embedded into its memory bank. Norbot discovers that in the darkest southeast corner of Tobor, there is a band of rebellious robots that fight each day, struggling for peace and freedom for all bots everywhere. He also discovers they worship the hand that once belonged to 'the one' that would some day be their saviour. Norbot realises it is his hand they worship and with a feeling of nobility, and a sense of responsibility, he realises it is his destiny to help them.

The evil Cy-bods still rule Tobor, but not without conflict. One element exists on Tobor that Mega-bite did not expect, the presence of H_2O. This can be fatal to Cy-bods, burning and decaying their components likes acid through flesh.

There are several pockets of resistance peppered across the homeland, still fighting the good fight. Some bots believe it is futile, while others believe 'the one' will someday come and save them from this evil tyranny.

This is simply an idea, a premise, or story overview, it's not a story. But it is the idea I have used to develop the game. My features, setting, characters etc. will all be based around my idea and the story elements will be designed into the game.

Summary

To summarise this chapter and as points of reference, here is a list of things we have discussed in this chapter.

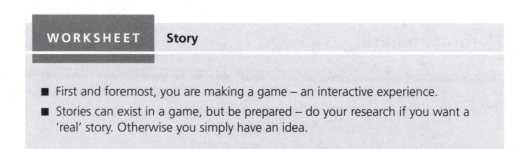

WORKSHEET   **Story**

- First and foremost, you are making a game – an interactive experience.
- Stories can exist in a game, but be prepared – do your research if you want a 'real' story. Otherwise you simply have an idea.

- When designing your story you should consider the following elements:
  - Setting
  - Structure
  - Genre
  - Story theme (not gameplay theme)
  - Defining complex characters
  - Emotion
  - Story dialogue (not real)
  - Audience expectation
  - Climatic incidents
  - Resolution

- If your game has story elements built into it and you have set your game in a real-life situation, be sure to do your research on the subject.

- Try and avoid FMV unless your producer is insistent, in which case, keep it limited to front-end and back-end FMV.

- Use real-time cut sequences wherever you can. Make them interactive and remove all exposition.

- Insist on having your dialogue written by a professional – it will add depth to your game.

- Insist on farming out FMV and possibly cut-scenes if your tool set is mobile.

There is a mountain of books on the subject of story. If you are serious about storytelling as a game device, study the art before embarking on your design. I have only scratched the surface and given you insight into how you can adapt stories to games. It is new to games, and it may be a little while before stories exist in games effectively.

CHAPTER 12

Design pitfalls

You've played them. I've played them. We've all played them. You know the ones I'm talking about, the games that excite nothing more than the static on your TV screen. What makes them so bad and why are they made? And once they are made, and everybody can see how bad they are, how do they get published? These questions roll around in the minds of many, but the answers are never forthcoming. Nobody wants to take the blame or be recognised for a bad quality or failed product.

I could give you a mountain of reasons why games are poor quality or never see the light of day, but this book is not about project management or scheduling, therefore I am only going to concentrate on bad game design. We have discussed many things that go into building a design; here we will discuss common mistakes designers can make and why a game design can go disastrously wrong during the design and development process.

When beginning a game design, it's safe to assume that if you don't identify your target audience and platform, your game could wander aimlessly, and possibly drift towards the foggy fringes of the hardcore gamers' market whereas you intended to target the mass-market, or vice versa. You could also assume that the lack of passion, lack of hard work and lack of vision can also see your design fail and die. Therefore we should leave the assumptions, and concentrate more on the specifics. I will also go into detail with some of the bigger problems a designer could face, and offer possible solutions to avoid these.

Your game never gets going

Often games will never see the starting block. The reasons are plentiful, from wrong place, wrong time, the team doesn't match the product or the marketing department can't see your game. But these are relatively minor reasons and although valid, it doesn't mean that your idea is a bad one or unworthy of development. In the movie and book world, they say everyone has a story inside them waiting to be written; the same can be said of games. To follow are some of the more extensive reasons why games don't get made – and the first one is rife!

Nothing original ... seen it all before

Plagiarism is a major problem in the games industry as it is in most industries. Very few games that come through development are totally content original.

The last game I can remember that was completely and truly original in game design and execution was Lemmings. Some people may argue that The Sims is an original game, but if you're an owner of a Commodore 64, you will most likely know of The Little Computer People™ as seen in Figure 12.1.

FIGURE 12.1 Little computer people

Although technologically crude in comparison, the idea was very similar. You had to take care of a little person who lived inside your computer, or so you were led to believe! You could play games with him as shown in Figure 12.2, he would get sick and when he wanted your attention, he would tap on the screen.

Hardcore gamers are having a hard time of late. They see their hobby being swallowed by mass-market clones that endlessly pour into the high street shops. But it's not so much the idea that has to be unique it's more the implementation of the idea. A recent game called Ico™ on PlayStation2 is very innovative, and uses some old-style gameplay techniques in a unique setting. You can have an idea and apply almost any genre of game to it. How the idea is conveyed and executed in the finished product is what will separate your game from the slush.

It's simply not possible to be innovative every time. In fact games that are innovative are rarely seen in today's high streets. This is largely to do with the high stakes involved in publishing. In the days of 8-bit gaming, games were developed at an alarming rate. Therefore, the chances of something

FIGURE 12.2   Game within a game

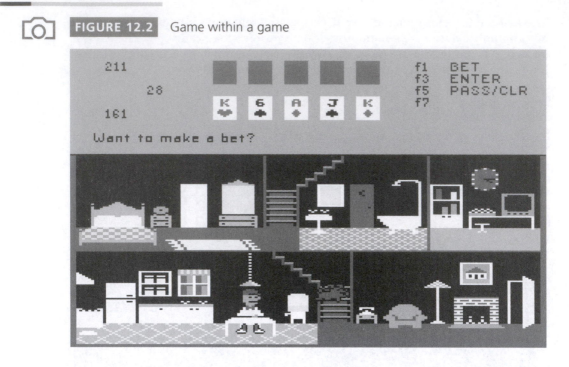

unique gracing the software shelves were very high indeed. Today, however, games cost millions of dollars to develop, the risks are higher, and publishers want to play safe and make money. There is little room for ingenuity in game development unless you can prove it before approaching a publisher, and then there is no guarantee of publication.

So how do you make your game stand out from the overcrowded slush piles, assuming you have hurdled the concept phase successfully, and are into pre-production? The first thing to do is define a prototype. You and your team should select the features of your game that convey the game's innovative qualities, which will subsequently reduce the risk for the publisher and prove the concept. Should you succeed and your game proves to be innovative, fun and marketable, it will certainly draw attention to itself and people will begin to talk about it. The uniqueness doesn't have to be the entire game, it could be a new interface strapped to a familiar genre, for example. Or perhaps it could come from the art department where the artists might create a new technique or visual style. Preferably it will come from the design department and you will have a special gameplay device or technique on your hands.

What is the game about ... I can't see it!

When somebody looks at your game, they need to be able to understand it simply by looking at it. This is a sad fact, but I'm afraid people in general have little time to explore a game's potential. You have to hit them with it. A publisher's marketing department often knows little about development and they don't understand why you are showing them untextured environments, placeholder graphics, little gameplay and bugs. This is often the case with work in progress, but marketing people don't want to see it ... don't show them. If you do, it could be a fatal trap for you and your team, and in many publishing houses, marketing departments have the power to kill a project if they can't see it. It's no fault of marketing; they are simply regurgitating what they have seen and been presented with. They know their audience and if they don't feel confident that they can sell it, they won't.

It's illogical, captain!

It often amazes me when you see a game design that defies logic. This is designing blind. You must be consistent and use logical puzzles or the player will not see your game. For example, if your character is a superhero and can smash through walls, throw cars and bend metal, do *not* let the player be stumped by a locked door. It's as plain as day, black and white, common sense. If your hero does have superhuman powers, a simple locked door that needs opening with a key is not going to work; the player will notice and feel cheated! He will try everything he can think of to smash down that door – because he feels he should be able to.

Bad design documents

I go into detail with design documents in Part 2, but I will cover the relevant issues here. Game design documents can reek of flaws which when read, make no sense. This can stop your game dead in its tracks before it gets out of the concept phase. These flaws can be anything including inconsistencies, bad layout, incomprehensible language, lack of detail, too much detail and many more besides. This can happen for several reasons. It could be that the designer has lived with it for so long that he has become blind to the content and can't see the wood for the trees. Or it could be that he doesn't have enough technical information in front of him to design his game accurately. To avoid this trap, share your work with your colleagues; remember, it's a team effort. It is really difficult to let go of something, particularly when it's only half finished, but honest feedback is really important.

It's mine ... all mine!

A common problem is that a designer takes on the sole responsibility of creating the documents by not involving anybody else in the design process. This consequently leaves the documents riddled with inaccurate information, no innovation and the lack of any realistic plan. The design documents should depict the entire game, the vision and more importantly the mechanics of your game. It will hold the stuff that makes the 'game' work and be fun. Therefore, accurate information and general feedback is essential when compiling the documents. You should *always* involve the team leads; they will know what is possible and what is not. This also depends what sort of designer you are and what experience you have. Some of the best designers I know were programmers prior to becoming designers. They are good because they understand the logic, the code architecture and technical capabilities of potential target machines. However, you still need feedback to be sure that what you are writing isn't nonsense.

Marketing transparency

Prior to preparing your documents, you must think about who will be reading them. If you're presenting to marketing, be sure the language is clear, accurate and precise. Remember, all they want to know is what the finished product will be like, not how many polygons are drawn, frame rate or what the special effects are going to look like. They want to be clear on the substance of the game. What is it about your game that is special, and what elements does it have that will sell it for them? Many people find it hard to grasp the concept that marketing needs a hook to sell a game. The game may be great, but if it's like a dozen other games with no clear hook, how are they supposed to sell it? You often hear developers say that if the gameplay is good then it shouldn't need marketing, it will sell anyway. No it won't. It will need exposure and to expose it, they cannot simply say it has great gameplay. Your game is the marketing department's tool. They will draw from it and create their own products, i.e. commercials and advertising. If you have to, create different documents for different audiences, but be consistent with your vision and convey it clearly in each document.

Foggy features

One of the most common mistakes a designer can make is being deficient in detail. Your design documents must convey *all* the game features clearly. Avoid using vague terminology. For example, if you've made up cool funky words for your items and features, you will need to describe what they are, what they do and where they fit into the overall structure of the game. By all means you can give them a name, but never assume the reader will know what the feature is by its name. Describe what it is and its function, using words everybody will understand. If you leave things open to interpretation, your game will fail to match yours and everybody else's vision.

I like it – so it must be good

I've mentioned this before, but it continues to be a big issue for designers. Design for your audience, not for yourself. If need be, get to know your audience. Designers will also design for themselves inadvertently. If you have a problem with this, go and speak to your audience and ask them what they like in a game. If your target market is 12- to 16-year-olds, for example, go visit a school and chat to 12- to 16-year-olds. You may even come away with an idea you never thought of. Authors do this all the time and they get so much from it. You must always keep your player in mind when designing your game.

Your audience will get bored with a game too, but the audience will determine how long that will take. Keep track of your design and make notes on how long you anticipate the player will take to complete each section. If your game is module based and linear, i.e. can be completed from start to finish in a predefined way, then your timeline should be no shorter than 10 hours of continuous gameplay. Anything beyond 25 to 30 hours is probably way too long for a linear, mass-market game.

Feature creep during production

Unless you have an experienced producer on your team, this can be a major problem, and is often the cause of a disastrous end or escalating costs. Features are continuously bundled into the design, milestones are missed, budgets spiral out of control and before you know it, you have a huge sprawling mess with enough disjointed features to feed the entire industry!

So how do you avoid this? This, like so many problems that can spring up during development, is not entirely your jurisdiction. You can help to channel the pipeline of clarity though. During pre-production, you will define your feature set that becomes part of the bible for your design. The producer will then create a schedule that reflects your design, and if the producer is worth the money he's being paid, he will have built latent contingency into that schedule. So, while in production, some bright spark will inevitably come up with an idea or a new feature for the game that will be tantalisingly irresistible to implement. If this happens, that new feature will begin to eat into that contingency. The contingency is there to bridge unforeseen hiccups, of which there are many, like bugs, flaky disc duplication, staff sickness, staff holidays etc. If this feature fudging happens too often, all the hard work the producer put into his production plan goes out the window and the game begins to slip. It is worth spending more time clarifying your design during pre-production rather than allowing features to creep into the game. While in production, be tough, avoid temptation and save the extra features for the sequel. Just say NO! The primary objective while in production is to work to a plan and stick with it. This doesn't mean your game can't change, it can and it will, but the changes need managing and monitoring efficiently.

Do not stray from your world – be consistent. When putting together your design, be sure the features you design all fit together and each one is a piece of the whole. This can be difficult, but try not to be influenced by a feature in another game just because you think it's cool, it will most likely stick out like a sore thumb. Designers tend to let their passion overwhelm them, without realising the consequences until it's too late!

It's too big!

The design document is now clearly defined, everything is in there, but it's simply too large. When creating your design, try and think how long each function or feature will take to design, implement, test and re-design. If you don't know, ask a producer or a programmer and involve your team. You will probably find you have way too much content. Be prepared to cut it out. You don't have to delete it forever. Perhaps you can use the excess ideas for your next game, or even a sequel if your game does well. Remember, the opposite can also happen.

Sprawling environments

As major mistakes go, the sprawling empty environment sits right next to 'not knowing your audience'. One of the reasons we create box maps and go through pre-production is to define the whole game and how it will work together to make an enthralling instance of interactive entertainment.

The world in which the game exists should be as big as you need to make it to convey your idea. No more than this. The player should never be able to travel too far without meeting his next challenge. Consider the rhythm of the game and check its consistency. Your game may be more packed with tasks and actions towards the end of the game than at the beginning, but the player should always have an objective and be clear what that objective is. If your game takes place in a city for example, and the player's task is on the other side of town, it must be placed there for a reason and you need to make the journey across town interesting for the player, otherwise you simply have a gigantic void.

One of the biggest problems in game design today is editing; we really are afraid to do it. The games industry doesn't understand post-production, but then again, we're only just coming to terms with pre-production! It costs so much money to create code, art and design, the last thing we want to do is cut it out. But look at movies for a good example. They chop and change large chunks of movie that cost hundreds of millions of dollars to make, and they do it to make the movie better. It improves the quality of the final movie and therefore increases income potential. If your game is full of blanks, chop them out. If your game has an obscure puzzle, chop it out or re-design it, don't jam the player on his path to glory. Play your game all the way through in box mode if you have to, but do not put blank spaces and annoying potholes in your world in an attempt to expand the play time.

Team relationships

For the benefit of the individual, I want to go into the relationships between team members. You may be thinking 'what has this got to do with game design?' Well, it has everything to do with it. Creating games is a team effort, it is no longer an individual event. And let's face it, you will have to eat, drink, and even sleep with these individuals for 18 to 24 months, working on the same project towards the same vision. That's two years of your working life per game – at least. Therefore, it is essential that you all get along.

Drive from the core

An efficient, well-motivated, creatively solid team that delivers product can be a valuable asset to any publisher or developer. However, depending on the size of your team, which could be anything from 10 to 40 people or more, it can be difficult to get to know everyone. Therefore a team needs to be well managed, or more time will be spent talking and socialising than actually making the game! Time is money and employing 30 creative people for two years is expensive, and people are usually the most expensive part of development. So if the budget needs cutting, you know what the management will look at first!

In every team there is a core. They are usually a small bunch of people that have the passion and determination of a raging bull, to drive the product through to the end. These people are usually paid the most money! They are the cornerstones of the development process and if they were to leave, it could have a dramatic effect on the schedule, the overall vision and consequently the game itself. If you are the lead designer, you will most likely be one of those people.

Weed them out

The producer needs to be vigilant and weed out any bad apples or lame wannabes. They will be there, they always are. They can sometimes pull the team down with them if you let them. I know what you're thinking, 'this all sounds very political'. The sad truth is these things can happen, particularly if there is no control over the direction of the team and the product. It is a creative process and creative people can be fickle and very stubborn. If you have strict control over the direction of the game, you remain focused and you have control over the schedule, you will soon learn which members don't harbour the same passion, or are simply lazy. They should be nurtured or extruded!

If other members of the team are not cognisant with the vision of the game, this could result in a shortfall in other elements that contribute to the design, thus letting the rest of the team down. Regular meetings and updates will help to maintain the consistency of the overall objective, which is – for every individual in the team – to make the same game.

You don't want to do it like that ... do it like this!

A 'know-it-all' designer is a bad designer. You should never swan around dictating to the rest of the team, preciously guarding your baby; remember, it's a team effort. When working with a team of professional people, you don't need to tell them how they should do their job. If you write your documents clearly and get your message across without patronising, they will respect you for that. Programmers and artists are fully aware of how to do their job, so do not preach to them. Remember, your concern, among other things, is the design and the functionality and vision of the game. Your prospective co-workers will write their own technical design documents and art style guides.

Listen to your peers and work as a team. Try not to alienate everyone around you or your development cycle will become a nightmare. You must get the team involved in the design. At the very least, make them feel like they are involved. Ninety per cent of ideas thrown at you should probably keep going into the wastepaper bin, but never tell them that. You make a note, smile and thank them. Whatever happens, do not let a programmer railroad you into anything. In the past, programmers have been guilty of designing to their abilities. If you can't create a particular feature, then harvest other opinions and perhaps somebody else will be able to do it. But be sure you have told programmer number one that you are going to do this.

Providing you approach game design in a professional manner and can work within a team structure, you will do well and so will your game.

Technological breakdown

Other elements of the game, beyond your control, may let it down, like the technology for example. If the technology has been designed badly or sits like a plate of spaghetti, you are doomed! If the technology isn't up to present-day standards, the quality of your game will suffer badly. The technology, to some extent, is blind to the outside world until you see it appear on the screen. Therefore, your technical director must have a clear vision of your design in order to plan and map his technology sufficiently.

Be sure to look at other similar products, particularly on your leading platform, and aim higher, or at the very least, at the same level. Remember, your game will take between 18 and 24 months, possibly more, to complete. A lot can happen in the world of technology in that time. You will only get to create two, maybe three games on any platform during its life-span. The console market tends to have a five-year life cycle while the PC market constantly changes. If you are designing a PC game, the highest spec PC at the start of your development cycle is usually the lowest spec at time of release.

Is he really a programmer?

Other technological disasters can come from incompetent programmers. The problem is it's not the incompetence that's the problem – they may just be badly placed by management. They may be very good programmers, but in their own niche. This rarely happens today, but occasionally a programmer will slip through the net who has no idea what he is doing. A good producer or technical director should be able to spot them early on, particularly if they begin to miss deadlines.

This problem is more likely to happen with artists. It has been known for an artist to get a job on the strength of other people's work. Of course this is pointless because he will soon be found out when the quality of his work doesn't meet expectations.

If you are a lead on a project and you have concerns over new staff joining, one way to quash those concerns is to ask to sit in on interviews. That way you can express your concerns before it's too late.

Publisher–developer relationships

This is not so much a design issue so I will only touch on this lightly. The relationship between a developer and a publisher can break down and subsequently bring your game to an end. This doesn't necessarily mean that the designer, or any other member of the team, is to blame for the cancellation of a project. So why do breakdowns happen?

Often, at the beginning of a project, a schedule is created to fit the publisher's needs rather than the game. Therefore, when the development studio fails to deliver promised milestones, or fails to meet quality expectations, a publisher can begin to lose faith in the product. This subsequently leads to a cancelled product.

Also, when a developer and publisher harbour different visions of the product, this too can result in the demise of the relationship. Whatever the reasons, it can cause major damage to companies, teams and individuals who have spent years of their life on a game only to see the project simply end. A loss of faith in the management will lead team members to move on and work elsewhere if this happens too often.

Summary

A game's demise is not always the fault of team members; more often than not, it is down to the management of a project. Be sure to plan well. Get along with your peers and resolve any problems as quickly as possible. Involve your team members in the design process and be sure everyone has a clear vision of the game.

CHECKLIST

- Drive your game and make it happen.
- Do you have something unique about your game?
- Is your game clear and precise, can the readers understand the content?
- Is your language clear enough? Did you get your message across?
- Are you being overly possessive?
- Is your game marketable?
- Are you designing for your audience, or is it for you?
- Size does matter – is it too big or possibly even too small?
- Get along with your colleagues or they'll get along without you!

CHAPTER 13

Player punishment

Chapter 12 discussed some of the reasons why a project can be cancelled before it reaches game status. This chapter is about how the player can be punished unjustifiably through bad game design, using the game's rules intentionally to do this. Bad game design can be identified in games that make it to retail and subsequently into the hands of the people that pay hard-earned money for them. Punishing the player, like so many other things in game design, can make or break your game. If the negatives outweigh the positives, it can come under fire from press and bad reviews, consequently dramatically affecting sales volume.

On the one hand you don't want to be too kind to the player so it makes the game too easy, but on the other you don't want to be too brutal. It's not just the legitimate game mechanics of punishing the player that can be unbalanced; the technology can punish the player also, like bad collision for example.

There is a fine line that runs through the objectives in your game; step on one side of it and the player gets punished, step on the other and the game becomes far too easy. You need to find that line, stay on it and follow it through to the end of your game.

If you remove one game element from a perfectly balanced game, it should break and fall over. Take Space Invaders, for example: what would the game be like without the bunkers perfectly placed along the bottom of the screen? Also, remove the larger power pills from Pac-Man and consider what would happen to that game? Both examples would punish the player without actually doing anything because they would become too difficult. Subsequently the player would become frustrated and most likely give up playing. As I said before, removing a single element from any game should upset the balance of the game, and make the game frustrating and almost unplayable. This is a good way of identifying any weak features in the game also. If you take them out and it has little or no effect on the game, it probably shouldn't be in there!

Implementing a bad save/load mechanism can also be a punishing ritual for the player. Save and load varies depending on the sort of game you are designing, but it should never be unfair to the player. We cover this in more detail in a later chapter.

Passive punishment

All topics discussed in this section are what I call 'passive punishment'. They are a collection of bad game design elements that punish the player unnecessarily, without the player doing anything wrong. Is it bad game design? Or is it a game that lacks certain elements thus upsetting the balance? Either way, they must be avoided. There are many things we could discuss when it comes to bad game design, but I have specifically chosen these because they focus on player punishment when the player is inactive.

I am going to cover many common flaws that designers have built into games that have left players wanting their money back. Many games are subjective to each player and may not necessarily be a case of bad game design. To differentiate between them I am going to focus on design faults and technical bugs that hinder the players' enjoyment. Often you will hear players disparage a game, but this doesn't necessarily mean it has faults. It's more likely they don't like that particular genre of game.

> **TIP**
>
> When you begin designing your game, be sure to study other successful games in the genre you are targeting. This doesn't mean you should copy them. In fact you should *never* do that. But do look at the structure of the games. Take them apart, reverse engineer it and make a note of all the pieces. For example, write down where items were placed, their value, purpose and then omit some design elements and see what effect it would have on the overall game. Reverse engineering is one way to learn from the masters and at a rapid pace. There are thousands of games out there, some superb, others downright dreadful. Play and study them all and you will learn not only what is good, but what is bad also.

Let's begin with some common design faults that are often found in computer and video games. Most of them can be found in most genres, but I will try and be specific where I can.

Where am I?

There are many ways a game can punish the player without actually harming him in any way. For example, allowing the player to wander aimlessly around a dungeon, with no apparent way out, is very painful for the player! If the walls and floors all look the same and there are no milestones or landmarks, the player will simply get lost. That is punishing the player, but more importantly, it's bad game design. Dungeon maze-like tunnels should be designed for the player, just like any other part of your game. Visual and audio references should be placed in the maze so the player can recognise his position in the world.

In a maze environment, you should try and avoid dead-ends where the player will be required to backtrack. This will allow the player to keep moving forward, providing a sense of progression, albeit perhaps a false sense of progression. This can happen if the player treads the same ground, i.e. going around in a circle, which is tolerable, providing he can recognise that he has been there before.

The maze needs to be challenging, but not confusing or disorientating. Allow the player to travel multiple routes through the maze, but include additional landmarks specific to each route. Your maze may not be dungeon tunnels either; it could be a forest, a jungle or a swamp for example. The point is that it's a maze and the player could get lost in it unless you give him some clues and a sense of direction. You might argue that getting the player lost is the whole point of a maze and you would be partially right. However, in an interactive gaming environment, players will get bored, feel cheated and walk away from the game if they are trapped or lost for too long. Therefore, a certain balance is required and you must help the players by giving them clues in one form or another.

One way to combat this would be to offer the player a map feature to help him navigate. Maps appear constantly, even subliminally, in our everyday lives. They appear in large office buildings, museums, amusement parks and shopping malls, and you can even find electronic map devices in cars. Maps aid navigation, so don't be afraid to use them. In fact, for any type of adventure-style game, you should insist upon it. The map doesn't have to show the entire environment at once; it can be revealed as the player travels around, providing 'feedback' as he advances, as in the example from Dungeon Siege (Figure 13.1).

Some players may choose not to use the map at all and that's fine, but at least the option is there for those who do need it! A map feature that reveals the area as the player travels through it still leaves room for surprises and exploration. If you provide a map, receiving it should be a reward and the player should have to earn it in some way. Remember, keep it consistent, in context and make it a reward.

Get me out of here!

Another severe form of punishment is freezing the player. When I say freezing, I mean placing a puzzle or obstacle in your game that has no logic, reason, is completely surreal or is just really hard to combat. Hardcore gamers will relentlessly pursue this type of punishment, but the mass-market will walk away in frustration. You must avoid that happening at all costs. If you can't re-design it, chop it out of the game. *Never* be afraid to chop blockages out of your game, it will make your game stronger. Remember, the player is playing your game to have fun, not to be punished.

FIGURE 13.1 Dungeon Siege map system

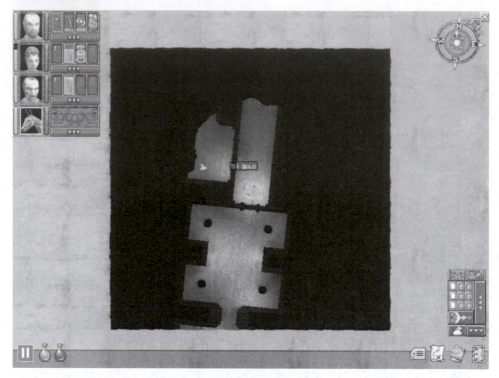

Puzzle design is an art form. Many years of game design will teach you how not to design puzzles, as well as how to design them well. You should never expect to simply begin designing perfect puzzles, it's a skill that needs to be learnt and mastered, as with most things in game design.

Many old 2D adventure games were full of puzzles where the player had to use several objects together in order to create a new one to subsequently solve a puzzle. Often, the objects bore no relation to one another and the solutions were blurry beyond belief. Consequently, the player would get stuck and give up.

Oh no – not again!

Loading and saving in games is a major issue when designing; be sure to give this a great deal of thought. Occasionally designers will decide they want to extend the playing time of their game and design a 'load/save' option that does exactly that. There is nothing worse than playing a game, getting almost to the end of a section and dying, only to start at the beginning again. This is a game killer because the player doesn't want to play the same thing over and over again. What can be even worse is that the designer forces the player to solve the same puzzles and collect important objects again and again. You should *never* do this because it can become very tedious for the player. Once a puzzle is solved it is no longer a puzzle, it simply becomes a chore!

Load and save can work differently on consoles than on PCs. In Dungeon Siege on the PC for example, the player can save at any point in the game, which is great. This might prove difficult on current consoles due to the limited space on the cartridge; however, there are several compression techniques a developer can use to crunch data and create smaller files. The Xbox has a hard drive built into the console and future consoles will undoubtedly have hard drives or some other mass storage device that will allow for larger save storage.

I am going to discuss different load/save mechanisms for different games on various platforms. Dungeon Siege has what I call an 'open' load/save option, allowing the player to load and save at any point in the game. When the player reloads a saved game, he will begin exactly where he left off, which is great for a game like Dungeon Siege on the PC. Figure 13.2 illustrates the open load/save function.

FIGURE 13.2   Open load/save

Game life-span/sections	1	2	3	4	5	6	7	8	9	10
Save locations										→
Restart points										→

The top bar represents the life span of the entire game broken down into clearly definable sections. You may have many more, or possibly less identifiable sections in your game than I have defined here, and each game will be different. Each vertical line represents a key moment in the game, or a threshold in the game cycle that the player will cross over. Along the 'save' row you will notice there are no restrictions or save points. It depicts that the player can save anywhere at any time and consequently, when the player restarts, the game will begin where he left off, as depicted in the 'restart' row.

FIGURE 13.3   Milestone load/save

Game life-span/sections	1	2	3	4	5	6	7	8	9	10
Save locations	∀	∀	∀	∀	∀	∀	∀	∀	∀	∀
Restart points	∀	∀	∀	∀	∀	∀	∀	∀	∀	∀

Figure 13.3 illustrates the 'milestone' load/save architecture. This structure of saving and loading forces the players to do so at specific milestones throughout the game as depicted in the 'save' row. Once the player returns to the

game, he will load and restart at the last predefined point the player saved. This method is synonymous with racing games, for example. After completing a track, the game will allow the player to save his progress and possibly open up further tracks for the player to explore. Some environment-based adventure games use this method also, but it can be frustrating for the player if the save feature is not evident at regular intervals and the player has to play for long periods before he is allowed to save. It can also be frustrating if the player-character is killed just before he reaches the save point and is placed back at the point of his last save.

FIGURE 13.4   Hybrid milestone load/save

Game life-span/sections	1	2	3	4	5	6	7	8	9	10
Save locations										→
Restart points	∀	∀	∀	∀	∀	∀	∀	∀	∀	∀

A preferable method of loading and saving is a hybrid of the first two options and used widely in console games today (Figure 13.4). In this example, the player has the option to save the game 'state' at any point while playing. This will preserve all puzzles and key objects retrieved by the player up to the point of the save. However, when the player reloads the game, he will begin at a specific spot, which is usually at the threshold of the environment in which the game was saved.

Why is this preferable? The player does not have to solve all the puzzles, find all keys or kill sub-bosses to get to where he left off. He will, however, possibly confront the antagonistic population again, but this is to be expected in order to maintain the player's interest. It is also preferable from a designer's perspective because the designer can plan his save 'states' and know in advance what will need saving at any particular moment. This is particularly useful for restricted save game cartridges.

Killing the player in a game

Here we move into something far more important for the designer – killing the player character. The moment in which the game kills the player character has to be justifiable. In other words, the player has to do something monumentally negative to bring upon his character's death. When I say character, I don't just mean the two arms and two legs kind. I am also referring to cars, tanks, squads of soldiers – whatever the player's controlling icon might be.

I have played many games in which the player is killed for simply existing, which makes no sense! In the days of platform games, more often than not the player would die if he missed a jump. This is not a crime punishable by death and it certainly is not fun. The player wants to be entertained not tortured.

I've also played many games where creatures become hostile when the killer trespasses onto their territory uninvited and they kill the player for that action. The player must be warned of this impending danger! This is called informative feedback; see the feedback techniques discussed in Chapter 6

Consider carefully how your character is going to die in your game, if at all. If your game puts the player in a racing car then it will be the car that dies – do it spectacularly so it's almost satisfying. If you have to kill the player character, don't do it too soon into the game. Let the player play and have fun.

If you insist on killing the player character, it's always good to give the player a 'chance' to redeem himself or bring his character back to life. Dungeon Siege does this very well. Because you control several characters, the player never loses until all characters are dead (which can happen). However, you soon learn to use the healing and resurrect powers of your magicians as soon as you are able to.

Zelda also does this very well. The player has the ability to carry bottles around with him. Inside those bottles he can store fairies. If the player has one of these on his person when he is killed, he will be resurrected with full health.

In Soul Reaver you never die, you simply reside in a spiritual state until the player finds a warp point. The designers built a 'chance' into the game to allow the player to return to the character's physical form. This 'chance' becomes part of the game structure and adds a fourth dimension to the game.

Giving the player this 'chance' allows him to step across a line that he would never normally cross, so therefore you have to limit the size of this chance. If you allow the player to activate his chance too often, the game will become easy, so ensure you resource or limit the 'chance' ability somehow. You must also consider your audience. If you are appealing to the mass-market, embedding a 'chance' system into your game is imperative.

Playing the 'chance'

Punishing the player is always part of the mechanism that kills the player-character. For example, reducing a 'life meter' or reducing one of the player's several 'life chances' are forms of punishment but the game isn't over until you run out of those chances.

There are many forms of 'chance' you can build into your game that would ease the punishment threshold. Tetris, for example, punishes the player. You may not think so, but the game also gives the player plenty of opportunity to redeem himself, but interestingly he only gets one life. The player begins with no wall and the player knows he has to keep the wall from reaching the top of the screen. As the wall creeps to the top, the player has plenty of time and plenty of 'chance' to reduce that wall before he is severely punished. The increased tempo (audio feedback) in the music is a warning that he is going to be punished unless he does something about it. Tetris is balanced to perfection and the rate in which the wall builds is also designed to give the player ample chance at the beginning of the game, but reduces that 'chance' factor as the player becomes more confident. Figure 13.5 illustrates the chance mechanism.

The flow chart in Figure 13.5 works from the moment the player does something wrong, but not, however, when the game design is at fault. The point at which the game punishes the player will very much depend on the balancing of your game to determine the severity of that punishment. You may also want to clearly define what determines bad performance from the player, thus justifying your punishments. Any ambiguity in this department will leave the player feeling confused.

FIGURE 13.5   Chance mechanism

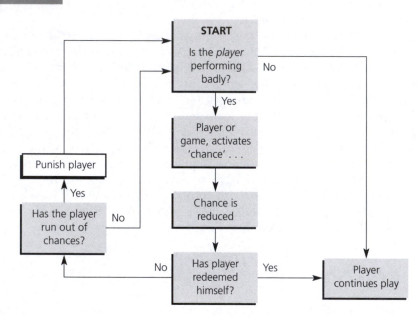

I have fond memories of playing shoot 'em ups from the 8-bit era, like Nemesis™ for example. It has what they use to call a smart bomb feature, which gave the player a 'chance'. The screen would fill with baddies, the player would become trapped and death was imminent, but then, at the last moment, when he knew there was no other option other than death, the player would activate the smart bomb, thus destroying all enemies on the screen in one fell swoop. This is a great tension builder and the release is placed under player control and often with dramatic effect. The smart bombs were limited and the player could only get a set number, which he would have to earn. Nevertheless, it gave the player a chance and allowed the player to get out of sticky situations spectacularly, at the press of a button.

Another form of chance is the shield function. This has been with games since day zero. It rarely gets mentioned as a 'chance' and I think most designers intuitively build it into their games as a defence mechanism. Most racing games will let the player crash and dent his car before it reaches a threshold and the crashing begins to adversely affect the player's performance, ultimately destroying his car. Shoot 'em ups often give the player the option of a force-field barrier and role-playing games gives the player-characters a traditional shield – all of which give the player a chance, pushing back the opposing forces, helping to shape and balance the game.

Punishing for existing

The player should never be put into a situation where he is being killed or punished for no reason. RPGs are sometimes guilty of this. The player can be walking through a forest, expecting opposition, when suddenly an arrow comes out of nowhere, with no warning and hits him, subsequently punishing the player for no reason other than being there. This, some people will argue is perfectly acceptable, but if the player can't see where the enemy is, or what is punishing him, he can't be expected to defend himself. It would be like designing a pitch-black tunnel into a racing game, and throwing in a few sharp corners for good measure – you simply wouldn't do it. The player should be forewarned of his opponents before venturing into the forest and at least given some clue as to what will be opposing him. This will give the player opportunity to arm his 'chances' and prepare his defence.

Another way to avoid unnecessary punishment is to allow the player foresight by feeding him clues and warnings. This can be portrayed using many devices such as maps or radar, for example. Defender™ did this particularly well by indicating enemies' positions on a radar to aid the player. Without this feature, the game would have been frustrating and much harder. Racing games often depict a rendition of the map on the screen, indicating sharp corners, other drivers and obstacles that may hinder the player's progress. Adventure games and RPGs do this through informative dialogue from other characters in the game. They may warn you of dangers up ahead, but won't give you specifics that might spoil the game. Allowing the player to store such information, along with quests etc., in a type of journal can also be beneficial and help the player through the playing field.

Traditional games allow the player foresight, such as Chess, Draughts and even games like Monopoly. The player is aware of his opponent's strategy and can possibly determine his next move. Therefore the player's vigilance allows him to plan his moves based on the opposing forces. When we drive our cars we are warned of any dangers, like low bridges, sharp bends and possible tumbling rocks. Armed with this information the driver has a better chance of evading danger should the need arise. Foresight is a form of feedback, and can be used to shift the balance one way or another.

Punishing the player for doing something right

How can a player be punished for doing something right? Believe me, it happens. Have you ever been playing a game and you simply fall through the floor for no reason or you get stuck in a wall and you can't get out? These are often the result of bugs, but they can destroy a game if they are left in. Bugs are not a result of bad game design, rather a result of bad technical design.

EXAMPLE   The invisible floor

There are some things that designers put into games that I consider design flaws. One in particular, or perhaps it's more of a pet hate of mine, is the invisible floor syndrome. This was rife in 8-bit platform games and does appear occasionally today. If a designer creates levels that have no floor, as I saw when working on a two-dimensional platform game once, it means the player can drop out of the gaming world into no-man's-land. In this case, the platform jumps were designed to severely punish the player if he missed a jump, giving the player no chance at all and dropping him out of the game. What made it worse is that not all the levels were like this and thus the game was very inconsistent.

Another design flaw evident in some computer games is the 'sudden death-trap' scenario. The player would be travelling through the game, doing everything right, when suddenly he is hit with a blow that kills him outright. Or he unpredictably falls down a hole and lands on a spike. If it's a racing game, the player may slide off a cliff on a sharp bend. The worst kind of all is the deliberate trap, when the player presses a button that activates a swinging spike ball, targeted right at the player. What are these designers thinking! This isn't fun. The challenge is absent, there is no way of evading the onslaught, thus survival is completely denied. The designer would simply be punishing the player for playing the game.

If you do have these sorts of traps in your game, give the player a warning. If it is the racing game, include a large bold sign along the track depicting the danger up ahead. If it's a trap in the floor, warn the player prior to venturing into the area and mark the floor differently to allow the player to learn when to look for these traps. If he then falls into them, then it's through bad gameplay, not from simply playing the game by the rules.

In retrospect it is easy to identify these design flaws, but to push games forward in design, we need to learn from the designers that pushed the frontiers of game design in the past.

Opposing forces

The opposing forces in every game will attempt to stop the player from fulfilling his core objective. The player however, must be able to defend himself or avoid in some way all offensive actions against him. If a monster starts clubbing the player with a weapon, for example, the player should be able to defend himself from this. If the player is put into a situation that he has no control over, and cannot defend himself from, this becomes very frustrating.

If there are weapons of mass destruction in a game, the player must be able to defend himself, or avoid being killed by them. This is part of gameplay and defence is part of the player's skill and judgement. A player should also be able to stop the event from happening to prevent further bombardment.

CASE STUDY	Pac-Man

What were the opposing forces in Pac-Man? Yes, you got it, the ghosts that chase you. It is an obvious question really, but now think about what defence the player has against these ghosts. They chase you round a maze and there are only four options for the player at any one time – move left or right, up or down. Remember the core objective of this game is to clear the arena of the pills that line the maze.

As the ghosts chase you, they can easily trap you in a corner. The designers, however, ingeniously placed power pills in each corner that, when collected, would instantly swap the forces of the game but only for a short period of time. The player becomes the opposing force or the antagonist, and the ghosts flee. This device is the player's defence against being trapped in the corners and dying for simply playing the game.

There was another little device that they incorporated into the game that helped the player flee from sticky situations – 'the magic tunnel' device. The player could dart through a gap in the side of the screen and appear on the opposite side. This too is a defence against the opposing force of the game. These are very small inclusions, but add so much to the gameplay, just like the kings in Draughts!

Summary

So, punishing the player is not always about game design, it can be a technical problem also. Whatever the cause, be sure to eliminate as many of them as you can. Punishing the player is also all about balance. You should only punish the player for the mistakes he makes, not from bad design. Design logically; the player shouldn't have to try and guess what you were thinking when you were designing the game, only what is provided as feedback from the game.

The player should have plenty of chance/warning that what he is doing is wrong and if he continues to do this, he will get punished for it. Allow him some foresight into the game so he can prepare himself.

When you are designing your opposing actions, ensure the player can defend against those actions. Give the player something to defeat that action, something he will learn to use skilfully in an interactive way.

CHAPTER 14

Characters in computer games

How important are the characters in your game, if indeed you have some? Are computer and video game characters becoming the stars of tomorrow? Or are they still simply computer images that serve as a vehicle for the gameplay?

Let's define the different types of computer game character and discuss each one in detail. There are many different types of player characters in video games. By that I mean they are represented in different ways and serve different purposes. Of course, they all exist as a vehicle for the gameplay. But at what level do you notice and care for your character?

The visual character

A character created for visual appeal is becoming an important aspect of game development in today's market-place. Or at least to the marketing and merchandising people it is. But is it important to the player? Yes, increasingly so, especially as technological capabilities increases and the market for games increases, because this growth consequently increases audience expectations, whereas in the days of 8-bit computers, four colours, a 32-pixel square grid and eight frames of animation usually did the trick! It was all in the game! Today, however, it is a different world.

As far as the game designer is concerned, first and foremost the character must be designed to perform its function within the game. It also has to be in context with the setting and the world in which it exists.

The process of visual character design

With the help of some friends and very talented artists from within the industry, I have included a process for creating a character for your game, particularly if it is a visual character. I know it's not entirely related to game design, but the imagery for the characters in your game needs to reflect the type of game it is, and include the elements and functionality you will expect for your design. You will need to give the concept artist a brief, which includes the characters' abilities and gameplay mechanics, in order for him to do a realistic rendition.

Research

The first stage in any design process is the research stage, involving examination of the given brief. The brief will most likely consist of a visual description of the character, a description of his characteristics and the mechanical design aspects, i.e. what he will be doing in the game.

An important part of this phase is to research other games and other popular media such as comics and movies, in order to get a clear picture as to how others have approached character design for similar briefs. This doesn't mean copy. Character designs often employ recognisable stereotypes. There may be a lot of debate concerning stereotypes and cliché, but the fact remains that the public at large are conditioned to recognise these stereotypes and can easily identify them as characters.

In fact, the reason many stereotypes exist is because they are taken from real-world observations. For example, why do mad professors have crazy white hair and mad staring eyes? The answer is plain and simple – Albert Einstein. People instantly recognise the visual connection and therefore the personality.

It is also important to know the physical demands for your character during gameplay, e.g. if it's going to be an acrobatic character who can cling to walls and somersault, it would make sense to look at a gymnast's physique. A lithe muscular physique would be needed for such a character to be believable.

Technical

Establish the platform and engine technology that you will be using. In most cases, the technical director should supply a polygon limit and texture size budget. This is crucial to comprehend, particularly from an artist's perspective because he will need to ensure the character is not beyond the technical boundaries of the target platform.

Visual design

The second phase of the design process will usually involve a gathering of team members for a brainstorming session. A number of sketches, born from the brief, will provide a variety of different angles on the character, featuring different costumes, props, hairstyles etc. At this stage it is a good idea to block out the overall shape and anatomy of your proposed character designs. Exploring a number of possibilities is essential at this stage. It gives the director or, as is often the case, the marketing team more options. Once an initial direction has been approved and initial feedback considered, you can narrow down your designs and focus and refine final props and a costume can be established.

The face is very important in forming your character. Most modern games involve cut-scenes and lip-sync so it is very important that your characters face reflects the appropriate attributes.

To make a character memorable, there are a few general factors that can help create a memorable and instantly recognisable design; for example, colour scheme and silhouette. Lara Croft is a classic example of this. Her colour scheme and pose make for a sexy, athletic and above all memorable design. The popularity speaks for itself. Simplicity can often lead to a more striking design. Superheroes can be recognised by simple colour schemes usually comprising of two or three main colours. The colours often become the character's signature – red and blue for Mario, for example.

A common mistake is to make character textures too detailed and fussy when in reality much detail will be lost on a limited TV resolution. Strong silhouettes are essential – nearly every great character design can be recognised by its outline alone. The character's pose is also essential in conveying personality and attitude. Look at the classic marvel pose for strong superheroes.

Another thing to consider is how your character will change and grow throughout your game, both emotionally and physically, and how that will affect what you see on the screen. Make sure your game design can support the designed character from the beginning of the game, all the way through to the end.

The result of creating such a hero provides a deeper connection between player and character and subsequently the game. The player will feel for the character on a deeper emotional level and become more involved. Pure visual characters also tend to lack a 'voice', like Crash Bandicoot and Mario who have no real story, in the truest sense of the word, attached to them but are great visual game characters.

The non-visual character

Because we have visual characters in games, it is safe to assume we have non-visual characters. The non-visual character shouldn't exist, but it does. It exists between the functional character and the visual character. It has none of the features we discussed above, but attempts to perform in the same manner.

These characters, you could say, were lost along the way. They may have begun as a central character that had identifiable characteristics, but somehow, often through bad design and story, became bland and ordinary, perhaps without a soul.

The functional character

The functional character can often be found in games like RPGs and RTS games. Although these types of characters are often artistically superb, their visual appeal is not the focus for the people that play them, but this doesn't mean they can't have character. Like all game characters, they serve a purpose, but the game is generally focused around the functionality of the character, i.e. they have little personality and story, but the character is the core feature of the game mechanics and it is their attributes and functionality that determine their characteristics.

FIGURE 14.1 Dungeon Siege characters

As seen in Figure 14.1, Dungeon Siege is a perfect example of characters that function as a game device but are also visually stunning. You know little about the characters' personality in the game, but you are fully aware of their capabilities as functional characters. They blend into the world of Ehb, and appear as though they belong, i.e. they are in context with their surroundings.

CASE STUDY   Pikmin

Another great example is Nintendo's Pikmin™. The player is in control of a space traveller named Captain Olimar, whose core objective is to get back to his home planet. However, he has been struck by a meteor and crash-lands on a strange planet, spilling the components of his craft across various hazardous terrains. Captain Olimar discovers the planet's inhabitants, which he calls Pikmin and which he adopts to retrieve the missing components of his spacecraft. The player achieves this by controlling the Pikmin indirectly through Captain Olimar and using the Pikmin's special abilities to perform a number of tasks. Of course, the Pikmin want something in return for helping Olimar and that is to help them rid their world of evil creatures, which is where some of the challenges for the player exist.

The Pikmin are a perfect example of functional characters that are appealing to the target audience, but are also designed to work as the core game mechanics that sit perfectly in the context of their world. The Pikmin do have character appeal, but they cannot speak; they are tiny creatures that grow out of the ground, they have tiny arms and legs and come in four different colours, and they can have leafs sprouting out of their heads! So what makes them appealing?

Apart from the aforementioned visual characteristics, they also have big wide eyes, a common feature in characters that are designed to appeal to children. The first thing that identifies their character is the sounds they make. I observed children playing this game, and it was one of the most significant tools used for communicating the way that the creatures felt. When Olimar pulls them out of the ground they make a sound that represents a sort of hello combined with a celebratory thank you, and this is great audio feedback, portraying the creatures' characteristics and appealing to the target audience. The children reacted in an emotional way to the tones and squeaks of the creatures, particularly when they were being eaten or killed by one of the monsters in the world, but the sounds also helped guide the children through the game through such audio feedback.

The second appealing attribute is their movements. The player controls Olimar, who in turn can control the Pikmin. Simply by pressing one button, all the Pikmin stand to attention, which is visual feedback and portrays the creatures' characteristics and respect for Olimar. There are many examples of this in Pikmin, which make the little creatures so very attractive as computer game characters.

They do have visual appeal, but the distinct difference between these characters and a character like 'Link' in Zelda, for example, is that Link is more human. In other words, children can relate to him on a human level and Link's personal problems become the player's problems. The emotion sits on a different level and is amplified by the fact that Link is personified.

The interactive story character

We touched on interactive story characters in Chapter 11, but here we look at them from a design perspective and the relationship between game, story and player.

An interactive story character has elements of the functional character with a heavy dose of visual appeal also. These guys are generally found in adventure games or action adventures. They need back-story, i.e. where they come from, what they do in the world in which they exist, fears, interests, family etc. Basically they need a personality for them to be believable. The visual character described above can go some way in defining the interactive story character, but you can only take the visual aspects so far before you need to look inside the character and pull out the personality for the player to truly see the story character and become emotionally attached.

If you are designing adventure games and have a central protagonist, then the game should focus around the central character's characteristics, and the puzzles should be designed around the character and the world in which he exists to convey coherency in the world.

Let's imagine a game that has a detective as the protagonist and the interactive story is set in the real world, as we know it. The challenges define it as an adventure game, and the puzzles all relate to the subject and context of the world of the detective, i.e. solving mysteries pertinent to the core objective. If the player were to suddenly come across a sliding puzzle room that when solved would unlock a door, it would be totally out of context. The detective would not do that in his world, it would feel wrong and the player would feel detached from his hero. Like most things in game design, you must be consistent with your characters and the challenges he confronts.

Norbot: first draft

FIGURE 14.2 Norbot

Figure 14.2 is Norbot, a first draft concept, without his attachments and missing components. He is not entirely as I imagined him, but he will grow with further renditions in Part II.

Norbot is a cross-breed between a visual character and a story character, but he has been designed with the gameplay in mind, which is really important. You will notice that his left hand is missing, which is built into the story, but has also been utilised in the gameplay with multiple attachments. Other game features that are missing include his bottom jaw, or a mouth attachment. Once he finds his voice, this will become an important part of the game. You will also notice the orange window in his chest, which is a slot for his heart, but the actual heart is missing in this concept.

The final rendition will have much more detail all over his body and many more attachments and gadgets that will aid him in his quest, but will be earnt throughout the game. The normal procedure would be to conceptualise the attachments and create a final draft of the character, prior to building the actual three-dimensional model.

Character persona versus game design

Let's go back to our detective. We need to somehow bring out the character traits in our hero, and reveal his personality. To do this, we need to give him choices and expose his strengths and weaknesses as a human being. Let's give him a fear and loathing of rats as one of his traits. Now to bring your character alive and make him feel like a real person, you should use that hatred of rats to bring out his personality and expose his weakness as a character. Remember, this should not be a weakness in the gameplay, but only within the story. You also need to remember that you always know what is going to happen in your story so you can be in complete control of your 'character'.

Most puzzles in games are a lock and key situation. The solution to the puzzle is the key to enable the player to move forward. Puzzles can be presented in many different ways, but adding characteristics such as your hero's hatred for rats will add another dimension to your game. It may also add a little comedic value. Perhaps he has to venture into the clichéd world of sewers to retrieve an important piece of evidence for a puzzle he is working on, but it is infested with rats. The character should let the player know of his fear by refusing to enter the sewer until the player purchases some protective clothing, a flamethrower, a gas mask etc. Retrieving these items may sound mundane, so be sure there is a fun aspect in earning these items, they should never be given to the player, as explained in a previous chapter. Once the detective reluctantly enters the sewer, you might begin to hear his thoughts, which is where the comedic element comes in. You might also want to add nuances in his animations that also let the player know he is afraid of rats. The possibilities are becoming endless, but there must be a good balance of character appeal and gameplay. If one overrides the other, then you may not get your desired result.

This is the stuff of great adventure games. The player's challenges reveal the characteristics of your hero, which are embedded into the gameplay. If you simply tell the player your character is afraid of rats and never use this in the game, then it's useless. Of course that is just one simple example, so let your imagination do its job and ensure you are consistent and in context with the world you have created.

Visual impact versus design

A well-designed central character can have a positive visual impact on a game, but are these characters necessary for gameplay to exist? The first response would obviously be dependent on what sort of game you are designing, but the answer is no – gameplay can exist without the perfect visual character. So why do we bother?

The answer is identification and branding. Gameplay should always be your first priority and the character should be spawned from the game design. If you're designing your game around a character that has already been conceptualised and approved as a visual masterpiece, you might well be limiting yourself and on a potential road for disaster. Licences do this and it can be said that many licensed games tend to be very shallow in gameplay and rely heavily on the brand to sell the game. Your original character is unknown and doesn't exist in any world. You have to create the world to fit the design of the character. You can create a box man as placement art, and put him through the paces of your design. It will act in the same way as your final character, but the visual aspect will not get in the way. Game design should always come first.

Creating the game design first will allow the character designers more scope with their design, and the character design will certainly benefit from a developed world in which to exist.

Market perception

Brands exist in every aspect of our lives, from the food we eat to the clothes we wear. Video games are no different. If you went onto the street and asked the general public to name three video game characters in quick succession, what would be their response? I'm sure Mario would be in there, as would Lara Croft and perhaps Zelda. Why? Because the characters are vivid, memorable and recognisable; they have become living legends in the world of video games and have traversed to other media.

If a chat show host were to interview the stars from video games, these three characters would be in his line-up of guests. One interesting observation is that all of these characters were born out of great games. The games came first and now, because technology has allowed it to happen, the characters have become the champions of their world. The designers have also been careful to carry the gameplay forward also, which is important for longevity, and the characters represent the quality of the products.

It's not easy to create new characters and even the masters get it wrong occasionally. So when you are creating your character and you feel it's at a stage that it can communicate to the target audience, put it to the test. Set it free and get some feedback. You may discover that the voice you have chosen is not right, or it does not have visual appeal at all. Perhaps the animations are quirky and are not working with the gameplay, or maybe, and this is one of the most common mistakes, your character is a visual replica of another character that already exists. If this happens, you could be in real trouble.

The replication often happens in the mechanics of the character, in that the characters often do things that have been done to death. This will inevitably weaken your character's appeal because the players will already have a character that does those things.

Effect of a central protagonist

The effect of having an identifiable, recognisable character can be a marketing department's dream come true. It will be branded and become an icon and legend in gaming history; this is something we all strive for.

However, for it to have any impact on the market-place at all, it has to meet the criteria of game character hero discussed previously, and this takes time, many game appearances and lots of money.

The effect an iconic character can have on a game that can convey the characteristics of that character on an emotional level, is to add significant depth to the experience for the player. Obviously not all games will have characters, and not all that do have characters will need the depth of character required for an adventure game, for example. Therefore, it's not a prerequisite of any game to have this level of detail with their characters.

Something else you should think about is that if your central protagonist is not human, you can still personify it within your game. You can still give it a character and it can still become a hero providing it is done well. Animals, such as Crash Bandicoot and Croc, are an obvious example.

Summary

There is a general belief that character personalities and plot are incidental elements of a game that should only be given a fleeting thought. This belief has grown from the inherent tradition that games are games, not movies or stories. But this is changing, and as we learn how to use our characters in a more creative story-interactive way, our games will become deeper, and will affect the player on an emotional level while retaining that fun aspect that games deliver. Technology is advancing and we can truly begin to bring pixels to life in games, just as Pixar have done in movies.

This extra dimension to video game characters will require talent that currently only exists in small doses, dotted around the industry. If you are going to survive in this field, then you need to bridge the gap and truly understand the elements that bring a character to life on the screen.

To follow are a few things you should ask yourself when you begin designing your characters. It will help you decide what level of detail your character will need or should have for your game.

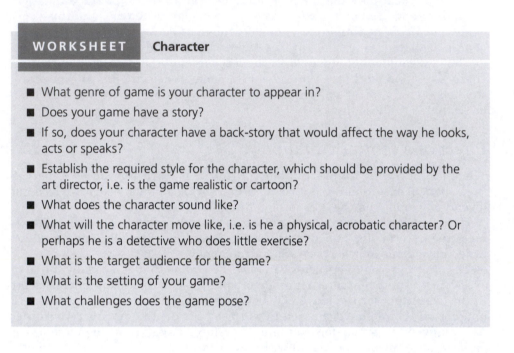

WORKSHEET   **Character**

- What genre of game is your character to appear in?
- Does your game have a story?
- If so, does your character have a back-story that would affect the way he looks, acts or speaks?
- Establish the required style for the character, which should be provided by the art director, i.e. is the game realistic or cartoon?
- What does the character sound like?
- What will the character move like, i.e. is he a physical, acrobatic character? Or perhaps he is a detective who does little exercise?
- What is the target audience for the game?
- What is the setting of your game?
- What challenges does the game pose?

CHAPTER 15

Interface

In our everyday lives we interact with thousands of objects without even thinking about it. We drive our cars, we operate lifts and machinery, we download our emails, make telephone calls and do even the smallest things, like opening doors and switching on lights, without giving them a second thought. Each day we are interfacing with devices that have been designed to work in the best possible way for human interaction.

So how do you feel when the interfaces to these devices are not functioning as you would like them to? Perhaps the lift has broken down, or the door handle has fallen off and you can't open the door. Maybe you become mildly frustrated. After one whole week of the lift still not working and the door handle not being fixed, then how do you feel? Angry?

One of my favourite observations is the shopping trolley scenario. The ideal scenario is this. You go to the supermarket and randomly pick a trolley. You push it around the store and collect your shopping, wheel it through the checkout and out to your car. Then you're on your way home, smiling and feeling great about your purchases.

Now imagine this. On the next trip, you pick a shopping trolley that has a damaged wheel. It doesn't go where you want it to go. It doesn't steer around corners and you keep crashing into the same person every alternate aisle as if the trolley is possessed. Frustration and anger overwhelms you and your shopping trip has turned into a nightmare.

Needless to say, I always check the wheels on my trolley before embarking on a potential shopping jaunt to hell! One important thing to remember, we can work around the sticky wheel problem by choosing a different cart, but the player can't do that with the interface to a game he has just purchased, so it's vital to get it right!

Imagine how a gamer feels when he buys a game only to get it home, drops the disc into the tray and bam! the interface is suddenly the challenge, not the game. Light switches can be fixed, door handles can be replaced and a wheel on a shopping trolley can be greased. Game interfaces are for life!

The interface to your game is probably the most difficult design aspect to perfect. The interface is the communication mechanism, the connection between player and game. It is this part of your game design that the player will judge first. Think of it as a relationship. It has to work both ways. Not only does the interface have to communicate with the game, but also the game has to provide feedback to the player based on the input of the interface. It has to be transparent, sublime and allow the player to control the game intuitively. The moment the player begins to struggle with it, you're in trouble. A lot of time should be spent on the interface and it should be functional as quickly as possible during the prototype phase.

In Figure 15.1 you can see how the interface perpetuates the communication in a gaming environment. If any one of those links is taken away or damaged, the player will become detached from the game.

FIGURE 15.1   Interface feedback

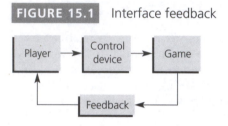

Defining the interface

So what is meant by interface? It is where two things interact or link. In the case of computer and video games the first link is between the player and a control device, which is generally a mouse and keyboard on a PC, or a controller on a console. This link is the only thing that every single game has in common. There are no sound-activated games in the market-place currently or for some time to come. The second interface link is between the control device and the game. It is this link that is the most important and the focus for the designer, as it characterises the gameplay and how the player will perceive and feel the game.

Depending on which platform your game is developed for will determine what device you use as your communication tool. The interface should be designed specifically for each platform and if you are developing cross-platform then changes may be required to the game design also. Planning your design for all potential development platforms at the start of your design cycle will save you time later, but you should never compromise one platform over another. Use each platform and control device to its full potential while retaining the essence of the game.

CASE STUDY   **Dungeon Siege**

Dungeon Siege has a familiar, yet perfectly unique and intuitive interface for a PC RPG. The two primary communication devices are the keyboard and the mouse. Generally, when playing the game, you have one hand on the keyboard hovering over a pre-defined set of keys while the other hand is on the mouse. With this combination, I find I never take my eyes off the screen while playing, which is how it should be.

Within some PC games you are presented with a plethora of keys to press in order to make things happen, which can be hard to remember and consequently forces the player to pause the game and look in the manual for the correct button presses. If this can be avoided then it should be at all costs. The player loses connection with the game, which will immediately shed points in the quality stakes because of this.

Dungeon Siege was specifically designed for the PC. We have already mentioned the eradication of load times, which are inherent in console games. But the devices used to interface Dungeon Siege have been utilised to their full potential. There is the obvious 'point and click' for navigating your team around the environment and interacting with the world, but it's the other little but crucially important things that make it easy to use and intuitive.

In Dungeon Siege you can control many characters simultaneously. Therefore the designers had to think very carefully about the interface and the control of so many avatars. They needed to make it as easy as they possibly could for the player. To achieve this they included many 'group' controlling elements to the interface. For example, a single press of 'W' on the keyboard enables the player to select and highlight the whole group. This can be useful if you want to get your party out of a sticky situation and move them quickly. With a single press of a key and a click on the left mouse button, 'all' of the characters can be moved from one place to another very quickly. Also, group selection is crucial in a combat situation. However, singular selection is also crucial for individual character control.

Pressing 'W' is not the only way of selecting the characters. A box highlighter can also be dragged around the group; not so good if they are apart from each other but useful for selecting two or three characters within the group who are close to one another. Drag and select is also useful for picking up a lot of items quickly. You can order many characters to pick up multiple objects lying around on the ground, which is particularly useful after a big battle.

The player can left-click on each character in the party individually. However, if this were the only way of moving the group, it would take the player so long to get anywhere that he would soon become frustrated.

Each character has a portrait displayed on the screen, which can also be clicked upon during play. This too is very useful for individual selection, particularly when they are off-screen. For example, Dungeon Siege allows you to purchase a donkey, which is great for carrying the plethora of items you collect along the way. However, there is a tendency to keep it at the back of the pack, out of harm's way, as a result of which he is often off-screen. Clicking on the Donkey's portrait and subsequently clicking in the environment among your party will order your donkey into view.

There are many other methods for easing control in Dungeon Siege, like accessing the inventory, for example. Pressing the 'I' key during play will reveal the inventory for the selected character. If the player has more than one character selected, then all selected inventories are displayed. This becomes very useful

▶

as the player progresses through the game and collects many items. It simplifies the transferring of items from character to another. The items are integral to the progression of the game and it's important to see what each character is carrying in their inventory in relation to what they are using on their person. Items quickly devalue as the player progresses. Therefore this item collecting and swapping is integral to character progression and part of the scoring element of the game.

Another useful button is 'J'. This will bring up your journal quickly and efficiently. The journal is a neat reminder of what tasks the player has done and what tasks he is currently doing. Journals are particularly important in a game like this, especially as the player can become engrossed in the combat elements of the game and the tasks become sidetracked, so a quick reminder is very useful.

So what does this tell us? All of these neat little interface inclusions allow Dungeon Siege to be accessible without a struggle and without confusing the player. The content of the game and the adventure are thrust centre stage and become the focus, not the interface.

Input devices

Here I will discuss the various devices traditionally used in computer and video games and how they are utilised for games. Although there are many other devices, such as steering wheels for racing games and dance mats for dance games, I will concentrate exclusively on the devices that are most common. There have even been some strange devices in the past, from various chairs that the player can sit in to control the game, to a device that sits on your head and reads the player's brain waves! Needless to say they have all failed for one reason or another.

Mouse

Let's begin with the mouse. It is a device that was not originally designed for use in computer games, and certainly not for 3D games because 3D games were not around when mice were invented. However, today it is one of two fundamental input devices used on a PC for every type of software, and I believe is just as suited to 3D games as it is for the traditional 2D games. Although you can purchase a mouse for some consoles, a designer would never design a console game based around a mouse, not even if he were adapting a PC game to a console.

Using a mouse to control a pointer on a flat screen is probably the most intuitive mechanism, except from directly speaking to it, for communicating with your computer, and has been present since home computers were invented. There has been no serious challenge to the mouse as an input device and that's probably because it is a device that suits its purpose perfectly.

As you well know, the mouse is held in one hand leaving the second hand free, and the mouse buttons are placed perfectly for the index finger and the middle finger to access. Little thought or effort is required to move the cursor around the screen. It's simplicity in its purest form.

So many different functions are assigned to the mouse, particularly in games. Using the mouse-pointer as a feedback device can be a very powerful tool in computer games. Simply by hovering the cursor over an object, vehicle or character etc. can feed the player with vital information. RTS and RPG games often use this technique to good effect. For example, if the player is controlling an army of men with the mouse, each man could potentially have its own life system. Therefore, by simply pointing at each man individually could reveal its health status. Or maybe you want to reveal its ammo status or magic level if it's a fantasy game. It is a particularly good feature that requires minimal effort.

Perhaps, for whatever reason, the units in your game all look similar, or are in the distance and are hard to see; therefore, pointing at them could reveal what type of character it is. This technique can also be applied to objects in a scene by moving the cursor over particular objects, which can reveal information relating to the object. You could take it a stage further and have the pointer image change shape. This is context-sensitive feedback, and can reveal an action that will be taken by clicking on the object.

So simply by pointing the mouse cursor at the entities in your scenes can provide informative feedback for the player, which is a very powerful tool in video games.

Combining the pointer with two mouse buttons amplifies the functionality of the mouse, but not so much that the user has to think about what buttons he should be pressing. When the user uses the mouse he is rarely conscious of the fact, except when it isn't working properly or the user interface is badly designed. 'Point and click' has been used in so many games to date and is a tried and tested form of issuing commands, from manoeuvring large armies and opening doors, to ordering a character to pick up an object. RTS, RPGs and adventure games use this type of input and combine it with the keyboard. Point and click is probably the most intuitive use of the mouse because it was originally designed for this type of functionality.

As I said before, the mouse is just as suited to 3D games as it is for 2D games, perhaps even more so. This is because the physical mouse itself exists in three-dimensional space and any movement of the mouse can be replicated in a 3D game, providing the mouse remains on a flat surface. First-person shooters take advantage of this technique. With one hand poised over the directional keys, the mouse can be used for steering and looking around your world simultaneously. Left and right usually steers the character and forward and back are generally look up and look down. The left mouse button is usually assigned to a weapon with the activation of it on the index finger (again intuitive) and jump is usually on the right button. In the first person type of environment, this is the most natural way to use the mouse as each movement of the hand is echoed on the screen and the player is directly linked with the movements on the screen. If the player moves his hand to the right, the character looks to the right and so forth. It is intuitive and simplistic.

If you are controlling multiple characters or vehicles, the 'drag and select' then 'point and click' method is the most intuitive method of selection. This can be seen in games like Command and Conquer where the player is required to issue orders to multiple units. Dragging the mouse over a group of units will draw a selection area, and everything within that selection becomes a collective unit (as Dungeon Siege illustrates in Figure 15.2). So, once selected, clicking in the scene will tell them 'all' to move to the point indicated.

FIGURE 15.2   Dungeon Siege drag and select

Perhaps you only want to lift and move an object from one place to another. This can also be a relatively simple task for a mouse. Simply click on the target object with the left mouse button, hold the button depressed, move the mouse to the desired location and release the button. This feels very natural and was a device used exceptionally well in Dungeon Keeper.

For RPGs, RTS, god-games and various other types, you may wish to shift your view-port around quickly, without fumbling with keys. If you are looking into your game and the desired location is out of view, 'pushing' the screen with the mouse pointer is a common method for shifting the view-port. As depicted in Figure 15.3, 'pushing' is achieved by moving the pointer to the edge of the screen. The view is then moved in the opposite direction to the edge the pointer is located. No extra buttons are required for this and is a simple and intuitive method for shifting your view-port around.

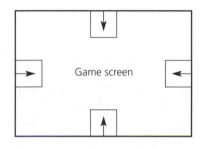

FIGURE 15.3   Screen pushing

One game that really used the mouse innovatively and successfully was Black and White. In this game the player could create miracles. This was achieved by simply gesturing with the mouse and was hailed as a unique game mechanic that was perfectly executed. The player would have to trace the shape of a miracle on the ground using the mouse. Once executed, it summoned the desired miracle into your hand (the player's mouse pointer). Of course, there are many rules attached to this ability, but the mechanic of doing this feels very natural because the player can control the mouse in real space to replicate the shape required.

A game before Black and White did something similar. Silve™, a PC RPG, used gesturing for its combat. The player could swing his sword by sliding the mouse round on the surface, replicating sword movements. This was great fun, and again used to good effect.

This three-dimensional motion, and the mouse pointer in general, is something that can't be done on a console and thus can separate PC games from console games and cause the most problems on conversion.

The invention of the mouse wheel has also become a blessing in disguise. It beckoned the game designer to implement a zoom function into many genres. Many point and click games have the facility to zoom, by simply rolling the wheel backwards and forwards, scaling the view-port in and out of the screen. This method is used in many three-dimensional RPGs and RTS games. Instead of locking the view-port to a fixed plane, this feature can immerse the player deeper into the game, allowing him to get closer to the action at the spin of a wheel. Many FPS games use this also, particularly those with zoom lenses on their weapons.

Of course, the idea of a mouse as a gaming device for the PC has proven to be successful in more ways than one. Using it intuitively and simply can provide a powerful tool for the designer and a manipulative tool for the gamer to poke and prod his way through a game. If you are using it to navigate, you should think about your camera view, but in most cases, the mouse will work logically no matter what view you are looking at.

Mouse uses

To summarise, here are a few uses the mouse can offer in a gaming environment:

- Feedback pointer
- Point and click commands
- Pick up and drop
- Drag and select
- Three-dimensional navigation
- Zoom feature
- Selecting

Keyboard

If you're designing a game for the PC, you will undoubtedly use the keyboard in your design. Therefore, it is crucial that you don't overwhelm the player by placing an excess amount of functions on it. Many games use the keyboard in conjunction with the mouse, but the keyboard, again, was designed for a specific task in its own right. One of the great things about Dungeon Siege is that almost all mouse-driven actions are replicated on the keyboard, so the player can choose the interface that suits him.

The secret of using the keyboard with your game (or any device for that matter) is simplicity and continuity. For example, 'I' is almost always 'inventory' with games that have an inventory. Why change it, why put inventory on a different key? It works and it's easy to remember. The directional keys have arrows on them. Use them for directional purposes. I never understand games that use a combination of keys in the Q, E, Z and C area as direction keys. It is awkward and one can never quite remember which key does what, particularly when you haven't played in a while. Dungeon Siege uses the arrow keys to rotate and tilt the camera in their respective directions, which is also intuitive. Having said all of this, the keyboard should be reconfigurable, selectable through the options. For familiarity and comfort, some gamers, particularly hardcore gamers, like to customise their interface to reflect the last game they played.

The keyboard is used for many functions in games, particularly on-line games, in which it becomes the primary communication tool. This is of course its traditional function.

Just like mice, keyboards are available for consoles also, but are rarely used and should not be considered for a console game unless you can convince the publisher to sell one with each game! Bearing in mind that you have about as much chance of seeing your game sold with a keyboard as of winning the lottery.

Controller

I would like to emphasise the differences between the PC duo, mouse and keyboard, and a console controller by examining a specific genre that has attempted to make a successful transition from PC to console interface. Currently, there are many first-person shooter (FPS) PC ports on consoles, such as Unreal®, Half-Life®, Quake III Arena and Deus Ex©. The FPS will exemplify the need to re-design a game when considering this leap. I'm not saying FPS games don't work on consoles, because Golden Eye on N64, among others, shows us that they do. But what I want to stress, is the need to rethink the design for the input device, and in many cases the game itself, for each version of a particular game.

Put simply, console controllers simply don't have enough buttons to map out all the functions one becomes accustomed to on the PC, particularly with these types of games. Controls such as hot-keys for weapons, jumping, crouching, secondary weapon firing/abilities, map, quick saving, options etc. take up many more buttons than your standard console controller has available. The weapon hot-keys alone can take up almost the same amount of buttons that exist on a controller.

On the PC a mouse is used to look/aim, whereas the consoles have to use an analogue control stick, which, as we've already discussed, is not intuitive. It simply doesn't feel as nice and it can be a fiddly affair.

Some developers have realised the need for a mouse and keyboard controls in some of these console games, and despite what I have said earlier some have included it in the console counterpart. Unreal Tournament for the PS2, for example, is compatible with a USB mouse and keyboard. For me, however, if I want to play Unreal Tournament, I will play it on a PC not on a console because it was originally designed for this platform and will ultimately provide the best experience. Also, one has to consider that a player plays a PC game usually sitting at a desk, while the console, more often than not, resides in the living room, which is not suitable for keyboard and mouse usage.

A controller is organically shaped, moulded to fit into both hands comfortably. Of course there is no perfect shape because hands come in all shapes and sizes, but you will notice that that all controllers have a similar contour. Buttons and thumb pads are also placed conveniently for fingers to access with ease. This is no revelation and may appear obvious. So why is it that some designers insist on designing the most awkward control combination they could possibly think of?

Console manufacturers tend to insist on certain buttons performing certain actions, which has to be adhered to, and rigorous testing is required to ensure standards are met. These control rules stem from the simplicity and continuity gamers require in their games. Gamers become familiar with the way they play and communicate with their console and want this consistency in their control mechanism. This in itself can be problematic when porting a game cross-platform, as the buttons you may want to use could be restricted for a particular use.

The controller has many names, like joypad for example, and although you can purchase one for the PC, it is primarily a console input device. This type of control has been around since the birth of consoles, but has evolved through the years to fit into your hands more comfortably. In recent years, many additional buttons and thumb sticks have been included to increase the experience and accessibility to games.

Contextual interface

An interface is all about communication and this is illustrated with a context-sensitive interface. A context-sensitive interface is an intuitive feature that enables the designer to include many functions on one button, as shown in the worksheet below.

A confusing interface can be an instant game killer before the game has even begun. Just like any aspect of game design, simplicity and consistency is crucial for a successful interface. If you are providing a context-sensitive interface, it must be self-explanatory when communicated to the player. You should keep wording simple and short, make icons clear and sharp and easy to understand. An ambiguous image for an instruction could be a potential block for a player.

As I said, be consistent. If you've used an icon for depicting 'opening a door' in one part of your design, be sure to use the same icon all the way through the game where a door can be opened.

WORKSHEET	Contextual interface

I have devised a simple test to give you one example of what 'context sensitivity' means within a game environment. Imagine for one moment that you are playing a game on a console and you're in control of a nondescript character, in a simple rectangular boxroom as in Figure 15.4.

The room has one locked door leading out of it. On the opposite wall from the door is a window. In the centre of the room is a table. Upon the table I have placed a lamp and a key and your character is standing in front of the door, facing into the room, opposite the window.

Note: you would normally have to think about many other things, like camera placement for example, but for this purpose, we will only focus on the contextual elements of the interface.

Here is a set of instructions, detailing what you have to do, but without any directions of how you actually do it.

Core objective: Leave the room.

Rule: If the player attempts to open the window, instruct the player that it is locked tight and cannot be opened.

Instructions:
1 Walk over to the table
2 Pick up the key
3 Turn off the lamp
4 Unlock the door
5 Leave the room.

As a test, write a simple walkthrough document, of no more than 300 words, describing how the player would move through the room and perform all of the tasks described above. The walkthrough must include the control mechanism and feedback that informs the player how and when he can perform tasks. The text should describe what is happening visually, as if every movement had been recorded.

FIGURE 15.4 Walkthrough scenario

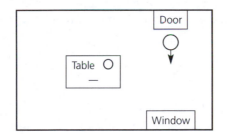

Here is my walkthrough in a contextual environment.

Controls

- The left thumb-pad moves the character around the room. Pushing it forward moves the character forward, left and right turns the character.
- The 'TBD' button is an action button. Pressing the 'TBD' button will instruct the character to perform many different tasks depending on his surroundings.

- The computer will automatically know which animations and actions to perform, in context with the objects highlighted.
- A target will visually highlight objects automatically that are interactive in the scene, as I move around using the thumb-pad stick.

Walkthrough

Using the thumb pad, walk the player to the window side of the table. Once the target has highlighted the pen, press the action button to pick it up. The computer will position the character and play the 'pick up an object from a table' sequence, and the pen will go into your character's inventory. Using the analogue stick, turn to face the lamp. Once the target has highlighted the lamp. Press the action button to switch it off. The character will automatically switch off the light. Once the tasks have been completed, walk over to the door using the analogue stick. When you reach the door, the handle will highlight. Once this happens, press the action button to automatically use the key to unlock the door, open it and leave.

Note: *I would like the action of unlocking the door, opening the door, leaving the room, and closing the door to be one continuous action with no delay or interruption from the player. Once the player has left the room and the door closes, the camera should cut to the other side of the door to see the door fully close behind the player. The player should be standing in front of it ready to be controlled once again. If the player attempts to open the door without the key, he will be told that it is locked and a key is required.*

End.

In the second part of the book, as an example I have included a walkthrough from a game I worked on; for legal reasons I had to change some things but the bare necessities are there.

The only limitation to a context-sensitive interface is your imagination and the genre of your game. There are innumerable actions you can devise for your game, but the method you use to activate them must be consistent.

Struggling with the interface

The player must not, under any circumstances, struggle with the interface. If he does, the game is doomed. The player must feel like he is in control of the game world at all times and the moment your interface becomes unresponsive, he will be pulled out of that world and most likely stop playing.

I recently played a game that infuriated me beyond anything I thought imaginable, and made my blood boil with frustration. I was happily tapping away at the controller, enjoying the game, until I got to this one room. It caused me to angrily throw the game-pad across the room and give up. It was a combination of bad room design and a lack of responsive controls.

The game in question (not named for legal reasons) has auto jump, which is fine and I personally like that. Like I said before, jumping is not fun so automating it is good. I also had weapons at my disposal, but for some unknown reason, they were useless in this one particular room. That was the first nail in the coffin.

I also had a feature that enabled me to sneak along narrow ledges with the character's back against the wall, which again, is good. In this one particular room, there were platforms suspended above the ground, attached to the walls and placed at various points around the room and all at the same height. I consequently *had* to negotiate them, jumping from one to another, in order to get out and move forward; there was no other way to go. To add to the difficulty of negotiating the character around the room, there were flying monsters that charged at me, but I could not defend myself against them except by moving out of the way. So far it doesn't sound too bad, but let's continue.

Many of the gaps between platforms were only just wide enough for the main character to leap-and-grab the edge. We call these 'critical jumps'. But in order to grab the edge successfully, I had to line up the character parallel with the edge of the platform and run straight towards it. If I were even a few degrees out, I would miss the jump and fall to the ground. If this happened it would punish me by decreasing my energy bar. Now, as we all know by now, jumping is not fun, but squaring up for the jump is just mind-numbingly ludicrous in today's world of gaming.

To solve this, the programmer could have easily included a piece of code that turned the character to face the edge if the character was slightly at an angle. But no, a repeated, infuriating bout of jumping and missing ensued, coupled with the occasional whack from a flying monster that I couldn't defend against. The flying monsters were not balanced to start with, in the fact they could fly and I had no way of killing flying monsters.

In between some of the gaps the designers put a sneak wall and I had to negotiate a narrow ledge instead of jumping because the gap between the platforms was too wide. Thank goodness for that, I thought. However, while on the ledge, the flying creatures insisted on battering me and there was no way of defending myself other than jumping down, which I really didn't want to do, as you can imagine! So I would take damage for no reason other than being in the wrong place at the wrong time.

If all of that wasn't bad enough, there was more to come! In order to square up to the edge I was jumping to, I had to position the camera behind the character, but there were a few critical jumps in the corners of the room that wouldn't let me get the camera into position, because the wall behind the character was in the way. Therefore it was guesswork whether you were square to the edge or not. To add insult to injury, the last jump was a 'critical jump' from a corner. The first time I missed, I was dumbfounded. I had to go back and do it *all* again!

This is a perfect example of how a player can struggle with the interface. It is a case of bad environment design, highlighting a badly designed control mechanism. The squaring up of the ledges should have been automated, the jumps should never have been critical and camera control and functionality should have been thought about a little more and I should have had a facility that enabled me to dispose of the flying creatures before they attacked me.

UI integration

So how do you implement an interface that works for your game? It's like most things in game development, it has to evolve and mature with each build of the game. The interface will need balancing as the features are implemented and tested. It has to be an ongoing process. It goes something like this:

1 Research interface methods that work pertinent to your product.
2 Create a basic overview of **UI** in the concept document, identifying buttons for key features etc.
3 Create a more detailed and revised version of the UI for inclusion in the full design document.
4 Implement UI into prototype and refine.
5 Harvest feedback from colleagues and target audience.
6 Update documents as you progress.
7 Repeat steps 3 to 6 until the game is complete.

This method of iterative development will apply to many aspects of your game, but we are only focusing on the interface here. Also if you have multiple platforms in progress, be sure to do this for all of them, not just one. It's unlikely that a prototype will begin on all platforms at the same time, until the fundamental risks have been solved, but it could happen if you were adapting an existing PC game onto multiple consoles for example.

The repetition through stages three to six are important, as this will refine the connection between player and game, and therefore will need to go through several iterations before a first draft intuitive mechanism is reached. If your project manages to rumble past pre-production and into production, it is very likely that more features will be added, balancing will be ongoing and the interface will also need further scrutiny.

Any graphics required for the UI should be left until the final control mechanism is reached. Placement art is usually used for the purpose of functionality testing and tweaking.

When designing your **HUD (head up display)**, avoid cluttering the screen and keep it simple. A cluttered screen can be a distraction to the game. PC games tend to do this more so than console games. This is generally down to the type of games that are played on the PC. Some games will insist on applying layer after layer of sliding panels and pop-up menus when it really isn't necessary.

So think carefully about the layout of your screen – if the player is required to click on the HUD to access inventory, for example, make it clear and simple. Be careful how you arrange your options, particularly where you place the quit option. Placing it next to another button that is used frequently would not be a wise decision.

Many console games hide parts of the HUD and other information off-screen until the player needs to see it. However, it is a good idea to always represent your character's health status on-screen, if indeed your character has that feature. With a press of a button, information can slide onto the screen and subtly slide off again once it is finished with. Games can activate this hidden information feature when actions are performed in a game.

Reconfigurable

A reconfigurable control system is less likely to be seen on a console as it is on a PC, although it does happen. This is primarily due to the type of games that

FIGURE 15.5   Dungeon Siege re-configurable keys

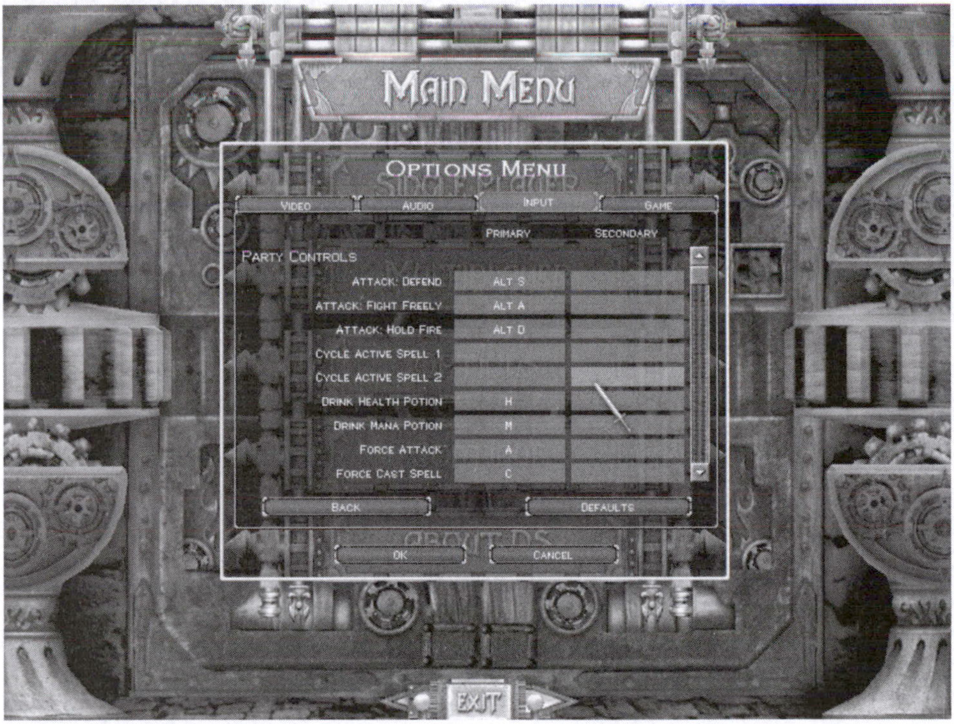

dominate the PC like RTS, RPG, FPS (First Person Shooter) and simulation games. These games in particular generally require keyboard input as well as mouse input, therefore a player will want to customise his keyboard and mouse to suit his own style of play. This can be especially important for people who are left-handed, for example.

An example of an interface to allow the player to reconfigure his keys can be seen in Figure 15.5 from Dungeon Siege. It allows the player to define his own hot-keys in order to control the game the best way that suits him. Although you can't see it on the screenshot, every key can be changed, simply by sliding the bar on the right of the window to reveal more keys. The default layout is usually the best way to play for most people and the designer would have initially applied the most common layout used by gamers. The most common set-up would be revealed during testing and focus testing and most other PC games will define many of the keys because they are familiar.

Another reason players like to customise their controls is for personal familiarity. PC gamers like to play their favourite games using the same control layout. If the default is not the desired set-up, the player will expect to be able to change it. They like to explore and take time to perfect the controls and make it feel as comfortable as it can be.

Controllers of the future

As you can imagine, predicting control devices of the future is purely subjective. One can look back and see how devices have evolved and project the same ideas going forward.

In the short term, I believe the functionality of the devices we have today will remain the same for the next generation of consoles, or at least remain familiar and will take us through to 2010. However, I see an emergence of wireless controllers, particularly on the PC. From a gamer's perspective this could be a good thing providing it's not restrictive in any way and still allows the gamer to interact and feel the games in the same way, or preferably enhance the player's experience.

I've always felt that a glove device that can replicate the motion of a mouse without relying on a flat surface could potentially be a controller of the future. Providing you don't have to hold your arm in the air for long periods of time, hand gesturing and finger movement would give the player a greater range of movement and control. If the issuing of commands was done intuitively, it would feel natural for the player because we use our hands more than any other part of the body.

Even though the trackball is an old device, I am surprised it hasn't been implemented in a controller. A track-ball controlled by the thumb could work particularly well in a three-dimensional environment, just as a mouse ball works for a mouse on the PC. Therefore, I can see a comeback for the track-ball, perhaps in the form of a 'thumb ball'.

Voice-activated control devices will eventually become an additional communication tool, but I don't think a player will fully control the game using the voice, as a game is all about interaction, and just using sound would detach the player from the game.

Summary

A good interface is an invisible interface, one that doesn't get in the way and become the challenge for the player. Study good and bad interface designs and learn from those who have got it right. If it feels right, then it probably is, but if you have to think about which buttons to press then you may need to rethink. Go through several iterations and never settle for the first one – there is always something better.

If you are porting an already developed game, be sure to re-design your interface. It will need to work with the target platform *and* the target audience and this can often mean re-designing elements of the game.

CHAPTER 16

Game balancing

What is game balancing? Balance is the precise coalescence of function and design. You may have noticed that I have discussed balancing at various points throughout the book. This is because game balancing is not just about modifying one element of a game. It's about finely tuning all the elements to work together as a collective unit, much like a beautifully tuned car. A car consists of many components and if one of those components fails or is badly tuned, the whole car will become unstable. When games are not balanced they too become unstable. It is defined in the playing and the player can feel it. It is ugly, clunky and really no fun at all.

Are difficult games badly balanced? It is very easy to make a game difficult, and if exposed to the right environment, I believe anybody could make a game really hard. Similarly, making a game easy can be just as accessible. However, both may cause a problem for the player, but it doesn't necessarily mean it's badly balanced. If the game is consistently too hard, the player will become infuriated and lose interest. On the other hand, if a game is consistently too easy, the player will get bored and most likely lose interest. But a difficulty level is purely subjective to the player. One player's difficulty can be another player's ease.

Balancing is mostly about making the game fair by giving the player an even chance of overcoming his challenges in a fun and interactive way. The player will have choices and make gameplay decisions throughout the game. All choices offered and decisions made should be credible for success. There should never be a right or wrong decision, only that each decision will lead him down a different path towards the core objective.

Pre-balancing

What obstacles do designers face when confronted with balancing their game? Balancing games is bad enough, but the designer will come up against some tough decisions before he can begin the arduous task. There are also many considerations you will have to take into account, of which many may have already been made when embarking on your design.

Development time

I mention this because it's usually one of the biggest influences on how much time you have to balance your game. There will be many people tugging at the purse strings, wanting that game finished and earning money as quickly as possible. Little do many of them realise that if they went that extra yard, spent a little more time honing and polishing, they would probably make more money.

To combat this scenario, you need to start balancing early. There is only so much you can do on paper before it needs proving 'in the flesh', as it were, and if you leave it too far into production, you will not have enough time. When I say early, I mean as soon as you have a prototype up and running; you don't need final graphics and state-of-the-art technology. You don't even need all the rules and features implemented, just the core systems that make the gameplay functional. However, you do need access to the core and be able to tweak the values until it plays to perfection. If it's simply numbers on a screen that represents your units and their values, then so be it, at least you can begin to test your theories.

Most programmers will set you up with this access. This is possible both on console and on PC and will enable you to modify the values that will alter your game's inner workings. This is game design, getting deep to the heart of the game and manipulating its characteristics. Like a surgeon in an operating theatre or a mechanic poring over an engine – it's game refinement.

Target audience

I've mentioned this all the way through the book, but you will need to consider your target audience before you begin balancing. In fact this consideration should have had an initial impact on the overall difficulty setting of your game when you began your design. If your audience is children, for example, then the challenges in your game will be much easier for the player than if your game was targeted at an adult hardcore gamer.

Whoever your audience is, balancing will not be any easier if they are young children or if they older hardcore gamers. Novelists and scriptwriters form a good analogy: they will write numerous iterations of their manuscripts before they deliver a final draft. Even then, the publisher will ask for more changes until it is honed to perfection. Writing for children can sometimes be much more difficult than writing for adults because your bandwidth is much tighter in terms of content and language suitable for children.

If you are designing an adventure game for a child audience, for example, then the words you use and the structure of your sentences will be very important, just as the gaming content, interface, challenges and the victory conditions need to be balanced with the audience in mind. With adult games, the bandwidth is much broader in terms of content and complexity of challenges therefore you have more choice, making balancing as difficult, but for different reasons.

Difficulty settings

What is an appropriate and satisfying level of difficulty? A simple answer for that is one where the player has an even chance of winning or losing. But I repeat, it is the player that will define how difficult the game is, not the game. The game can be set at a particular difficulty level, but if the player is not adept at playing games, he will find it more difficult than a gamer who plays games often. So this is one aspect of a game that can make balancing difficult. The only way to combat this is to define your audience at the beginning and balance your difficulty setting at that level, consistently, throughout the entire game.

Some games will have a difficulty setting built into them. These settings are basically global modifiers that change the internal settings of the game. Take an action adventure game, for example. You may have a challenge where you have to gain access to a building, but to do this you may have to get past several armed guards that will shoot on sight.

Let's assume our imaginary game has three difficulty settings – **Easy**, **Medium** and **Hard**. A game's difficulty default is generally set at medium, but the player should have the option to change this, usually at the start of a game.

> **TIP**
>
> Never give a player the option to change levels during a game because it could be used as a cheat to get past certain parts in the game.

If the game is set on easy, there may only be one guard guarding the door that is relatively easy to shoot. However, on the hard setting there may be three guards that are a little more difficult to kill and require a slightly different strategy. This can be achieved by giving the guards a set of attributes that can be scaled based on the level of difficulty. On easy, the player may be able to get closer to the enemy and the guard may be easier to shoot. On hard you could increase the guards' motion detection range, make them harder to kill and possibly even turn on the guards' usable shield. You could even make them immune to certain weapons by changing their clothes, like a bulletproof vest for example.

All of this takes time to create during production and needs to be decided early so it is designed into the game from the start.

Even though you may have various levels of difficulty, this does not guarantee a well-balanced game. As illustrated in Figure 16.1, you can see that if you have a particularly hard puzzle or perhaps a particularly hard sentry to sneak past, it will cause a spike in your game, no matter what level of difficulty the game is set at. If the game is set on the easy setting and you hit that tough spot, you can see the difficulty setting will increase during the game, which is not the desired result. This will echo through all difficulty levels, making it hard, extremely hard!

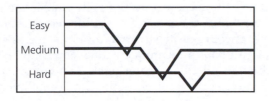

FIGURE 16.1 Difficulty spike

Multi-player

Making the game fundamentally fair for all players is vital. If your game supports multi-player, it must give each player an equal chance of winning. Each player must have the same level and value of components at his disposal as every other player. Even if you have designed different armies that look and act differently, they must be equal in ability and functionality. One player should never have the upper hand.

If a player discovers a unit that has superior strength to his opponent's units, he will undoubtedly use it against him to win every time, shifting the balance of the game in his favour. This is in fact utilising a cheat in the game and this is what makes computer games so different to external games. Computer and video games cannot generally be fixed, unless via a downloaded patch off the Internet, which simply should never happen or be relied upon by the developer/publisher.

Testing balancing

The only way you are going to tell if your game is balanced or not, is by playing it. A good designer will play his game and subsequently yield success from doing so. How do you know if the elements of your game are working if you don't play it? You don't is the answer.

I mentioned that you should begin testing early and this is true. The good thing about starting early is that you can test new theories, which may lead to new ideas for your game that you may never have thought of otherwise. Experimentation is great in a creative environment, providing it is controlled and managed. If you try new things out you can always change it back again if it doesn't work. Dispel the weaknesses of your game and build on the strengths, and the more time you have doing this, the better your game will become.

Work with your producer and/or keeper of schedules to ensure they have allowed time for balancing the game. This is game design; without balancing you have just the paper it was wrapped in – dull and lifeless.

For richer and poorer

You must have heard the expression 'the rich get richer and the poor get poorer'. Although this tends to happen in real life, you cannot let it happen in your game, it simply encourages frustration and in some cases anger!

Racing games often adopt a technique called 'catch-up'. For example, if the player falls too far behind the leading pack, the computer will adopt the 'catch-up' mode, modifying the opponents to allow the player to catch up with them. A similar thing will happen if the player gets too far ahead; the computer will modify the opponents to become better drivers and slowly catch up the player. This can be a tricky affair, because you have to be careful you don't get into a situation where the player finds it difficult to shake the pack and get ahead, or allow the opponents to get so far ahead that the player will never catch up. You also have to be careful that when the opponents are modified, they are never modified beyond the extremities of what the player could achieve, otherwise that would be unfair. Again, it comes down to balancing and setting the limitations to allow fairness. The player will still need a challenge, but not so much that it's too easy or far too difficult.

In this situation the player will have more fun if it is a close, competitive race. This can be said for most games. Competition is what games are about, so if it's too easy, there is no competition and if it's too difficult, it is simply annoying and frustrating.

You must also be aware that the player could use the 'catch-up' technique to cheat if he becomes aware that it's happening. The player can deliberately perform badly in order to slow down the computer-controlled cars, then, towards the end of the race, the player can play well and race ahead to win the race. To avoid this, you have to be careful that the window you open for the player to play catch-up is not too wide but subtle – and never modify the player controls during a game, as he will notice!

The brick wall syndrome

The brick wall syndrome is a situation where the player has got stuck and hit a brick wall. He has to make a final decision to get past this one bottleneck in the game, but he doesn't know what it is. Perhaps it's a puzzle with an elusive answer, synonymous with adventure games, or maybe it's a boss character that's a tough nut to crack. Whatever it is, remove the blockage, flatten the spike and make it easier.

If you balance your game, you will weed out all of your brick walls and smooth the path through the game. The more you play, the more you will find and the less there will be in the final product. Make it easier for the player by modifying the challenge or decisions the player has to make to enable him to progress. And remember, all decisions should be fundamental to the game and help the player progress further into the game, never backwards.

Where's the challenge?

As well as brick walls, you have to be careful that you avoid free fall. This can happen when the player can walk through the game, right to the very end in no time at all. It is better for the player to reach the end wanting more than to find it very difficult, but to allow him through with little in the way of challenge has the opposite effect.

You must increase the level of your challenges as the player moves through the game, subsequently making the reward much higher each time. Never stagnate your challenges so they are the same throughout the game. The player will get better at playing and require bigger challenges. A stagnant game is a boring game and one of many reasons why gamers never finish them.

Summary

Game developers have, in the past, tended to focus on technology and art, which are important, but it has been at the cost of gameplay and the void of any real game balancing. Technology and art are external elements of games and as soon as the player has seen them, he looks through them, into the game, searching for that magic ingredient called gameplay.

Remember to place your challenges in such a way that the player is always moving forwards towards a single goal that contributes to the core objective. Each challenge should lead to the next and every decision the player makes should never be wrong.

If you have not spent time balancing (designing) your game, then the magic ingredient may require a little magic of its own. Find the time, even if it's your own time; it will make all the difference.

Many gamers now adopt a try-before-you-buy attitude, particularly now they can rent games from their local Blockbuster. So if they find a dull game, they won't buy it. If they find a challenging and interesting game, they will more likely buy it than keep renting it.

CHAPTER 17

The future of gaming

Where are games going? Can we see a trend in gaming history that will lead us to see the future? I have been making games for twenty years, and in that time, one thing has remained consistent: 'gameplay' rules! If anything will remain in games of the future, it will be the paramount importance of gameplay, because without it you simply have no game at all.

To create coherent masterful gameplay for future games, we need great innovative designers. Games will grow and evolve and become technically more challenging, which will subsequently open up new avenues and inspire new design possibilities. Innovative and creative designers are the key to games of the future. They will need to see beyond the murky repetitive residue of today's games and create the uniqueness that was once computer and video games. If we neglect the future by failing to offer new avenues for new designers, the industry will stagnate and the same repetitive drivel will continue to spew onto our game store shelves.

New inventions such as the Internet and broadband have given designers the capacity to build perpetual worlds that are populated with avatars controlled by real people from all over the world. These are games that can live forever, that have no end but permanently exist in the digital universe.

Game development companies will come and go, technologies will live and die and game designers will grow old and grey, but games will go on forever. To a certain degree we can predict future games. If you look at the last twenty years, games have remained fairly consistent in terms of genre, themes and ideas. The little plumber who kicked off big-style back in the 1970s is still here today, as are most of his relations. They keep within strict boundaries and design constraints, but creativity and technology has allowed the games to mature and grow with time. Racing games are still racing games, although they are depicted in three dimensions and are faster and more realistic. Football games still have the same rules, attract the same people and sell the same millions.

An increase in hardware technological capabilities has allowed the player to experience games from a different place, and I'm not talking about a geographical place. Games deliver feedback at a different sensory intensity from games of old, but some people would argue that technology has destroyed games. But surely, that is pure nonsense? It is simply a greater challenge today to create something outstanding than it was in the days of 8-bit gaming. Because of the lack of technology and the simplicity in hardware capabilities in the 1980s, the focus was on gameplay and not the features of the rendering engine and the rate at which data can be pushed around. Currently small teams struggle with the might of technology, while larger more experienced teams flourish and reap the benefits.

Although Tetris is a masterpiece, the original game could not be sold today as it was then, unless you bundled it with a plethora of other games. Over the years it has been dressed up and emulated, but it will never be as successful in today's market as it was when it was originally released. Will we ever see another Tetris in our time? Expectations are higher, technology is more advanced and gamers want a bigger challenge. Tetris is possibly a game that you might play on a handheld while on a train, but for a next-generation console it is too light.

Although history tends to repeat itself, at best we can only truly guess at what lies ahead. We can certainly learn from our mistakes and build upon our successes, but we have seen the simplicity of Space Invaders and Pac-Man become a distant blip in the light of games like Halo®, for example.

To illustrate how much and how quickly technology has evolved, the Commodore 64, around in the early 1980s, had just 64 kb of memory and only a portion of that was accessible for games, unless you switched out its operating system. Today, a save game cartridge for the Sony PlayStation2 has 8 Mb, just to store *save data* from games today!

Where are we now?

That's a very good question. I can only answer that at the time of writing and it appears that the industry is again going through a transitional period. The last big transition, from two dimensions to three dimensions, saw gaming technology take a massive shift, while the skills of the development industry struggled to catch up. Today we are seeing a quality shift. The benchmark for justifiable publication has risen to such an extent that developers are finding it difficult to adjust and deliver the standards expected of them. The art and technology content is racing towards movie quality. Consequently some small development teams have become huge unmanageable teams and some small companies have diminished under financial strain, while the larger companies that can take the financial impact simply get fatter.

So what about the games themselves? Well … I can honestly say that the majority of them have become repetitive and boring. They are beautiful to look at and run at super-smooth speeds, but they are simply iterations of the last generation of games. Each game looks like the last and originality and innovation is a rare find indeed.

How did we get into this situation? Like I said earlier, games have become large and complex, so large in fact, that it costs enormous amounts of money to develop them to the required standard. Therefore the risk for the publisher to fund and publish such a game has also increased dramatically. Consequently, there is little room for those riskier original products that might have become the next big hit. The industry simply can't afford to take those kinds of risks anymore. Publishers can only afford to fund safe products; products they know will make them money, which are usually either sequels or licences, of which the stores are full. And if you're a developer, publishers will want to see your game almost complete before they will fully commit to it.

In reality, the increase in quality has been getting progressively more evident since games began. It's no real big surprise that we find ourselves here today and I believe there is still yet more to come before the industry finds a steady plateau and balanced business model in which to exist. TVs can only display so many pixels and colours before the player no longer takes notice of an increase in technology. Sound also has a technological ceiling which it cannot go beyond. Therefore, creativity and game design will become the most important aspects of game development.

While games move ever closer to movies, the games industry will adopt a movie industry-style production structure if game development studios are to survive. Compared to movies, game development is in its adolescence and the industry still has years of growth ahead of it. As games get bigger and more complex, there will be a greater emphasis on game design and we will rely less on art and technology to sell games. The audience will get bored of the same derived content and will stop buying them and look for something else to do!

One overriding aspect of game design that we will see in games of the future is games that require multiple human participants in one form or another.

MMOG (Massive Multi-player On-line Games)

It's certainly a mouthful to say! But what are they? It used to be that it was only role-playing (**MMORG**) games that were played across the Internet, but now, it can be any genre of game you like. A hardcore gamer will most likely be familiar with them, but the general games-buying public has yet to grasp this concept. Massive multi-player on-line games have certainly arrived and they are growing in numbers at an alarming rate. With help from other uses of on-line functionality, on-line games will someday replace the traditional publishers and high street game stores. You will simply switch onto the net and have access to your TV, music, movies and games etc. accessible from around the globe.

Right now, the general public or mass-market is not ready for this type of gaming environment. The thought of speaking to hundreds of strangers around the world frightens a lot of people. The potential of exposing yourself to the world is mind-blowing for those who rarely use computers, let alone play games. There is a huge leap from surfing the net for information and jumping on-line to play a game and communicate with somebody you have never even met.

There are several MMORGs currently out there, making large corporations huge amounts of money. For around ten to thirteen US dollars a month, you can play Everquest, Asheron's Call© or Dark Age of Camelot, to name but a few. If you are a child, you could hook up and play Disney's cartoon game with all your friends, which is fun for children and, more importantly, very secure from unwanted communication.

Designing these types of games is a whole new ball game – completely different to designing games you find in your local games store. The first obvious difference is the fact that you play on-line, usually with thousands of other people from all over the world. I played one of these games for almost two years and found that it had addictive qualities I hadn't experienced since the days I first found video games. The gameplay fundamentals are the same but the mechanics and structure are different in that it's perpetual, usually free roaming and often unpredictable. There is also the social aspect, which literally adds a whole new dimension to the word 'interactive'.

The interesting thing about playing with real people is that they are completely unpredictable. You could be in the midst of a great battle and they will suddenly drop off-line, which immediately shifts the perspective of the gameplay, usually from fighting to fleeing!

You have to think differently when designing these games and think big, because like Everquest for example, you can design a situation where a group of 20 or 30 people can fight a huge monster, and you have to cater for all of them and reward them all based on their contribution. Not an easy task, but that is just one of many aspects of on-line game design. These types of games will become more popular in time, but only when the mass-market accepts the new virtual world that is growing and spreading across the Internet.

Episodic gaming

Episodic gaming is a format that has not been fully utilised in any innovative way, but I believe it will become a gaming format of the future. The format has relied, and will continue to do so, on the Internet as a vehicle for distribution to keep the costs down, but the format also has other benefits that have yet to be utilised.

This type of gaming is in its infancy. There are only a handful of games that have been developed as episodic and none have been truly successful to date. A recent TV show, 24, will no doubt rejuvenate the episodic formula on TV. It typifies what could be achieved with games, in that it is one plot, with a beginning and an end, spread across 24 episodes, slowly building, twisting and turning, revealing its characters over the duration of the show, unlike traditional episodic shows that have their own isolated storylines.

The episodic game can follow a similar mould to 24, in that an episode of the game is developed and introduced to the player at any one time, rather than the whole game. The opener to the game is usually given away free, and contains a hook to encourage players to jump on-line and download subsequent chapters.

The business model is new and therefore risky, so there is a level of resistance to developing this type of game. There is a temptation for developers to develop this way because they get to make the game at a steady pace rather than the traditional 'all-in-one-go' scenario. It is also tempting for the player because it means he can play before he buys and if he is hooked, he can continue to play by purchasing iteratively and having the option to drop out when ever he chooses.

There have been a few attempts at episodic gaming in the past with games like Origin's Wing Commander: Secret Ops and EA's Majestic, both having failed. The former was simply too much of a download for computers to handle at the time, and people could not, or would not tolerate such a waste of time. The latter failed for a different reason in that the game would contact the player by any means possible, fax, phone and email, which became too obtrusive for players.

The current batch of consoles is teetering on the edge of delivering episodic gaming and there is a curious buzz about the gaming format from various key figures in the industry. Consoles are ideal for this, although an Internet connection and a large storage device such as a hard drive will be required. Consoles are a mass-market format and the majority audience like short bursts of gameplay that can be picked up and put down.

It is also financially attractive in that it doesn't require a massive initial investment for the player, for which could potentially be a bad product. If the player enjoys the game, he can acquire additional episodes as and when they appear. However, this puts the onus on the developer to develop quality products for fear of losing their revenue stream.

Unlike a perpetual world such as Everquest and other MMORGs, episodic games have a predefined beginning and end and therefore the player can simply stop playing if he is bored with the game or there is no pull. This is a common flaw in many games that are bought off the shelf, which will need to be addressed in episodic games if the format is to blossom. Once the formula *has* been defined and proven, the player's perception of gaming will change forever.

Social gaming

What is social gaming? Multiplayer has traditionally meant that players compete against each other. Social gaming requires the players to work together as a team against another opposing force. Social gaming often requires the Internet and can also take place on a potentially massive scale requiring large groups of people. Multiplayer games are played across the Internet also, but social games are few and far between off the Internet.

A simple definition could be: *Social gaming requires multiple human beings to participate and communicate in a computer or video game to reach a collective core objective.*

Social gaming is not so much a genre or a format as it is a tool to create and force social challenges. Although I've mentioned it before, Verants' Everquest is a good example of social gaming. To describe the complexities and the attraction of so many players to this game would need a book all of its own, but they do play together and all participants fight against the inhabitants of Norrath and Velious, the world and moon in which the game takes place. These games generally require human-to-human co-operation for the challenges to be overcome.

As technology constantly offers new ways of communication, social games are, without doubt, going to become extremely mass-market. With the emergence of Xbox live and other console Internet connectivity it will slowly seep into our homes like TV and radio, but it will bring with it interactivity. At no time in history has this type of gaming been available on such a massive scale.

So how will this affect games in the future? I believe that social gaming will become a major focus for development. It takes interactivity to a new level for the player and someday we could have our own world existing online that can be explored from the comfort of our own homes. Of course gaming is about challenges, and social gaming will offer a different type of challenge based on human–human communication and co-operation.

Party games

Party games are becoming very popular. Nintendo are masters of party games – Mario Party and Monkey Ball, to name just two superb examples of this genre. Party games are a type of social gaming but they do not require the Internet to play them. Some people might call them multi-player games. However, Command and Conquer can be played as a multi-player game, but it's certainly not a party game. Party games will be played, as the name suggests, at parties, family gatherings or summer barbeques and will essentially be a group event played purely for fun and nothing more. The challenges will be simple and obvious and they will be played in the living room, on a console, by the mass-market.

With the appearance of more of these types of games, more peripherals may also appear, such as the dance mat for the recent batch of dance games (which also fall into the category of party game).

The design process of the future

With the emergence of new styles of games, a new type of industry must also emerge. Games have and will always continue to grasp major licences due to their almost guaranteed volume of sales, particularly major movie licences. This trend is already beginning to reverse and we see games being made into motion pictures, like Tomb Raider for example. This I believe will become more prevalent but as the two mediums slink ever closer, games will require more content and detail, and the quality benchmark will continue to rise.

Consequential effects will be: games will be made like Hollywood makes movies. Small production houses will pop up that specialise in different fields of game development, such as game design, character design and animation, environment creation etc. Game studios will harbour core teams that manage the games, but outsource to specialist studios. This will also make the game business a financially better place to be for developers. Developers will not have to house hundreds of staff that sit around surfing the Internet during, and more specifically, between projects. This down-time costs developers money that they could otherwise invest in the initial design and pre-production stages of a game, allowing them to experiment with their creativity before any major investment is made.

There are risks involved in this model, but providing they are managed efficiently, it could work. However, this type of infrastructure doesn't exist at the time of writing, and developers will need to get savoir-faire in terms of cross-studio project management.

This type of scenario could also inject renewed vigour back into the industry and the people that work within it. Working within a specific field of games, such as art and design, will mean that practitioners will not spend many years working on one project and will most likely find that they will work on several projects in close succession.

Once developers have that infrastructure in place, investors will see a business structure and model that can work more effectively than the current publisher funding model, and more investment will come into the industry, subsequently providing developers with financial stability and independence from publishers. Consequently, developers will take on the pecuniary risk of pre-production, and eventually production also, while cultivating a formal structured approach to game design and development, reminiscent of Hollywood. The resulting situation will allow developers to spend more time on building, moulding and perfecting gameplay and the interactive experience without the publisher pressure of release schedules.

One area of development we need to invest more time in is planning. We need to find a way of improving our planning and scheduling. As games and teams get larger, it's not going to get any easier as the industry currently exists. The infrastructure I mentioned above will go some way towards doing that. The satellite service studios will be independent and will not get paid until the work is complete, to spec and of a high standard. Therefore this will encourage better management and asset control. We should never be afraid to plan; in fact it is vital we do. Think about it, what industry spends millions of dollars developing a product without a plan? Architects design their buildings by drafting plans. They lay out streets, and even generate pictorial examples of the proposed site. It's the same with cars – designers conceptualise them and then build a prototype prior to going onto the production line. Design–plan–prototype generates a snapshot of a product that can be sold to the highest bidder. In game development, it is at this point the publisher should get involved, and the developer can choose which publisher is right for the product, if indeed the publisher need get involved at all!

Summary

We are on the brink of a new world of games and interactive experience. Below is a list of ideas for the future, based on what we have seen in the past and what we see today. Needless to say, the games industry has only truly begun its journey and it will be here for many years to come. It will constantly evolve and reinvent itself and the gaming experience with each wave of technology. But one aspect of games that will always be there is gameplay.

PREDICTIONS

- A social gaming environment will emerge and breed a new type of gaming environment.
- On-line gaming will crawl out of the hardcore gamers' corner and become mass-market.
- Social games will become more popular.
- Party games will also become more popular.
- Episodic gaming will eventually find a business model where it can exist.
- New types of interface that allow the gamer to experience games on new and different sensory levels will be designed for the new gaming world.
- The games industry will reinvent its financial and development infrastructure.

PART II

Documenting the design

CHAPTER 18

The creative process

I want to discuss areas of development that other authors rarely mention, but do exist behind the façade of game development. These are the parts of development we in the industry take for granted and do not acknowledge to be part of the process at all. The 'creative process' *is* exactly that. Although the process can sometimes be anarchic, there are familiar spikes and troughs we all pass through on our journey to the finished product.

The game development industry is a rewarding place to build a career, but it can be cruel at times. It can also be unpredictable, pushing you in directions you never thought you would ever venture, and it will allow you to work with people from all around the world. It is a place where immortality is possible if you hit the right notes and score a top ten hit. Your game could be revered for years to come, immortalising your creative genius for all to see.

In Part I we explored the components of the game and studied techniques used to create gameplay. In Part II we will be going through the motions of scribing those elements and techniques into design documents to familiarise yourself with a process. It may not be *the* only process, but it will give you insight into how it can be done in a development environment. It is depicted purely from a design perspective and therefore a programmer's and artist's creative process may appear slightly different.

The creative process – what does this mean in the context of games, and does it really exist? Next to movies and the music industry, the games industry is one of the most expressive and creative industries you can work in. However, the creative process for many in the industry is a little vague, and currently there are no standards. I wrote this chapter based on my experiences over the last twenty years and from the experiences of others. It is intended to demonstrate one way of creating a game design from idea to prototype, but it is not intended to be the only way. I will also cover each section in more detail in the following chapters.

Before we begin discussing the process and creating actual documents, one thing must be clear to you. Every development studio and publisher has a different approach and format for documentation and development. There is no singularly defined creative process. This inconsistency has plagued the industry since game development began. However, some believe it is this tightening of the process belt that is squeezing the creative juices from the soul of the industry. On the contrary, anarchic development is one of the reasons why so many studios have crumbled and fallen. We need a structured, focused, organised development environment, but we also need the space for creativity and it is this 'structured creative process' and development environment that I believe will prevail, as explained in Chapter 17.

Other industries use pertinent terminology consistently from one company to the next. The only realised consistencies the games industry has are the platforms we develop for and the commercial software we use to create and manage our products. The process and structure of game development varies enormously, but this is beginning to change and will continue to change over time as successful standard industry practices begin to emerge.

Often you will find, within the confines of individual companies, standards and procedures already exist, and some of the larger more established companies have game development and publishing down to a fine art, or so they believe. One thing about managing a creative environment is that you have to be creative with your management techniques. No two games have ever been the same in my experience, but there are some fundamentals that the industry uses from one project to the next.

Begin at the beginning

So you have decided that game design is what you really want to do and by now you should have an idea bubbling away in the old grey matter. This is where you start – with an idea that will eventually spring forth into the foray of game publishing and stand proud, head and shoulders above the competition. It has a core feature that you have never seen before and will push your game into the forefront of interactive entertainment.

Let's pause for a moment and look at your core idea as if it belonged to somebody else. Are you sure the idea you have is really good? You need to be sure that it is worth spending a substantial amount of your time on and it will convince others to invest large sums of money into. Perhaps you know somebody who can appreciate your idea? If so, discuss it with them and get some feedback. It's always reassuring to get good honest feedback from somebody who will tell you truthfully if the idea is worthy of the initial treatment. They may even have suggestions and ideas that you may not have thought of. Another thing to remember is that an idea is only theory until it is proven practically or commercially. If it's already proven, then you have a good foundation to build upon, which is the difference between an original idea and a licensed product.

You may discover that your idea is not so original after all, and somebody has actually done it before. But that shouldn't stop you from moving forward with it. Remember 'ideas and themes': as long your idea has been improved over the original and offers something new and challenging, then it's not a bad idea. However, it is unacceptable to rehash the same idea over and over again with no improvement on the game mechanics and challenges.

Figure 18.1 shows the life cycle of a game through the eyes of a designer. I have tried to be accurate with the time-scale for each stage, but it can vary depending on the type of game and the company you work for. There are many aspects of game development that co-exist alongside this timeline and many things will happen as the game is developed. Many departments, from programmers and artists to marketing, will all have their own milestones and requests, which will take place alongside your design goals.

| FIGURE 18.1 | Creative process timeline |

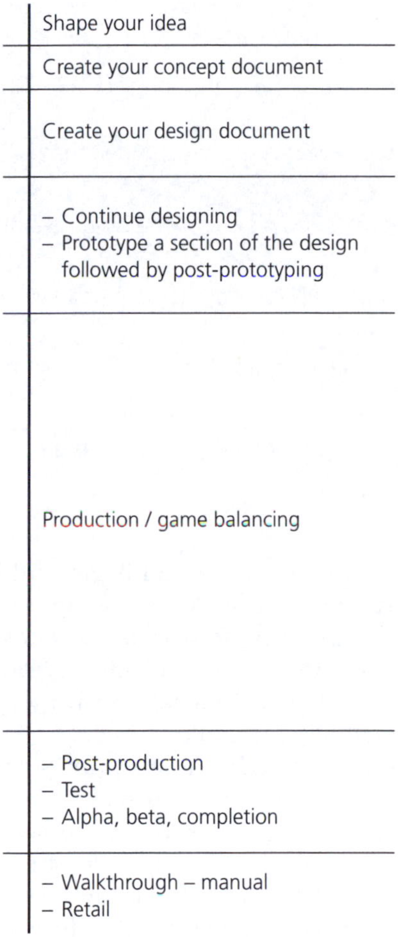

Shape your idea

Create your concept document

Create your design document

– Continue designing
– Prototype a section of the design
   followed by post-prototyping

Production / game balancing

– Post-production
– Test
– Alpha, beta, completion

– Walkthrough – manual
– Retail

Shaping your idea

Once you are confident your idea is strong enough to warrant spending more time, you need to consider how you are going to make your idea 'fun'. What challenges can be born out of your idea that pulls the player towards a core objective?

Once you start shaping your core idea, the next thing you need to do is determine your target audience. If it hasn't done so already, a mental picture of your game will begin to form and it's at this point you can begin to create your documents.

WORKSHEET   **Defining your product**

- Consider who your target audience will be.
- Be confident the idea is worth spending time and money on by gathering feedback from colleagues.
- Establish an overall core objective from your idea that will be used as a nucleus for the rest of the game.
- List the types of challenges the player will be doing as this will help determine the genre of the game.
- Determine how the player will control the game as this, too, will help determine the type (genre) of game it is.
- Define any unique features that are essential for gameplay to exist.
- Consider the theme of your gameplay (not the graphical theme).
- Solidify and clearly define your idea in a two- or three-page document.

You can work through the list above and begin making notes. Some people do a work-up document or a high concept document, which is basically an electronic form of your notes, organised into a two- or three-page document. This becomes a starting point for your concept document. Your high concept document should convey your initial ideas, your target audience and it should explicitly capture the spirit of your game.

If you get stuck, don't procrastinate, do your research. One reason why people procrastinate is due to the lack of research. Your brain needs nourishment, just like any other part of your body, and unless you feed it, it becomes stagnant. Play good games, play bad games, read comics, books and magazines that are pertinent to your game – it will help you focus your ideas.

Although we've established that documents differ in format depending on which company you work for, there are three important ingredients that are required for your documents that are essentially prerequisites:

1 Viable content
2 Coherent language
3 Neat presentation

You may think this is obvious, but I can assure you that some of the documents I have read resemble nothing more than a garbled meaningless hash of mumbo jumbo. First of all, viable content is an imperative, not an option. Also, the reader needs to be able to understand what he is reading and therefore coherent language is also an imperative. Neat presentation never harmed anyone and can only serve to show your professionalism.

I have worked in some companies that never create documents and begin building the game from word of mouth. Yes, believe it or not, this really does happen and more often than not it ends in disaster. There is no direction or cohesion. The documents give it that cohesion and focus, and it provides a reference point for the team. Design documents are the instructions on how to build the game. They are alive, growing and always present. The people concerned can begin to touch and feel your game and begin to understand what it is about, as soon as you begin to write your documents.

Chapter 19 discusses the content of your concept document and uses the example game Norbot as an illustration. When you begin your design, you should start by involving others in the design process. Unlike novels and scriptwriting, which can be lonely ventures, game design is a team effort and a game can no longer be conceived in isolation.

Who is involved in the creative process

There is a saying within the industry that we should never design by committee. To some extent, this is true, but if you have a blend of like-minded people with the same goals, it can only serve to bring spice and flavouring to your game. It is at this point you will determine which people are rowing in the same direction.

Once you have bandied your idea around with trusted colleagues, you will undoubtedly be itching to get going. So who should be involved in the process of putting it together? By now you should begin to harbour questions about technology, art styles, whether the mechanics you want are possible on the target platform. You might also be wondering about secrecy and protecting your idea. I'll let you into a secret. Nobody is going to steal it – what motivation would they have? Perhaps it would make the perpetrator look good in front of his boss? Or maybe he is moving jobs and you're afraid he will take it with him. OK, let's assume they do steal your idea, then what? Somebody asks them to talk about it or write it up, but they're stumped. They don't know the details, the mechanics or the characteristics of the game, as you do. You can almost guarantee that if you gave the same idea to two different people and ask them to make a game from it, the two games would be vastly different. The chances of it being similar increase depending how close to the final product you are. It is more likely to happen once the game is released rather than at this early stage. If you are really concerned and need peace of mind, there are a few simple things you can do to ensure it is safe. Of course if you are an employee, it is highly likely the company will own your idea through your employment contract. Once the paranoia is removed, you can concentrate on the game itself.

- Print your name clearly on the front of the document and also include it in the header or footer of every page.

- Include a '©' symbol on the front of the document to let others know that it is a protected idea.

- Once you have the fundamental idea typed up, put it in an envelope and send it to yourself. When you receive it, do not open it! Lock it up in a safe place.

The first meeting

The first meeting should take place with key people who will form your team and perhaps key members from other teams. Prior to calling the meeting, create a one-page document that describes what the meeting will be about and your objectives for the meeting and hand it out to the attendees. The team might consist of a technical director, lead programmer, art director and lead artist and almost certainly other designers, particularly if they are going to be working on your idea. When you call this meeting, you should have clear aspirations for your game – as if you can almost see the game working in your mind's eye.

Once in the meeting, you should discuss your idea and thrash out any potential technical and art constraints that are related to the game mechanics you are proposing. The constrictions will obviously be limited at this stage, but there may be obvious problems with some of your proposed design elements. You must try and keep the meeting focused on your design and avoid letting it turn into a production or technical meeting, which is often the case, hence the focused one-pager you did initially. Discuss the core game idea in as much detail as you can and you will find, more often than not, the team will have many complementary ideas of their own, which is great and is exactly what you need. It is essential to write everything down, no matter how ludicrous it may seem at the time; it may come in useful later.

The worst thing that could happen is that you call a meeting with no plan. I have sat in a room with a team of creative people and you could have heard a pin drop. Not everyone can or wants to contribute. You will also get an idea of how keen individuals are to work on your project should it get the green light.

Once the meeting is over, use your minutes to compile a document of everything that was said, and in particular, any ideas that came out of your initial idea. Update your two- or three-page document that you originally compiled based on the first meeting. You should have a good vibe as to how people feel about the idea, whether it was good or bad, and don't be disheartened if it gets dropped right away; this does happen frequently. It is simply impossible to make everybody's game.

If people are buzzing, asking questions and generally feel good about it, then you know you may have something that could potentially be a great game, and you can move on to the next phase – creating your concept document. You should have the following information at hand at this stage:

- your initial two- or three-page treatment;
- more ideas, perhaps incorporating some from your colleagues;
- feedback, notes and research that will help you refine your ideas;
- your audience definition;
- a list of the types of challenges the player will face;
- your genre definition;
- your leading platform whether it's PC or console;
- the scope of your game;
- a proposed list of team requirements.

The concept document

I cover the concept document in great detail in Chapter 19, therefore I will only touch on it at this point. Needless to say, you need to create one. Perhaps when you had the initial meeting, the artists were inspired to draw some concept sketches of your main character, or some neat features that you described. If your idea is unique and inspiring, they will most likely be asked to conceptualise for you. If you are lucky enough to have this resource, milk it for all it's worth. Once you have concept drawings, include them in your document. Remember, games are a visual medium and a picture speaks a thousand words. A cliché I know, but it is so true in this industry! Imagine trying to describe your character in a design document. Wouldn't you rather place a picture of it in front of the reader? It's easier, cleaner and less complicated than a page full of words that could be interpreted in many different ways.

Once you have read through the next chapter, think about whether you have included everything the readers need to know about your game.

Concept approval

Let's assume here that you have completed your concept document. Providing you have included all the relevant information, you can now set it free. Put it out to the people that need and want to read it. One of two things will happen – it will either flourish, or it will wither and die. After which, you must be prepared to accept the fact that your game may not get developed, but with each step you take, you are getting closer to the end.

Who will read your concept document? Management, producers, directors and leads will all evaluate your proposal. If your concept has been requested for a licence, or a sequel to an original product, the chances are it will get immediate attention. If it was requested for an original concept, it may take a little longer for decisions to be made. The riskier the product, the more cautious they will be with their finances and decisions. If your game is one of your own original ideas, it has less chance of even making it into any meeting unless there is a slot for development. You must also bear in mind that a game takes between 18 to 24 months to develop and therefore the chance of your idea being heard is minimal.

The design document

So you've made it this far, everyone is getting excited, but now the backbreaking part of development begins. Using all of your previous notes, research, feedback and concept document, you will now begin to build the blueprints for your game.

What is the main purpose of the game design document? The document will be used as an instruction manual on how to build your game, not how to play your game. This segregation is important. A manual has its own audience – the player. A design document is written for the development team, instructing them how to piece together and structure the game. It is not intended to sell anything to anyone, unlike the concept document. If you are thorough, it should take you around four to six months to complete the first draft, but it obviously depends on the sort of game you are creating.

You might be thinking creating this document is a lot of work; if it's only for the development team then why should I do it? You might also be thinking that they should know the game and you could get away with not doing so much work because you are part of the team. Don't make this mistake. You need a design document just as you need your brain to think! One of the most common causes of failed development is ambiguity and lack of communication. If your team begins developing your game (I don't mean the technology), before you have completed your design documents, it is highly likely that it will not meet expectations and many people on your team will be pulling in different directions. Fifty per cent of the overall time of creating your game should be used designing, planning and prototyping your vision.

A perfect example of good planning can be seen in engineering. Prior to any labour commencing, an architect will plan a building right down to the mortar that holds the bricks together. He will create blueprints that define the boundaries and the layout. The blueprints will go into finite detail, depicting water pipes, electrical points and the architect will even define the materials it is to be built from. Often a miniature model will be created to show what the building will look like on completion. It will go through various authorities for building application and authorisation and only then will the creation of the physical building commence. It should be the same with game development, and if any part of the process is missed, you could end up with a disaster on your hands.

The design document should describe your game in every detail, from the innermost workings to the outermost visual feedback that will be illustrated on-screen. No stone should be left unturned, or somebody else will turn that stone and implement their own interpretation.

Not everybody will read the design document and some will read only parts of it. The leads, directors and producers will read all of it as it's in their interest to get it right. Once again, the leads will also provide additional feedback on the completed design document. Artists might only read the sections that are pertinent to the work they have been allocated, but everybody should see at least some of it and you should know all of it inside and out.

Other parts of the process can commence at this point. Artists will define the visual style and theme, and subsequently conceptualise the entire content of the game. This will include environments, characters, vehicles and all objects, particularly key objects that the player will interact with. The game setting will be visually evident and defined as a whole. The lead programmer or technical director will also create a technical design document that describes how the game will be technically built. This will incorporate all high-risk aspects of the game and solutions as to how they may be overcome. This will subsequently lead to prototyping high-risk technology, which should be complete by the time 'game' development commences.

Keeping documents live

Before we move on, a word about all those documents you have created during the initial design phase. Once the first draft is complete, you will need to keep them live throughout production. There is one fundamental reason for this. There is no way you can predict your game is going to work as you have written it. The game will evolve and mature, therefore all documents will need to be maintained throughout the development cycle.

There are other reasons why this should be done. When you are designing your game, it is highly likely that you did not think of everything. Someone will read it and say 'what about this', in which case you will need to update your documents. There is a difference between someone finding a major flaw in the design and somebody wishing to add to the design. Don't be pushed into feature creep.

Another good reason to have up-to-date documents at the end of development is this. If your game is successful, you may decide to do a sequel, in which case, the majority of your work is already done. With minimal work, for the sequel you can take the design document to the next level.

Also, perhaps the publisher has allocated conversions to another team or developer. If this is the case, they will need to evaluate the design in order to determine whether there will be any major changes for market realignment. Console manufacturers often prefer their game to be better than any competing format, which is not always possible, particularly if you are working downwards in technological capabilities.

Of course, once you have created your documents, there is no real way of knowing that it will work as intended until it is implemented. So how can we prove it will work before we spend colossal amounts of cash on it? One way, which has become a prerequisite, is to create a prototype, which takes us into the next part of the creative process.

The prototype

Now we can move onto the prototype. It is around this time your team will begin to grow – primarily the leads, but others may also join, depending on the schedule for the prototype. For the programmers in particular, this will be the fun part. But it is usually this part that gets everybody excited and where most work *appears* to be done.

So why do we create a prototype? Although you have sold your game at concept to get to the prototype stage, you now have to sell the prototype to move into full production. Not only will the prototype prove your concept, it will be used as a tool to convince investors to continue investing in you, your team and the game.

Here are some other reasons why we create a prototype:

■ to implement and prove high-risk technology;
■ to prove the concept;
■ to prove the gameplay and features through a series of defined challenges;
■ to prove the interface;
■ to prove the art style;
■ to define a schedule for production;
■ to reduce the risk of spiralling budgets;
■ to harvest motivation and enthusiasm among team members and the development company.

These are all valid reasons for creating a prototype. However, the prototype should be a snapshot of the game as if a slice were lifted from the final game. If your game were a racing game, perhaps your prototype would be a race, with one of the best cars, in one of the settings described and illustrated in the design document. Or maybe your game is an action adventure, and therefore your prototype would depict the action and the adventure aspects of the game. It should have a beginning and an end that allows the player to play towards a clearly defined objective, comprising many challenges. The level of difficulty should be balanced around the middle of the game. Developers tend to develop games with a high difficulty level. One theory for this is that developers have a tendency to design for themselves rather than the target audience. Therefore, balancing the prototype towards the middle of the game will allow the developers to make it easier or harder if required to do so. It should also begin with a splash-screen and relevant options if the player can modify the gameplay. You as the designer should play it as early as you can, as often as you can, working with the team to make it play and feel like the game you envisaged it would be. If the team have been following your design, it should be very close to your design document.

The development duration of the prototype phase varies enormously and can depend on many things. If it's a sequel with new features, this will be much quicker to prove than an original idea that has been designed from scratch. It also largely depends on the company you work for, but four to six months is about the average, depending on the game. Most of this time should be allocated to building the game and making it feel great.

One of the biggest challenges I have experienced is creating the feeling of power in a fighting game, because the gameplay for this type of game relies heavily on the animations and feedback being just right. The speed, pose and effect of each attack will determine the feedback the player gets after executing each command. If it's too slow, it will feel sluggish. If it's too fast, it won't look impressive and if you have no key frame poses, the animations will look poor. So it's important that time is built into the schedule to allow the programmers, artists and designers to build *the gameplay* and not just the assets, which is what most development companies do.

Post-prototyping

Once the prototype is complete, there should be time for reflection. Stand back and take a look at the prototype and determine what changes you would like to make going forward. It should be focus tested by the target audience to determine whether or not the design is actually suitable for them. This will also highlight any potential problems the game may harbour, and now will be the time to weed them out and correct them. Perhaps one feature of the game didn't turn out as you had expected and further tweaking is required. Some companies will allow for post-prototyping, but not all. Some would rather just get it out the door and get a product finished, rather than work on the quality of the game. This is often determined by the budget the developer has to work with versus the value of the product to the publisher.

Development

If your game is to go forward into full development, it is this phase that will cost the majority of money for the investor. The team will rack up to full capacity and the rest of the game will be built.

Once you step into full development, the chances of your game being published will increase dramatically, but there is still a risk that it will get shelved. It is less likely to happen today due to developers becoming more knowledgeable in the assessment of risks and the overall management and scheduling of projects.

Whether or not your game is going to be shelved is the last thing you need to be thinking about. You should be ensuring the design is adhered to. Let the people who run the company deal with the politics and financial worries; you should just concentrate on your game.

So where do you begin? I can guarantee there will have been changes to the design during prototype, and therefore your documents should reflect those changes. You need to update your documents to ensure there is no confusion as the game is being built.

Once you have updated your documents, there are many tasks the producers could assign to you. For example, scripting. This is always a bigger job than most people care to recognise. Learn C++, as this is the language the scripting engine will most likely be based upon. You might also be creating and editing box maps, ready for artists to apply their magic to the game. Box maps are an important phase in development because this process will have an enormous effect on the gameplay and the overall feel of the game.

One part we should never forget is balancing the game. So many games fail because of fundamental flaws left in them. To avoid this, there must be people playing the game at all times and as early as possible. Feedback should be delivered to the team in a controlled and managed environment. You need external testing because you will be too close to the game at this stage, but you should possess the ability to recognise and extract the valid points and act upon them.

Taking the game from beginning to end, with a well-balanced set of challenges that produce a rhythm and a consuming quality is one of the hardest jobs in game development. It requires so much time, skill and an innate ability that few humans possess. But it is this balancing that will determine the quality of your game. Your game may have a high-quality concept that has taken it into production but if it then becomes fuzzy and confusing, it will stumble and fall.

This phase will test your stamina to the limit. The workload will seem immense and the pressure and expectation to produce a quality game can be an enormous burden for some people. Perseverance will reward you, however, not through monetary gain, although that helps, but through the satisfaction of producing something amazing that has spanned two years of your working life.

Post-production

This rarely happens in game development. Or rather, it does happen, but is never acknowledged. Somebody once said to me that post-production in game development is balancing gameplay. This is partly true. Balancing should happen continuously throughout development, through post-production, onto the end when the producers are peeling your fingers off the keyboard. Post-production is also about cutting out the blank spots, the poor elements of the game, the bits that don't belong to the whole. Post-production affects every aspect of game development including the programmers and artists, not just the designers.

One of the most difficult parts of game development is cutting out code, scripts and artwork that have been lovingly crafted – but it has to be done. Think back to Tetris one more time and think what you could edit from that game. There are no blank spaces in the gameplay and there is nothing you can point a finger at that should not be there.

Be sure you have the ability to edit your game. By edit I mean delete chunks of environment, move collision, add and remove objects, creatures and trigger zones and edit creature behaviour and stats within your game. You may be thinking that your game is shrinking when you're doing this, but the phrase 'less is more' is certainly relevant here. If the game works the same without it, you don't need it in there.

When discussing your schedule with the producer, be sure to mention post-production. Your game will benefit from it in the same way a movie benefits from the editing room. However, convincing a producer that you require this time may not be easy, but if you have planned the production carefully to start with, it should not be a problem.

The walkthrough

Once your game is complete, it is often requested that the designer create a walkthrough. This is not a manual, nor is it a design document, but a set of instructions depicting one linear way of playing the game. Of course there may be many ways to complete it, but this will describe just one. It is born out of the final design documents and the physical game itself. A better description of this would be a transcript, which describes every event the player needs to do to complete the section of the game. The producer often requests a walkthrough so he can provide marketing and the press with the knowledge of how to play the game.

Below is an excerpt of a walkthrough I created for a game I worked on in the past. For the sake of copyright and legal issues, a number of things have been changed, but the essence of the document is still intact.

EXAMPLE   **Walkthrough**

You may create separate documents for different parts of the game, therefore you should begin with a header section that looks something like this. Also, don't forget to format the document with page numbers etc.

▶

Game title: Title
Date: 1 June 2004
Area 1 / Sector 1
Version: 1.0
Author: It is important you put your name here because there may be several designers working on level design and scripting, and anyone of them could create a walkthrough document.

***

Setting:

A dark London residential street. It's late on a clear moonlit night and the hero has just left his place of work – The Jugglers Tavern.

Hero:

Stig Streak
We had multiple heroes in this game; therefore I had to define which hero is being used in this particular section of the game.

Adversaries:

- Shadow Shifters
- Redcaps
- Hood Stalkers
- Boss character 1

This will inform the reader which creatures he will encounter during the walk-through.

Player controls:

- **Walk** – Partially pushing the control stick in any direction causes the hero to walk.
- **Run** – Pushing the stick fully in any direction causes the hero to run.
- **Jump** (1st level jump) – by pressing the 'jump' button (re-definable).
- **Double jump** – Perform the 'jump' when standing against a wall. Pressing the jump button a second time will cause the hero to perform a second jump off the wall. At this stage, this double jump allows him to reach areas up to three metres high.
- **Activate/Use/Action** – The contextual button can be used to open doors, pull levers, press switches, pick up items, etc. The game will inform the player what actions are available to him as he plays the game.
- **Pick up and walk with object** – The hero is able to walk around, albeit slower, when carrying an object. The player cannot run while carrying an object.

- **Throw object** – When carrying an object, the hero can throw it at enemies and other parts of the scenery by pressing the action button.
- **Shoulder barge** – By pressing the 'Barge' button while running, the hero will perform his barge attack.
- **Combat** – The hero will be able to perform his combat moves, defined later in this document.
- **Hero Talk Button** – The player can press this at various points throughout the game. It will instruct the hero to talk to the player pertinent to his surroundings. This can be used for hints and tips or as a vehicle to reveal the hero's characteristics.

A cut scene shows the hero being forced to walk down an alley due to roadblocks. The street beyond the roadblock is busy with traffic and all seems normal. Cars are going past, people are walking by and the usual London street sounds can be heard.

The camera cuts, the player is looking out of the alley as the hero walks into it (enemy's viewpoint). A wall, covered in purple slime, suddenly bursts out of the ground, trapping the player in the alley (scripted). The camera view is switched to 'player cam' and the player can now see down the alley.

Alley atmosphere:

It is dark and the giant buildings are distorted and looming overhead. Steam is spewing from vents in the ground and red lights can be seen flickering further down the alley. The world has become twisted and evil. The music has changed to a sinister track depicting tension, and the player can hear the hero's faint heart-beat. This is a place where the player meets evil.

The mentor character (defined in the design document) appears from nowhere in a burst of magic, and charges the hero with magic power. The hero thinks he's dreaming and the player can hear the hero's comments as he talks to himself.

The mentor equips the player with an electrified baton (important item), which has the ability to spark and glow when close to enemies. The mentor also informs the player of his first challenge.

Note: *Magic is* always *green and evil is* always *purple in the game. This keeps consistency for the player.*

The only direction the player can go is forward, into the darkness, down the alley. The atmosphere is tense, implying anything could jump out at the player at any moment. The corners are dark and things can be seen shifting around in the shadows.

Challenge 1:

The hero is under player control and armed with his baton, illuminating the immediate vicinity (dynamic light). The player should run down the alley, passing the lit fire drums and other alley clutter. Deathly screams will be heard in the distance as if

▶

coming from further down the alley. The hero's baton will spark brighter and lighter (detects creature – feedback). Suddenly a haunting scream is heard (same warning for player each time this happens) and a Shadow Shifter leaps from a dark corner:

- Using the 'earth smash', the player, with one hit, can smash the creature with his baton and send it hurling through the air. If the creature hits a window, it will smash leaving a hole. If it hits any clutter in the alley it will scatter it, possibly destroying it. If the creature hits a wall, the creature will simply explode into a purple haze and a shower of particles, leaving a wispy glowing green pod of magic energy for the player to collect. On first encounter with the green magic pods, the mentor can be heard, but not seen, explaining the pods' function. The hero will look around and appear to be wondering where the voice is coming from.

- If the hero doesn't hit the creature, it will attack the player once, draining health, then scuttle off into the shadows and then repeat the attack sequence again.

Note: *The magic pods are a resource for the magical weapons. If the player uses a special move with his baton, like the 'earth smash', where the baton is smashed on the ground causing a magical shockwave that emanates from the point of impact, it will deplete the magic energy reservoir. Collecting the magic pods will replenish this reservoir.*

Pressing the context 'hero talk button' reveals the hero's jovial curiosity in the situation.

Challenge 2:

The player should now move further down the alley and around a corner. It opens to a smaller, darker and more twisted walled clearing. All round the edges of the clearing is clutter and high walls that are blocking the hero's path.

- Garbage dumpsters
- Burnt-out cars
- A flickering neon light over an odd, distorted-looking door
- Crates, boxes and piles of junk
- Water dribbling from twisted drainpipes

As soon as the player steps into the clearing, the dumpsters begin racing towards him. The player should move out of the way to avoid being hit by them. (*This scene will inform the player that the dumpsters can be moved around*.)

Two Shadow Shifters emerge and start circling the enclosure. One attacks the hero, while the other continues to circle. The hero can dispatch them in the same fashion he used earlier – using his baton. If not he will get hurt just as before. Once the first creature has been dispatched, the second creature will begin attacking. Dispatching the first creature will leave a green wispy magic pod for the player to pick up.

Warning: If the player does not pick up the magic pod, after five seconds (TBD), the remaining creature will pick it up and bring the first creature back to life.

Dispatching both creatures leaves two magic pods for the player to collect.

Challenge 3:

The player now has to push the dumpster against the right-hand wall. It can then be used to negotiate a route onto the rooftop, as the player has come to a dead-end and cannot otherwise progress.

The rooftop is a large flat area with high walls all round and water towers located nearby. Windows can be seen along the right wall as the player moves forward. As soon as the player moves along the rooftop, smashing glass will be heard and shadow creatures will begin pouring out of the smashed windows in the wall.

The hero has to defend himself by pulling off quick successive baton moves, sending the creatures flying through the air, in turn smashing anything they meet. Pulling off special moves (such as the 'ground smash') will dispatch them quickly, but will deplete the player's magic reservoir, so be sure to collect the magic pods.

Challenge 4:

Once the rooftop combat is over, the mentor will appear once again, and create an energy rip. This will allow the hero to replenish his health. The rip appears in mid air and the player has to walk near it to suck the energy from it. As the energy is sucked out of the rip, it will reduce in size and eventually disappear.

Note: These rips vary in size. As the game progresses, they will become larger and more frequent, allowing the hero to draw more energy.

On the other side of the rooftop, the player can jump down off the roof, through a gap in the wall to his left. He has entered an enclosure that appears to be under construction. Piles of wood are scattered around and scaffolding towers over the player. Large vents can be seen in the floor, steam is pouring into the air and a bricked-up arched bridge can be seen up ahead.

As the hero walks or runs over the vents, creatures are seen to scuttle past beneath. Once again, the hero is attacked, but this time the monsters are bigger and more evil than before. They are big devilish Redcaps that jump down off the bridge, each brandishing a big spiky cosh.

Three Redcaps can be seen; although bigger and heavier than the Shadow Shifters, they can trot at a fair pace. It will take more than one hit to kill these creatures. The player should dispatch them using his combination moves and baton specials. Three successive non-special hits of the baton followed by a special will kill them. Only one Redcap will attack the hero at any one time and they will defend themselves, so be aware of the attack pattern.

Hitting these creatures with the 'special move' will send them hurling through the air, and on impact with the scaffolding, will cause it to tumble and crash to the

▶

ground. The piles of wood and general clutter will be sent smashing around the environment if hit by either the Redcap or the player.

On killing the Redcaps, the hero will need to negotiate the remaining scaffolding, jump over the bridge wall and **end Area 1 / Sector 1.**

Stream Mission / Sector 2 from disc.

Area 1 / Sector 2
Challenge 5:

The hero can be seen jumping from the arched bridge into the alley. Twisted cars are parked along a wall, but they are covered in purple slime, as if they have been possessed. The music from the first challenge is still playing. The player must walk around the corner where he will find two trucks parked up. The headlamps and grill on the front of the trucks look like evil, distorted faces.

Suddenly, the trucks burst into life. The headlamps illuminate, lighting up the area and the engines roar, pouring smoke into the sky from the exhausts. Suddenly, they start moving backwards and forwards erratically, which blocks the player's path. Redcaps emerge from behind the player and start attacking (the same attack pattern as before). The player has to kill the Redcaps and demolish the trucks. Once the trucks have been sufficiently demolished, they will explode causing a section of wall to collapse.

Note: *Upon killing the Redcaps, they will drop green wispy magic pods.*

Set piece 1 (Challenge 6):

Note: *We concluded that the combat needed breaking up with set pieces, to offer variation in gameplay. The underlying rule was that it had to be done with current technology.*

Once the hero walks through the hole in the wall, he finds himself standing at the end of a very long narrow alleyway. It is filled with obstacles that appear to be blocking his path. Once the player moves into a specific zone near the first obstacle, the environment will suddenly begin to shake (screen shake – feedback) and the player will see the ground starting to fall away behind him into a fiery world below. There is no way back for the player and he has to run forwards before being swallowed by the eroding ground.

Tension and pace is the key here and the music portrays this. The player can see the metal girders, wooden fences, crates, burnt-out cars etc. blocking the route, arranged in such a fashion that it forces the player to think about his route down the alley. He has to smash his way through the wooden sections using his barge attack and avoid the metal girders or the player will lose time and possibly his life!

As the player successfully reaches the end, he will see a fire escape and a large *wooden* door several floors up – it is the only way out of the alley.

The player will have to rush to the fire escape, up the steps and smash his way through the door using the barge attack. Once completed he will suddenly appear in a *pocket of 'REAL' world*. The player has entered a small grubby apartment, with a loud TV in one corner and a fat man screaming at him to get out. The language is garbled speak. It's the angry tone that's important.

Note: *The pockets of real world are safe havens for the hero; the baddies can't hurt him while he is in these sections. The mentor will appear and create another energy rip. This will allow the hero to replenish his health. The rip appears in mid-air and the player has to walk near it to suck energy from it. As the energy is sucked out of the rip, it will reduce in size and eventually disappear.*

Upon investigation, the player soon realises that the door he smashed through has vanished and is now a solid wall.

Pressing the context 'hero talk button' reveals the hero's jovial curiosity in the situation.

The original document was obviously much longer than this and took the player right through to the boss section. The document assumes the player is familiar with the product and interface. This is evident in the fact that I have given no explanation as to who the hero and the mentor are and the situation they are in. The designer does not need to include this type of information in the walkthrough because the reader will be presented with this type of information also, but in separate documentation as an overview to the game. This can be extracted from the design document.

Marketing and press coverage

So you think it's all over! For most of the team, it is the end, but for you, the work lingers on! Depending how high profile your product is will determine how much work you have to do at this point. Marketing will have a list as long as your arm requesting screenshots, video clips, walkthroughs etc. and you will be asked to do interviews for on-line and off-line magazines.

Of course, this privilege is only bestowed to the leads on the team, and someday that could be you!

Summary

This is just one process, but it is a process that has worked. Things can go wrong during the process that might kill your game, but don't be disheartened by that, it happens to us all. Potentially damaging incidents may materialise that are beyond your control. However, all incidents need managing to minimise the effect on the creative process, bringing them to a resolution as swiftly as possible.

There is a misconception that games are made just by programmers tapping at keyboards and crunching numbers. How wrong this is. The journey is indeed a creative one. A game needs to be crafted, moulded and the elements honed until it becomes an entity that takes on its own characteristics.

CHAPTER 19

The concept document

The concept document, sometimes called the overview document, is where your physical design truly begins. For consistency, we will always refer to it as the concept document.

This is the document that will sell your game to the investors who will pay to have your game developed. This is the first document people will read and for many, the only document they will read, therefore it's very important that it serves its purpose well!

The purpose of this chapter is to explain why you need a concept document, what should go into it, and how to format it in the best possible way.

Are games ever developed without a concept document? For sequels that have little change from the original game, the designer will jump straight into revising the original design document. A designer that has an impeccable reputation and is simply trusted by the publisher to create a masterpiece may get away without creating a concept document. This honour, however, is only bestowed on a handful of designers around the world.

So why do I need a concept document?

The primary function of a concept document is to sell your idea and vision of the game. This may be to internal colleagues within a development studio, or it may be to a publisher who has requested it for a particular project.

A good example of when a concept document is required is when a publisher acquires a licence and is unsure in which direction to take it. The job of the designer would be to write a concept document that captures the essence of the licence. Perhaps you have several ideas of how you would like to develop it and you would like to give the publisher several options. Of course most of the time the publishers will know exactly what they want, but not until they 'see' it!

If you decide to do a concept document for each idea you have, each document should be significantly different, i.e. each one should perhaps portray a different genre and direction for the licence, but more importantly, each document should explain why the licence will make a great game and what features and challenges you can pull out of the licence that will prove that.

The concept document should obviously reflect an abbreviated version of the game. The reader should ascertain how the player is going to play the game and what unique features there are, if any. He will be able to play the game in his mind's eye, simply from reading the concept document. If you leave gaps in your design, the reader's imagination will most likely fill them in and he will begin to harbour preconceived ideas on what those blanks should be, so you should be as clear and precise as possible.

Formatting your document

The layout and presentation of your document can be very important. Often designers will write documents that tightly fill the pages with text. Here are a few tips that will make your documents feel bright, well organised and easy to read.

TIPS **Formatting**

- Use 1.5 or double-spaced lines. This isn't crucial but I believe it makes the document look less crowded and is less likely to make potential readers shy away.
- Include a front page with a title, date, version number, author's name and contact details in the centre of the page. If you work for a team, the company and game logo (if you have one) should also appear on the front.
- Include page numbers in the header or footer on the right-hand side and include the title on the left-hand side. This helps to re-organise the work if the pages are loose and become separated.
- If you wish to include concept drawings with your documents, do so, but don't swamp your document with variations. Embed them into the document, but ensure the text surrounds the images neatly. Swamping your document with images will detract from the text and often the reader will stop reading to look at the pictures, which is not the desired intention. You can use specific informative pictures and diagrams effectively, depicting particular features you intend to include, but it should only really be done for informative purposes rather than dressing up your document. Remember it is an informative document, not an art document.
- Use a clear font (like this one), which is *easily* readable. Designers are guilty of trying to be over-creative with a custom font that they think depicts their creative genius! What it actually does is make the documents hard to read and the reader will give up. No one will judge you based on the type of font you use except if it's unreadable!
- Clearly label everything that the reader might find ambiguous and use clear headings to introduce each topic.
- The concept document should be around 15 to 25 pages, depending on your game, but don't go overboard and drown it with technical detail. People want to read your design, not a technical handbook.

Creating the document

We are now going to create a concept document for the example game Norbot. As I do this, I will explain each section of the document as we go along. Some sections are self-explanatory and need little or no explanation. It is as important to mention the things that will *not* be in your design as much as it is to mention what will. In Norbot, there will be no multi-player, for example. Never assume anything; this will minimise questions later. There is currently no 'correct' way of writing your documents, but the documents do serve a purpose, and the audience do require you to include certain elements.

Norbot: concept document

The first thing you will create is the front page, which might look something like this. You can include an image in the background, but make sure it is high quality and depicts the 'game'. You will not get extra points for including an image here, so if you feel it may detract, leave it out.

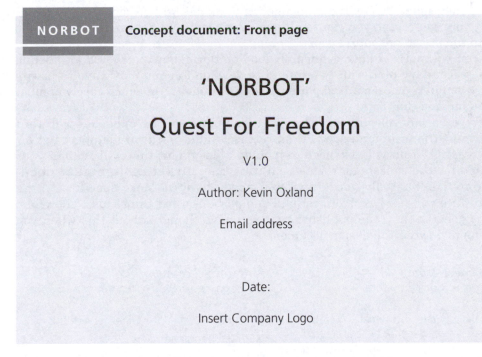

NORBOT	Concept document: Front page

'NORBOT'
Quest For Freedom

V1.0

Author: Kevin Oxland

Email address

Date:

Insert Company Logo

A title, whether work in progress or not, is important, and just like every other word in the document, it should say something about the game you are proposing. If it is a licence, then perhaps your title has already been decided for you. Next, your concept document will inform the reader what platform your game will be development for, and the genre you feel your game will fall into.

NORBOT	**Concept document: First page**

Title: 'NORBOT'
Format: Lead – Console 1 (Console 2, Console 3)
Genre: 'Norbot' is a character-based action adventure with emphasis on interactive story. The player controls a robot called Norbot and the action will consist of combat, puzzle solving and adventure, and there will be an element of stealth using set pieces.

The visual style will be rich and colourful with a cartoon feel to it, which will appeal to the primary target audience. There will also be an element of comedy in the game, which will be delivered through various robot characters and through the feedback.

As I mentioned before, the challenges in the game will go some way to defining your genre and you can see I have justified why I believe this game falls into the action adventure genre.

You will notice I have defined my lead platform, but you should also define any secondary platforms you intend to develop for. You may have to justify why you have chosen a lead platform to the publisher, in which case you must also include that here.

If you are developing for PC as your lead platform, the publisher will want to know the minimum spec PC on release, and a hardware support list for your game. You will also need to include a document that will realign your game for the console market – I call this the **market realignment document**. Undoubtedly your game will need changes. More specifically, the interface will need a major overhaul and perhaps other things also. Therefore, it is good to show the publisher that you have thought about this when you come to do your full design documents.

Game: *Norbot*		**Platform:** *All consoles*	
Age	*Core audience*	*Other games played*	*Secondary audience*
11+	Male and female. A casual gamer that typically enjoys playing action adventure games	■ Mario ■ Crash Bandicoot ■ Luigi's Mansion	Older fans of this genre

Market research:

Action adventure games are one of the best-selling genres of video games. However, in recent times, there has been a tendency for these games to be repetitive in nature, offering nothing in terms of original game design elements. Norbot offers several original game features that would appeal to my target audience. Norbot is also a character-based game, and will stand out as an original and highly competitive contender in the popular character stakes. It offers potential for merchandise and spin-offs. To underpin this potential, cross-platform development will be pivotal in the development process.

The interface offers a context-sensitive control mechanism and therefore will be intuitive to the mass-market and appeal to a younger audience. The game will portray positive values for younger players and deliver family values. All weapons will be designed for defensive purposes and projectile weapons will disable foe in a fun and perhaps comical manner to reflect the target audience.

Other activities my audience will typically participate in:

My core audience might be found partaking in family activities, like bowling for example. My core and secondary audience will read teen magazines, listening to popular music particularly chart music, read Harry Potter, attend the cinema, and read computer and video game magazines. They are most likely to own a PS2 and/or a Gamecube.

In the other activities section, you can be more specific than I have been here. For example, if your game is based on a particular sport, you should include the most popular shows on TV, the best-selling magazines in the sport you are targeting and other specific magazines read by the same audience. In your documents, you can actually name the movies, music and magazines to build a clearer picture.

Your reader will begin to build a picture of your game in his mind. Every word that you type will influence and prod their thoughts and imagination. The 'secondary target audience' defined above will plant images from another game into their minds, so beware of what comparisons you make to other games or it can lead to false expectations.

Languages:

English, French, German, Spanish and Italian
Japanese (TBC)

> **Territories:**
>
> North America, Europe and Japan (all formats)
> NTSC and PAL

Here I have defined the languages the game will support and in which territories the game will be developed for. This is important for the publisher to know because it enables them to calculate the cost of the product, taking into account any text translations and dialogue, marketing, packaging and distribution costs etc. Some publishers are not too concerned about this at this stage, but will certainly want to know going forward.

Expanding the idea

Although important, you have so far only summarised superficial elements of your game. Now you need to look into your game, and expose its internal organs. You have your idea and you are sat in front of your word processor, but your idea is just one line, so how do you expand it? You need to sell it, make the game sound like the best game ever to grace the shelves of any store by communicating the features, mechanics and unique qualities that will separate your game from the rest. Remember, it's a tough market and your game needs to stand out.

NORBOT   **Concept document: Page break**

Game overview:

'Norbot' is a character-based, mass-market, third-person action adventure, set in the fantasy kingdom of Tobor. It combines action, adventure, puzzle solving and set pieces, with a narrative to match, which complements the gameplay, offering a durable blend of unique game mechanics and third-person action adventure. A unique approach to interactive storytelling is also proposed in the following document.

This concept document depicts a single player game with no multi-player functionality. An additional design for arena style, on-line, multi-player game, using different robots and features is currently being drafted. This will make up phase 2 of the development process. The idea of building custom robots using different components will migrate to on-line perfectly, lending itself to custom robot, arena-style battles unlike anything seen before.

Core objective:

The player must guide a robot (Norbot), from his imprisonment at the recycling factory, by whatever means available to him. The player will take him across post-war robot cities, treacherous bot-bug infested swamps and fiery oceans, to name but a few, to confront Dr Mega-bite *and* retrieve Norbot's missing hand. But the journey is perilous and Norbot will confront the most evil Cy-bods ever created.

The player must use all of Norbot's functioning robotic attachments to succeed, including his heli-blades that enable him to fly; his boot boost-thrusters that will give him that extra lift and distance and his shields and lasers should he need to defend himself. These simple attachments will not last long against the might of Mega-bite. Norbot will need to upgrade and seek additional devices, attachments and resources on his journey if he is to succeed in his quest for freedom.

Norbot has one *big* problem. He has been stripped of his vitals. He has no soul. Nor has he a heart, a personality, a voice, a memory bank or a sense of direction. He has been stripped of his organs and exists in a state of perpetual gloom and requires initial guidance. However, once his vitals are restored, Norbot will become fully functional and with each vital found, will aid the player on his quest, maturing the gameplay and narrative as the player advances.

Gameplay theme:

The gameplay theme is robotics and this will be used to create the challenges within the game. It will be a constant theme throughout the game and everything will be designed around it including the interface, the world, the features and the inhabitants. The antagonist and protagonist are both robots; although the enemy are part organic Cy-bods.

The theme itself lends a wealth of ideas to the game, as robots are generally made up of switchable components. The idea of component robot architecture will be used as a unique feature in the game, allowing the player to customise Norbot.

Game structure:

The game will take place over numerous major environments, each broken down into three to four sub-sections. The environments will be designed around a hub system to give the impression of a free-roaming world. However, access to each environment will initially be limited and only accessible once the player obtains the ability to access them, consequently unlocking different areas of Tobor as the player progresses. Each environment will get progressively harder and require the player's newly acquired features to combat them.

Within each environment, there will be a number of sub-quests for the player to complete. These will vary from disabling Dr Mega-bite's enforcements, to freeing prisoners and disposing of the enemy forces, to name but a few. The environments will also contain various set-piece puzzles that have to be solved to earn major appliances and other rewards.

▶

The occupied world of the game will be divided into good and evil, portrayed using visual and audio feedback for both world characteristics. This will provide a clear contrast between good and evil and will inform the player when danger is imminent, inducing an emotional reaction. Data streaming will also be used to convey a feeling of continuity when the player travels from one environment to another.

Norbot will begin as a standard robot, originally manufactured for the service industry by the Obo-Tec Corporation. As the adventure unfolds, Norbot will systematically change into a powerful all-round robot that is capable of leadership. His character will grow from a withdrawn static individual to a charismatic, dynamic and masterful leader. This can only be achieved once the player finds Norbot's vital organs.

The player's abilities and game features will evolve and grow at rhythmic stages throughout the game, subsequently rewarding the player. We will also build in a performance-related score system that will encourage the player to do his best and get the best score. At the end of each environment, a few simple stats, like the number of enemies disabled and the number of freed robot prisoners will be tallied up and multiplied against remaining health to give an overall score for each level. This will encourage the player to perform his best and motivate forward motion. At the end of each section, an overall leader 'rating' will be given, ranging from rookie to leadership qualities. This will also give the player incentive to perform well.

Distinctive features:

- Unique character development and visual character growth
- A variety of unique sub-games
- Data streaming between locations depicting a seamless perpetual world
- Customisable robots
- Distinctive robot gadgets that provide a unique gameplay experience
- A profound, gripping story that will lure the player through the game
- Unique character/player interaction forming a relationship

Here I have simply given an overview of the game scenario, the 'core objective' and a basic structure. There is little mention of game mechanics and features, but it gives the reader a notion as to what kind of game it will be.

In the next section, I have described some of the gameplay features found in Norbot. However, your game may not be character based, in which case you can modify this document to suit your own needs. Perhaps the player will control cars, or command an army of tanks and soldiers. Whatever it might be, describe the features of the controlled device and describe how those features will interact with the world. You don't have to go into great detail of stats etc. at this stage, but give a clear depiction of each function in the structure of the game.

NORBOT | **Character features**

Norbot is a robot and has been installed with the very latest Toborian hi-tech, state-of-the-art features. He has the capacity to install many components using the empty user ports on his person. Obo-Tec robots are designed to allow them to upgrade themselves and have the ability to change limbs if the need should arise (left hand).

One feature that will be an ongoing development is Norbot's character and his relationship with the player. Most interactive story-based games let the player control a computer character on an adventure with little or no connection between them on a story level. To develop a true interactive story, I feel the player should become emotionally attached to Norbot on a deeper level and experience the adventure *with* Norbot rather than looking into the game as in most games. Although the game will be third person and the player will guide Norbot, Norbot will interact with the player and communicate his feelings about the actions and situation he finds himself led into. He will speak to the player, passing positive comments when the player makes a good decision and mocking the player when he makes a bad decision, subsequently providing feedback. A simple 'Quickspeak™' language will be built into the game allowing the player to communicate with Norbot with simple questions and responses. When Norbot wishes to speak to the player, on occasion he will grab hold of the camera and pull it down towards him and speak into it as if the player were there with him. The blend of this level of story interactivity and gameplay is unique and offers a wealth of possibilities.

Norbot can relay game state information to the player and remind him of quests, providing hints and guidance explicitly without any need for extra windows and menus. The possibilities for this are endless.

Movement:

For movement, Norbot can walk and run, but he can also adopt many components. For example:

- **Heli-blades** (upgradeable): When activated, these will allow Norbot to fly for long periods of time, but they will suck power, therefore the player will need to obtain power to maintain usability. The blades will be awarded to the player at a specific point in the game to avoid overuse.

- **Boot-Boost thrusters** (upgradeable): Horizontal and vertical thrusters for precise and quick burst manoeuvring working in conjunction with gravity – fitted as standard. Again, requires power so the player will be required to replenish his power source at regular intervals.

Standard components, such as the thrusters, are not designed for combat use or to be utilised in a hostile environment, and therefore, they will not last the distance of the adventure. The player will need to upgrade or even replace them if he is to make it across Tobor safely. Many more transport and movement devices will

▶

be designed into the game, such as a teleport mechanism in later stages of the game for example.

Visual aids:

Obo-Tec designed Norbot's model to function effectively in the dark. He has been equipped with the following capabilities for that purpose.

- **Infrared lenses:** These are embedded in Norbot's eyes. They will allow the player to see clearly in the dark by going first person while stationary. They also have zoom control to allow the player to zoom in on distant objects.
- **Lumi-light:** At the time of Norbot's design, Obo-Tec had only just invented Lumi-light, which was a feature that all customers demanded. It has the ability to light up the surrounding area around a robot, enabling them to function in the dark while moving, unlike the infrared capabilities. A thin flexible strip filled with liquid Lumi-light is fitted into every limb of the robot. It is light sensitive and activated automatically when the light drops below a defined level.

Shields and weapons:

Norbot also has standard lasers and shields, but because he was designed by Obo-Tec for labour purposes, they are only capable of defence and are not used for destructive purposes. However, all weapons are upgradeable and Norbot is capable of attaching more powerful weapons, which will be necessary if he is to succeed.

- **Protective shield** (upgradeable)**:** This will be Norbot's first level of defence. It can only withstand a certain degree of impact, and therefore, anything more than this initial impact level will penetrate the shield causing damage to Norbot. The shield, when hit, will reduce in effectiveness and an auto recharge time period will be required.
- **Invisibility cloak:** This reflects the surrounding environment off his shiny outer skin, giving the impression of being invisible. This has limited use and is most effective when Norbot is standing still. However, heat sensors can still detect Norbot! This is not a standard feature.
- **Laser** (upgradeable)**:** This is very basic and requires a lot of power to create a powerful enough laser to destroy anything. Under normal conditions, it would only be used to open or seal metal packing cases and other such packaging material.

Map features:

Norbot has the ability to track and map his surroundings. As standard, he has only been programmed with the map of his local surroundings, but he has the capacity to store much more information.

- **Track and map:** Norbot can only map his surroundings as he travels around, storing the data in his 'memory banks' (once he finds them).
- **Motion detectors:** This allows Norbot to detect any movement around him or within a certain distance and works in conjunction with the map.

Additional components:

Norbot also has various data ports that are empty at the start of the game. He can attach various devices and additional weapons as he finds them. Norbot also has an extendable intelligent cable (intellicable™) that can jack into data ports in and around the environment. Norbot will find these data ports scattered all over Tobor, allowing him to access information relating to each zone and the data on the inhabitants.

- **Lock-picking device:** These are electronic codes that the player will find on his journey and use to unlock security locks using Norbot's extendable intellicable.

- **Toontonium discharger** (upgradeable)**:** Toontonium is the power source for Tobor and it just so happens that the Kingdom of Tobor is rich in Toontonium. The discharger can emit a quick, high-powered burst of Toontonium that can blow lights, security cameras and other toontonic devices in the vicinity. Once upgraded, this can also be used as a close combat area weapon – if many robots surround Norbot simultaneously, a larger Toontonium surge will send a burst of energy at the foe, taking out their circuitry, disabling them.

- **Toontonium outrider:** This is a tiny self-contained, intelligent ball-like object that can travel around with a robot and act as a companion or third eye. They also have many sensors on board allowing them to detect motion, organic material etc. and send the data back to Norbot. These were invented by the resistance and will be available at later stages in the game.

- **Water guns** (upgradeable)**:** It just so happens that the biggest fear of all robots is water. It has a cancerous acid effect on a robot should they come into contact with it. The resistance forces have utilised this fear and are developing water weapons as a cheap source of defence against Dr Mega-bite's army.

- **Water bombs:** These can be placed in the world and activated, but Norbot must move out of the way when it explodes. Water is showered into the environment in all directions and will harm any Toontonium-powered object within range, but they have no effect on the environment. All bombs are magnetic and can stick to anything metal in the scene.

- **Toontonium bombs:** These are far more powerful than water bombs and can cause damage to the environment. Again, these are magnetic.

Inventory system:

There will be an inventory system to manage all objects and components Norbot can collect. Spaces will be allocated for every component available to the player and will be visibly evident when the player accesses his inventory. This will also give the player a progression meter as the slots are filled.

The inventory system is accessed through the menu system, however, components can be selected from the game screen (see control mechanics).

This has now given the reader a better understanding of the features of the game and how the player will control Norbot. The functionality of the above features will be designed in detail in the full-design document, but at this stage, the reader only needs an overview of the features. Therefore, the above information is enough to satisfy that. You may also include any images that relate directly to each feature, but remember, do not swamp the document with different variations and a plethora of pictures otherwise the game will get lost in the wash and appear tenuous.

Player mechanics

We have discussed some of the features that will appear in the game, now we need to address some mechanics, or inner workings of those features. These will give the reader an idea of how the player will communicate with the games features to overcome the challenges presented to him. For example, damage control, how the player might die, what rewards, scoring and feedback the player might receive, environment interaction and any additional camera viewpoints that are required for gameplay features, to name a few. Of course, the contents of this will completely depend on the sort of game you are developing.

The mechanics of a game are exactly what the term implies – the inner workings. The mechanics of a car are the engine or the working components, enabling it to function and move from one place to another through interaction.

NORBOT	Player mechanics

Norbot is a robot and therefore all player mechanics are kept in context with the robotic theme.

Norbot damage control:

The player will not have lives in the traditional sense. He will have one perpetual life, but his character will have a Tootonium power bank (hit points) that will be present on-screen. When the player receives damage, his power bank will be reduced, but the player will be able to replenish his power bank using Toontonium outlets and other forms of Toontonium power resources strategically placed across the world.

Norbot also has a separate power supply for his components and doubles as a backup life support. As a life support, it is automatically activated should his main bank of life Toontonium reach zero. This ensures Norbot's life is maintained in an emergency. However, this power supply is minimal when functioning as a life support, because it is reduced constantly at an increased rate due to the supply demand for both Norbot's life and powering his attachments.

This back-up device gives the player a second 'chance' to find and refresh his main power supplies. An alarm will continuously sound, informing the player that he has limited time to find power. This incessant alarm should induce a sense of panic into the player until power is collected. When power is collected, Norbot's life reservoir takes precedence over attachment power and is replenished first.

When Norbot's life-power is below 50 per cent and the player obtains Toontonium then this is refilled first.

If both of Norbot's power banks diminish to zero, Norbot will die and the game will restart at the last saved game-state and the player will restart at the last restart point. It is believed that inducing this method of damage control will force the player to think and plan.

Reward/scoring mechanism:

There will be a scoring mechanism embedded into the game. This will be done in several ways. At any one time, the player will always have at least one task activated that has to be completed and facilitates his core objective. As each task is complete, a record of this achievements will be stored in Norbot's data banks for the player to access and examine at will, providing progression feedback for the player.

The player will be rewarded with an abundance of items and attachments. These range from small Toontonium power cells, to the larger mega-attachment weapons found in various locations throughout the world.

An obvious growth in abilities and strength will be evident, feeding the player's hunger for fulfilment. This will be evident through feedback in the form of special effects, visual treats and significant landmark player appraisals through the unique Quickspeak system.

Environment interaction:

The environment will be interactive. If an object exists in the world it will serve a purpose rather than simply existing. Norbot will have the ability to open doors; pick locked doors; access data banks via computer terminals placed throughout Tobor. Using the terminals will allow Norbot to access cameras placed around the world and spy on enemy placements. He can also save his progress and download additional information on his surroundings, like a map, for example.

Explosions will damage the environments and destroy objects close to the explosion. The environments can also harm and thwart Norbot's progress, like fire and water environments in particular.

Norbot can drop Toontonium explosives that destroy parts of the environment. Damageable sections of environment will be visually evident for the player to easily identify them.

▶

Map feature:

At any time throughout the game, the player will have access to his map feature. The map is a standard feature with the Norbot model. When the map is activated it will display the surrounding area and show areas that have been travelled by the player. It will also identify all access points and terminals in the area.

With a simple upgrade, the map will also allow Norbot to scan the area for movement. This will allow the map to display any objects or enemy robots that are moving in close proximity.

Saving and loading:

Computer terminals will allow the player to save his progress. The terminals will be placed strategically in order for the player to access them at will.

When the game is saved, the state of the world will be saved to avoid puzzle repetition and frustration from the player. The player can travel back to any terminal and save progress anytime the player wishes to do so. When the game loads, the player will begin next to the last saved terminal. This will also be the case when the player restarts the game from being killed.

Camera views:

The primary game view will be third person with the camera trailing Norbot. Control will be given to the player when the primary view is active.

There are additional cameras in the game, such as the first-person mode where the player can look around using the robot's first-person mode. It has a zoom function, which allows the player to look into the distance at potential problems.

The player can also look around at sections of the environments using the computer terminals. This will allow the player to, pan around them and peek at unexplored places. This feature will allow the player to plan his moves.

For copyright reasons, I cannot use the correct technical terms specified by the console manufacturers. In Table 19.1 where I have written button #number etc. you will need to specifically identify which buttons you want the functions to be attached to. At this stage, and during prototyping, your initial choices will be preliminary until you can fully play the game. If your game reaches development, the controls will most likely change as the features emerge and are tested. However, it is important to have an initial control layout in order for the team to begin prototyping.

The console manufacturers have specific technical requirements when it comes to which buttons do what. They too like consistency across products that are developed on their consoles.

| NORBOT | Control mechanism |

The controls are designed to work on all console controller pads. No PC game has been planned.

Norbot will be flying as well as walking and running. When on the ground, the buttons required for the movement of Norbot and the camera, is the same when flying, i.e. left is still left etc.

When the player activates something in the environment, like a door, or console for example, it will be done using the context sensitive button #4. This will be known as the **'Use Button'**.

You can use a table like the one below to assign buttons to actions or you can create your own. Of course, it will be pertinent to the controls you decide to include in your game. It's always good to pick up a controller and imagine playing your game with the controller in your hand. If it is a PC game, then have a keyboard in front of you and press the proposed key as you play the game in your minds eye.

| TABLE 19.1 | Preliminary controls |

Action	Control
Walk/move forward	Lightly push the left stick up
Walk/move backwards	Lightly push the left stick down
Walk/turn left	Lightly push the left stick left
Walk/turn right	Lightly push the left stick right
Run forward	Push the left stick fully up
Run/turn left	Push the left stick fully left
Run/turn right	Push the left stick fully right
Strafe left/right	Hold Button #5 and press left stick left / right
Activate selected feature	Button #1
Move left through features	Left pad button
Move right through features	Right pad button
Fire weapon #1	Button #2
Power-up weapon #1	Press and hold Button #2
Fire weapon #2	Button #3
Lock-on target	Automated

▶

TABLE 19.1	Preliminary controls *continued*
Action	*Control*
Look around	Right shoulder Button #1 + left stick (only when standing. Up, Down, Left and Right to look around.
Zoom when looking around (right shoulder button #1 depressed)	Right stick up zoom in / Right stick down zoom out
Context sensitive **'Use Button'**	Button #4 (see environment mechanics)
Menu / inventory / pause game	Button #6
Access map	'Left Shoulder Button' will activate the map window. A subsequent press will deactivate the window

Weapons and weapons mechanics

Here I will list the preliminary weapons proposed for the design and the functionality of each weapon. I do not need to go into any detail regarding hit-points, range etc. in this document, as this will be included in the full design document, but the reader will want to know how the player will interact with the weapons.

NORBOT	**Weapons and weapons mechanics**

There is one fire button for each of the two weapon slots. Pressing each of these buttons once will activate a weapon. Button #2 is for the primary weapon and button #3 is for the secondary weapon.

To change the weapons and allocate a different weapon to each button will require the player accessing his inventory and changing the allocation.

Weapons will be powered by the Toontonium energy bank and will only stop working when the energy pool diminishes. The only exceptions are the bombs, which are self-powered and explode shortly after activating them. Bombs are resourced and will need to be collected by the player, just like Toontonium.

Considering the target audience, the accuracy of weapons will be very generous, and a simple targeting system will be used to avoid the player having to carefully line up the character to hit a target.

Friend and foe

Within the document, you will need to list the good guys and the bad guys. Here we are just going to list a few and give them some background. In the full design spec, we will detail their function in the world, how they die, hit points, weaknesses and strengths, attack patterns, inventory, power resource etc.

Here I have only mentioned a few of the main characters in the game. There will be much more than this in a final design document and described in much more detail, but this will give you an idea of how to present them initially. They will also be conceptualised by an artist, therefore in order for him to do that, he will need a much better description, particularly the gameplay features they perform within the game.

NORBOT	Friends and foe
Friends:	
Norbot	**Norbot** is the primary protagonist, which the player will control through the adventure. Norbot is a service robot, but has the capacity to be upgraded using the Obo-tec component architecture.
Teefour-T4	**Teefour-T4** is a mentor character that helps Norbot begin his adventure. Knowing that Norbot, the owner of the hand, has been dumped for recycling, T4 gives up his existence to find Norbot and deliver the important message from worshippers in the South. T4 also gives Norbot several objects at the start of the game.
Spark	**Resistance Learder #1** – Holding up on the edge of the fiery lake (gives you a weapon).
Bits	**Resistance Learder #2** – Holding up in the south on the outskirts of Mega-bite headquarters (gives you final weapon for Mega-bite confrontation).
Foes:	
Dr Mega-bite	Mega-bite is the main antagonist and comes from the kingdom of Bootoon. Bootoon has been drained of its Toontonium, which powers all robots, and he now seeks a new Toontonium-rich kingdom to conquer.
Tronn-01 (wip)	One of Mega-bite's henchmen. Tronn is a boss character and will attempt to stop the player in an arena style battle.
Trinn-02 (wip)	The second of Mega-bite's henchmen. Trinn is another boss character and will attempt to stop the player, but in a different style to Tronn.
Tripp-03 (wip)	The Third of Mega-bite's henchmen. Tripp is a boss character and will also attempt to stop the player but different to both of the previous bosses.

▶

Drones	Patrolling guards. They are armed and can detect movement at different ranges depending how close the player gets to Mega-bite.

Story premise

You will notice I have put the story overview near the end of the document. I do this because it's the last thing people want to read in a game design document, if at all. Some may skip it and not read it. The emphasis should be on the game, not the story elements. The core objective should be the common goal for both game and story, bringing them together at the most pinnacle moment.

NORBOT   **Story premise**

Norbot is a lonely robot, glumly sitting among a robot-recycling scrap heap destined to become a cube of mangled metal. He once lived a fulfilling existence serving his master, until one day, the robot wars came. A race of evil Cy-bods, created by Dr Mega-bite, invaded his homeland, the Kingdom of Tobor.

In the midst of battle, an enemy laser blew Norbot's left hand clean off. It could so easily have been more, perhaps even fatal. In the chaos that ensued, he was eventually scooped by the Cy-bod-tec disposal-squad, stripped of all his vital components and dumped in the recycling factory.

While Norbot mourns his beloved kingdom, another more dishevelled robot is dumped on the heap next to him. The heavy crashing triggers a message embedded into its memory bank. Norbot discovers that in the darkest southeast corner of Tobor, there is a band of rebellious robots that live each day, struggling for peace and freedom for all bots. He also discovers they worship the hand that once belonged to 'the one' that would some day be their saviour. Norbot realises it is his hand they worship and with a feeling of nobility, and a sense of responsibility, he realises it's his destiny to help them.

The evil Cy-bods still rule Tobor, but not without conflict. One element exists on Tobor that Mega-bite did not expect, the presence of H_2O. This can be fatal to Cy-bods, burning and decaying their components likes acid through flesh. There are also pockets of resistance scattered across the kingdom, still fighting the good fight. Some bots believe it to be futile, while others believe 'the one' will someday come and save them from this evil tyranny.

Story elements:

The story follows Norbot's journey from the recycling scrap heap, to the southern tip of Tobor. Norbot will be portrayed as a lovable cute robot alone and vulnerable in his world. It will toy with the player's emotions making him laugh, gasp and possibly even cry. There is a dark and serious undertone to the story, portrayed through the presence of Dr Mega-bite and his henchmen.

The player will need to reveal Norbot's true character by finding his vital components. For example, to hear Norbot speak, he will need his voice box; for him to remember his past and reveal secrets to the player he will need to find his memory chips. There are many more components of Norbot the player will need to find. They will be tied to the game's architecture and the structure of the story, binding them together into a unique interactive experience.

Environment features

Depending on the type of game you are creating, you should give an overview of the world in which the game is set. You should identify any game features of your world and give some examples of the environments that will be in the game.

NORBOT   **Environment features**

The player will guide Norbot across many types of terrain on his journey. From his humble beginnings at the recycling plant, to the stronghold of Mega-bite. The world in general is a hi-tech world with little organic matter, but is torn and twisted from the wars and the brutal strength of Mega-bite and his army. Norbot will fly across the great fiery lakes, negotiate through a dilapidated robot city, escape from a recycling factory and penetrate Mega-bites fort to name but a few locations.

Look and feel:

The game will have a cartoony feel to it, while retaining the three dimensions in which the game exists. Norbot is a relatively small robot and the feeling that he has stepped into a BIG world will be portrayed through the art, the dynamic camera views and the cut-scenes.

The two sides of good and evil, dark and light, will be portrayed in the art and the player will know what part of the world he is in.

The concept document is done – now what?

Well, it's almost done. Accompanying the document, you will need to include proposed budgets for the development of the game. A clue as to the amount of dialogue – if any, sound (music and effects) and a proposed head count for your team. They may also need team information such as skill sets, hierarchy, names etc. Another member of the team, such as the producer, may compile this sort of information, but it will be born out of your concept document.

Ok, so you have the first draft of your concept document complete and ready to show everyone. You will be nervous, especially if it's your first document and you wonder what everybody will think of your ideas. Don't fret; you will soon know if it is a really good idea, everyone will tell you. They should also tell you if it has any weak spots or elements that need further fleshing out.

You should show it to as many people as you can before handing it to the boss. Hand it out to friends and colleagues who will give you honest, constructive feedback. Listen to what they tell you, take on board the good and bad comments and make lots of notes. Put your concept in a drawer to cook for a day or so and then do a second draft. You will often find that you think of new fresh ideas and some of your original ideas were not so good. Keep doing this until you either run out of time, or you are completely happy with it. It is rarely the latter!

TIP

I always carry a small notebook around with me and record any ideas that pop into my head. I then type them up later when I get to a keyboard.

The presentation

Everybody involved in making the game should read the document and give you feedback. One thing to bear in mind is that you should never become obsessed with feedback. You will never please all the people all the time, it simply never happens. Never compromise what you feel is a great design feature, just because Joe Bloggs hates the idea. People who need to read your document will include the producer, art director, technical director, before ending up with the prospective publisher or investor, but not before a final revision – V1.0.

If there is to be one, who does the presentation of your design? It's often not the designer, but more likely to be the producer or the project lead that will perform this role, while the designer waits in the wings with gritted teeth. A pitch is an art form and should be left to the people that are good at it. It mostly depends on the sort of person you are. If you are confident and can talk the talk, then you may be the person to do it and more often than not, the designer will know more about the game than the producer, but may quiver and fumble under the spotlight.

There are many tools the presenter can use to help pitch the game to the people that matter. Storyboards, props and even a clay model of your central character can be a good device. With one game I was involved with, the designer commissioned a friend to create a model figure of his main character. The marketing people loved it because they could touch it and see potential merchandise standing in front of them. When props are presented, touching them becomes irresistible and it instantly gives your game a physical presence, even at this early stage.

If you insist on presenting your idea, practise first. Present the concept to your team, present it to another team and feel comfortable with what you are saying. Marketing people are very good at presenting – it's what they do. You should find some marketing people and present it to them too. They will give you some feedback, both on your presentation skills and on the market potential for your game idea.

Summary

So that is the concept phase of your design idea. 'Norbot' is no great shake-up of game design, but the purpose was to show you what is required of a concept document. All concept documents will be different for every game proposed, but the type of content and structure can be similar. When you do your concept document, be sure to cover all aspects of the design, but be as brief as you can be without holding back the essence of the game, and give plenty of examples. The detail will come in the full design spec – if it gets that far.

I showed some colleagues the 'Norbot' idea after I typed it up and I had some very interesting feedback, which I actually took on board. You can read about that in the next chapter.

I left the above concept document in its initial state because it's important for you to see the transformation and the spiralling growth of an idea from the first draft to the final design. If I included all the changes I wanted to make, you would never see that growth and transformation clearly.

CHAPTER 20

The design document

In Chapter 18, we discussed why we need a design document and who will be reading it. In this chapter we are going to discuss the format and content of a design document. There are two things I need to make clear before we begin.

The first is that a game design document created for each genre will have a different content and structure due to the nature of each genre. A racing game design document, for example, will vary somewhat to that of an RPG design document, as you can well imagine. There is no set way of creating a document for all games, however there are many common elements to all design documents, which we will discuss here.

The second thing is, unlike the concept document in Chapter 19, I cannot write a complete design document for inclusion in this book – it would simply take too much time and too much space. Before we begin, here is a reminder of some of the things you will have done prior to reaching this stage of your design.

CHECKLIST

- You have expanded your idea into a potential challenging interactive experience and created a two- or three-page overview to portray the essence of your game.
- You have researched your topic.
- You have written your concept document and included all relevant information.
- You concept document has been approved.
- You have included your team members in the design process and gathered their feedback.
- Having completed all of the above, you should know the scope of your game and have identified all the risks.
- It has been officially acknowledged that you can continue with your design document and spend the next three or four months creating it.

Remember, the design document is the bible for your game and should remain live throughout production. It is the instruction manual on how to build the elements that make up your game, the inner workings and mechanics of your vision. You are not using the design document to sell your game, it will only be used by the development staff and therefore it should be created for them in mind. The language will be different to that of the concept document in that a technical/game register can be used. You can compare it to a movie script in that it's written for the director and everybody who works on the movie, to use for their guidance.

The game design document follows up the concept document. Creating a design document can be overwhelming to a designer who has not written one before, so help from colleagues will be essential. The concept skims the surface of the game, highlighting the features and content overview. The design document goes into every nook and cranny, detailing everything from the rules, the interface, creature attributes, stats, the physics of vehicles if it's a racing game, to the inner workings and solutions of every puzzle and more, all clearly documented and illustrated.

Expanding the concept

You can use your concept document as a starting point for your design document. However, you will not need to include things like: lead platform, target audience, languages and territories. We are dealing with the game content now, nothing more than that. As I have said many times, the format of documents varies from game to game and company to company, so it may be worth asking the programmers and artists how they would like the information presented to them and in what format. This may already be standardised within the company, but if not, it would be worth asking. Some teams prefer it to be on-line via an intranet, while others like a neatly printed document so they can make notes on the pages as they build the game. Others prefer nothing at all and like simply to be told what to do.

I revealed my example concept to some of my colleagues, obviously explaining the purpose of the document. Here are just a few of the more interesting and constructive comments I received.

You can see they're not all positive comments but are constructive, which is what you need. With this feedback in mind, I would, in normal circumstances, revise my concept document to reflect some of the ideas put forward.

NORBOT   **Concept feedback**

- 'The concept of controlling a robot is a great idea and could be used to better effect, including more technological features, for example audio zoom for sensitive hearing as well as zoom lenses. This audio clue could be great for dark areas or claustrophobic environments where visibility is poor.'

- 'I think you should use the idea of customising your robot from the start of the game – let the player build his own robot from the beginning. This will make it feel more personal and unique.'
- 'The story is a little clichéd, but a great idea.'
- 'I would like to see a lot of variation in the evil robots. Robotics allow you to create some interesting combinations and your imagination is your only limitation.'
- 'One of the oldest toys I can remember is a toy that can be taken apart and put back together again. Having this ability in a computer game will give it an innate appeal to your target audience.'

How big should my design document be?

There is no preset answer to that question. The design document needs to be big enough to describe the whole game in every detail, so there is no set size. Every game design you create will be different to the last. They usually end up around two to three hundred pages, but there also exists many offshoot documents that accompany the design document. This very much depends on the type of game you are designing. A character-based game might include documents like these:

Design document offshoots

- Concept document
- Design document
- Character/cast list and descriptions
- Animation lists and/or motion capture lists
- Cut scene descriptions
- FMV descriptions
- Dialogue script
- Music and sound FX lists
- Story and structure

When all of these documents have been created, they will make your design very big, and because each document is specifically informative rather than design documents, they are generally created separately, but as part of the design document process. It makes life simpler if, for example, when the audio engineer asks what sounds you require, all you need to do is give him the audio document. Sounds aren't usually generated until well into production, and often placement sounds, like so many other things in game development, are used prior to final sounds being implemented. Therefore, the sound engineer may also require the design document and possibly a copy of the game. This will allow him to keep the sounds he creates in context with the game.

Keeping the documents separate also helps the developers find the information they need quickly, without wading through a mountain of paperwork.

Structure

The structure of your documents can be very important to the people that will read them. All of the development staff rarely read the whole document, but will read sections that are pertinent to what they are doing. The worst thing you could do is drop a document as thick as a telephone directory in front of every person on your team; they will never read it. It's too overwhelming and a complete waste of trees! This is an obvious case of information overload. It will end up beneath their monitors, in the bottom drawer of their pedestals or being used as a giant doorstop.

So how do you prevent that from happening and get them to read your design? The first thing you might consider is to break down your document into digestible sections. This will have more benefits than you think. The first thing you, as the author, will notice is that it's easier to manage and schedule the creation of your documents. Psychologically, creating smaller documents will seem less daunting to you than one hefty tome. You will know how long one to ten pages will take to write, but when you think of it as a whole, there is no way you can accurately determine a realistic timescale.

You will find that 'bite size scheduling' is common in different areas of game development due to the size and complexity of a game. The player will only see the final complete article, but the amount of elements that go into making that article are probably thousands, from the tiniest texture to every function of code written by the programmers.

The other benefits of 'bite size documents' will go to the people that read them. When they need to access and read a specific element of your design document, they can dip in and out with ease, without feeling overwhelmed and without having to search for the information they are looking for. If your document is on-line and viewed in a web browser, you could also include hyperlinks to related sections of the document. For example, the chapter on player mechanics will go into a lot of detail about how the player controls his hero etc. But you should not include a list of animations; this would make the document fat and indigestible. Your animation lists should be separate and part of your animation document. A simple link will give the reader the option to go there if he needs to. If it is a printed document, refer to the list or document in the text so the reader can easily find it.

Remember, if people only want to know your target audience or get an overview of the game, they can read the concept document; that's partly what it's there for. The structure of your design document might appear something like this.

WORKSHEET   **Design document structure**

Do remember to include page numbers in the header or footer, your name, and the name of the game.

Front page:

■ Title, version number, author, copyright and date. You could include imagery, but it's not essential because the team already know what your game looks like!

Contents:

■ Self-explanatory, but do ensure it's hyperlinked.

Objectives for the game:

■ This should describe what you want to achieve with the game, the overall vision and philosophy. Make a statement about what you want to achieve for the player.

General overview:

■ Perspective, i.e. third person/first person, or perhaps there are several viewpoints. Is it single player, multi-player or both, the player's role within the gaming world and an overview of the challenges the player will encounter.

Player character (or characters)/mechanics:

When I use the word character, I am of course referring to the entity the player could control, whether it's a car, plane, an army or a single avatar.

■ Initially describe the character(s) the player will become from start to finish.

■ What is the player's motivation for playing?

■ Describe the mechanics of character growth both in appearance and functionality.

■ Lives, hit points, health system.

■ Movement through all environment types such as land, water, air and any special movement features relevant to your game.

■ Administering actions and special items such as inventory objects the player will use for gameplay such as weapons, and all of the object's mechanics and resources.

GUI – Graphical User Interface:

■ All front-end menus including title screen, options, save / load, inventory system, map function, HUD layout, game over screen, pause screen, etc.

User interface:

■ Controlling the player characters, activating and controlling weapons and items.

Game structure:

■ Progression, mission / challenge structure, implicit and explicit rules, puzzle structure, reward system, difficulty settings, saving/loading, pace, rhythm, victory conditions, chance element, all types of feedback, scope.

Missions / challenges in detail:

■ Using the rules and structure previously defined, you will need to describe every mission and challenge, documenting how the player will achieve the victory and failure conditions.

Feature set and mechanics:

■ All items and attachments like weapons, for example, and more specifically in the case of Norbot, heli-blades, thrusters and let's not forget to document the feedback for those items.

Game environments:

■ Size, environment structure, features, interaction (for example, how will the player know what to interact with to open doors, switch on lights, activate lifts etc.), feedback, damage limitations, weather, time of day, day and night conditions, special environment cameras, special environment features such as gravity, a word about collision, special lighting required for gameplay purposes, boundaries.

Creatures and behaviour/AI:

■ Details of all characters that are not directly controlled by the player. Including class, structure, purpose in game, movement, special features, intelligence and behaviour, hit-points, inventory, dispatching and re-spawning.

Sound:

■ Musical scores, sound effects, sound design and mechanics used in the gameplay.

▶

Multi-player:

- If your game relies heavily on multiple players, you will need to repeat all of the above in the context of multi-player scenarios. You will also need to deal with communication and social interaction between players, gameplay balance and distribution of all items and objects between multiple players.

Peripheral documents:

- Include all the documents detailed previously if they are not included in the design document.

You may not require all of these elements in your design and you may require additional sections. This of course, is just a template. If you're designing a racing game for example, under player mechanics, your hero will most likely be a car or several cars. Also, under creature behaviour, it might say 'car opponent behaviour'. You have to tailor it to the style of game you are creating. Some of these elements may not even be relevant to your design.

At this stage you will almost certainly have concept work available to you, but you do not need to include it in your design document. Remember your document's audience, they will know the graphical style of your hero and environments: you don't need to tell them that. You can, however, include it wherever you need to show something for informative purposes, like a map for example, but don't swamp your document with images, it will be big enough as it is. To illustrate structures and interfaces, you should use diagrams if it will make understanding your system easier.

Design elements in detail

It's fine giving you a template for your document, but it's little use if you don't understand what is required to fill the pages. Therefore, I am going to pick out some elements of the template and provide examples in order for you to get an idea of the level of detail required for your design documents.

One of the hardest to determine is the non-player controlled characters in your game and how to document their behaviour etc. The first segment below is an example of how I documented my characters in Norbot and this is the Drone character mentioned in the concept document.

 ### Character values

You will notice here I have included the name of my drone and where in the game they will appear. I have also defined that this is the easy setting of the game. This may be relevant if you have varying difficulty levels in your game and you need to define different attributes for each level of difficulty.

For clarity, I am using metres and seconds to define my measurements, for distance and time.

NORBOT   Drone – Type Guard #1 (Model D-G01)

The Drones are guards and exist as various types in Norbot, which have varying capabilities. They generally patrol the environment searching for hostile intruders and have the capabilities to exterminate. Type #1 is the basic model and can be found in the early part of the game.

Mission 1, 2	Easy
Hit points	50
Motion detection range (metres)	5
Line of sight range (metres)	15
Audio detection range	–
Detection cone angle (degrees)	90
Action delay timer (seconds)	3
Patrolling movement speed (metres per second)	0.5
Detected player speed (metres per second)	1
Weapons max range (metres)	10
Weapons min range (metres)	1
Weapons accuracy at max range (%)	50
Weapons accuracy at minimum range (%)	80
Damage inflicted at max range	10
Damage inflicted at minimum range	20
Shield capabilities	Yes
Shield hit points	50
Resource drops	Yes
Weapon details	(include link)
Animation details	(include link)
Feedback details	(include link)

All of these attributes will need balancing once the game is working and are only preliminary. They will also be entered into a database that you will doubt have control over. Let's go through each one in a little more detail so you understand why I have included them in my chart.

- **Hit points:** These are fairly self-explanatory and determine how much damage the drone can take before it is taken out of service (dead). This will need balancing against the weapon I have. For example, I may have a homing missile that can do 100 hit points of damage on impact and therefore will be dead with one hit. On the other hand I may have a weapon that only does 10 hit points of damage at this stage in the game, and therefore, it will require five hits to take it out of action.

- **Motion detection range:** This is how close the player can get to the drone before it detects the player's motion. The detection will also be cone based and visually represented on the screen. This will allow for some stealthy challenges in the game.

- **Line of sight range (LOS):** The type #1 drones have better visibility than motion sensors and therefore can detect the player at 20 metres.

- **Audio detection range:** Some robots will have audio detection capabilities and hear you coming, but I decided that this level robot doesn't have that feature.

- **Detection cone angle:** From a singular point at the front of the drone at an angle of ninety degrees, a cone will be drawn to define the area of detectability. Figure 20.1 illustrates the line of sight detection for the drone. My figures in the above table determines that if the player steps into that cone, the drone will detect him and perform the necessary actions I will have defined in another section of the design.

FIGURE 20.1   Line of sight detection

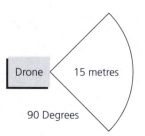

The singular point on my drone will most likely be the head, which will move from side to side as if scanning the area. The cone can also be seen on the map feature which will aid the player avoid detection. This scanning from side to side will add to the difficulty for the player, but can be adjusted by modifying the numbers in the table.

- **Action delay timer:** In some cases I may want to delay the drone from shooting at the player. This can be used for balancing the game to make things easier or more difficult simply by modifying a number. Robots in the later stages of the game will almost certainly have a zero setting here.

- **Patrolling movement speed:** This is how fast the drone moves around the environment when simply patrolling.

- **Detected movement speed:** This is how fast the drone will move if he detects the player. You will see that he can move twice as fast when in action mode. In the documents that define this character, I will explain that this drone will revert back to patrol speed if the player is out of sight or out of motion detection.

- **Weapons max range:** I have kept the weapons range below the detection range in order to give the player a 'chance'. The AI will determine that in order for the drone to shoot the player, he will have to move closer to him based on the range the weapon has.

- **Weapons min range:** This works in conjunction with weapons accuracy. According to my table, anything closer than one metre will get hit every time (max damage, 100% of the time).

- **Weapons accuracy (max and min):** This defines the probability of the player being hit by the projectile. The closer to the drone the player is, the higher the probability.

- **Damage inflicted (max and min):** This determines how much damage a direct hit does to the player. Again, more damage done the closer the player is to the drone.

You will notice that I would include links to other parts of the document that refer to this particular character and any separate documents that may be relevant also.

Every character, good and bad, and object that exist in your game will require this attention and for every difficulty level. If the player can interact with the entity, which he should be able to if it's in your game, then it will require this treatment in your game design document. The more detail you go into, the better the programmers will interpret it and portray it as you imagined.

Creature behaviour and rules

In my creature behaviour section, my drone section might read something like this.

NORBOT	Drone: Type #1

Unit Game name: Model D-G01

Description:

Type #1 is a drone guard and will be found in the recycling factory environments. It is an old robot and moves around on tracks unlike the modern limb-based robots

▶

such as Norbot. It is equipped with a basic Toontonium-powered laser, which rarely kills with just one hit, but can cause serious damage. The upper body sits on the track base and can rotate. It has two arms and can direct its weapon using the arms without turning its upper body. When patrolling, the head of the drone does a repetitive 180-degree scan as it moves along. It has LOS and motion sensors.

Movement:

The drone will follow a pre-defined path around the facility at a pre-determined speed.

Events:

- If the drone detects the player, the AI will trigger the drone to investigate and track the source. Its speed will increase (defined in the stats) and it will find the quickest route to the player until it is close enough to attack the player with its weapon.
- On entering investigate/track mode, the AI will trigger an internal alarm, that will trigger and pass player co-ordinates to other drones within 20 metres. This will trigger multiple events. The alarm will also be heard by the player for feedback purposes
- When the drone is firing, it will continue to move towards the player using the find-path until the player is out of sight or stationary (hiding).
- If the player moves while being tracked, the drone will do its utmost to keep the player in its LOS and/or motion detection cone, by moving accordingly (chase the player). This chase effect will be done by passing the player's co-ordinates to the drone, enabling it to move towards the player giving the impression of intelligence.
- If the player is out of the drone's LOS, but within motion range, the player could remain still to avoid being detected by the drone's motion sensors.
- If the drone takes damage, it will recoil, reduce in hit-points based on weapon used by the player, and activate its shield. The drone cannot fire while its shield is activated. After four seconds of shield activation and no fire, the drone will lower its shield. The shield can be destroyed based on the pre-defined shield hit points.
- The drone will become inactive (die by explosion) when all shield and drone hit points reach zero.
- The drone will drop resource items.

The events described above will most likely be driven by scripts, which is a simple language understood by the game, not the computer. We will go into this in a little more detail in a subsequent chapter.

Just by outlining what needs to be defined for one of my characters, you can project the amount of work involved for a whole game. Obviously the character AI will cover all characters but the character tables will make them individual.

Once you have done all of this, there is no way of knowing that your rules will work until they are brought to fruition. Once they are functioning, these tables will need modifying and balancing, which is the most difficult part of game design and where the real work begins.

Document storage

Although not relevant to the actual creation of the documents, it can be problematic for a team if your documents are named badly or fragmented and stored all over your hard drive. You must make a space for them that everybody can access, name them relevant to the content and, above all else, keep them up to date, including a change order document so the team know what has been changed and when.

Create a single directory called 'GAME-design-documents'. There is a tendency to name things in development that is purportedly comedic, but is often offensive. If your document is about mission structure, you'd be expected to call it that, not some obscene reference to male or female sexual organs! Yes, this does happen.

Be sure to make regular back-ups if the company you work for is not doing it automatically. There is nothing worse than losing documents through viruses or a corrupt system that requires a re-format of the machine!

Formatting

The formatting of your design documents should be the same as your concept document for consistency. Consistency is a common theme in game design, therefore it should be applied to your documents also. If you are breaking down your document into several smaller documents, be sure to keep them consistent also. Make sure the headings and sub-headings in your documents are clear and relate to the contents. If there are any dependencies, be sure to mention this at the beginning of the document and include links to them.

Embed tables, diagrams and charts into the relevant sections of the document; the reader will not want to search for them.

Live and kicking

Once you have completed the first draft of your document, you shouldn't consider it complete. This is a common mistake in the games industry and your work will have only just begun. Work usually stops on the documents because of scheduling issues, therefore updating and modifying the documents always becomes a lesser priority than anything else. Design documents should always remain live, and you need to update them constantly. If something changes in the game or something is cut out while in development, it may have a dramatic impact on other aspects of the game. Therefore updating will highlight any potential problems down the road.

You may also want to consider the fact that the lead designer could decide he didn't want to work on the project anymore and leave. This could potentially put the game and team in trouble, and somebody else would have to take up the design reins; without up-to-date documents this could be problematic.

Consider the design documents as a temporary storeroom for the components of your game, i.e. the first working version in which elements will come and go, change and evolve as time progresses.

Summary

As you can see, creating a whole design document here is almost an impossible task and would make the book twice as big. But not only that, game design is not just about creating documents. You need all the other elements that go into making a game whole. Game design is also about implementing and balancing your initial paper design, while bringing together all other components of the game such as art, music and sound effects, through the vital coding efforts of the programmers.

Some people question the creation of documentation and ask why we can't simply build the game in the computer iteratively. There are many reasons why we create documents, but one of the main reasons is this. The rules of most computer and video games are hidden inside the computer. The developers can see them clear as day, but the players can't. Therefore, the design documents allow the developers to build the game for the player, and the game will subsequently portray those rules to the player.

CHAPTER 21

Tools of the trade

There is a common belief that designing games is simply about coming up with great ideas and being able to do things better than the last person. Coming up with great game ideas relies on the designer having a good imagination, which is an innate aptitude in most people, but having this single ability is certainly not what designing games is all about. Transferring those ideas into an engrossing marketable interactive experience is really what it's about and it can be a tough brief.

Like most jobs, it can be an arduous task and the designer is required to use a multitude of tools to do his job and deliver his vision to many different audiences. The tools you use are the interface to your talent and should not be underestimated or compromised in any way.

Learn to use them

If you are already working in the games industry, perhaps you're a game tester or an artist aspiring to become a game designer. If so, you will have more access to designers than people outside the industry and therefore you should ask the designers directly what tools they use to build a design.

The first and most obvious tool you will need is a computer. Without a computer you have little or no chance of becoming a designer. Handwritten documents are simply not even considered in the advanced technological world of game development. It would also be advisable to own at least one console, but preferably you should be able to experience games on all consoles, although this can be an expensive pursuit.

The software tools a designer could use can vary from 3D applications and 2D visual aids to word processors, flow-chart and database software, but the first and most obvious tool a designer will use is a word processor.

Office tools

Creative writing will be one talent that you will use time and time again as a designer. You will need to be able to use a word processor and all its functions. You need to be able to type but not necessarily 60 words a minute! You also need to understand how to format and style your documents and insert images. You will also undoubtedly use tables at some point in your design. Don't simply rely on knowing a few functions of any tool, learn to use all of them; it will show when you create your documents.

Another office tool you will most likely use is database software such as Microsoft® Access. A database is one link between designer and programmer – generally used to input game data that can be modified by the designer and used by the programmers to feed the game's entities as shown in Chapter 20.

Excel can also be used to create spreadsheets or worksheets. I have used it to create and define my missions/environment structure. Not only does it let you type and create documents, but it also allows you to input figures and you can ask it to do calculations, which can be a great feature when you are balancing your data.

Front Page is basic web page design software, but it can also be a useful tool for structuring and trying out **graphical user interfaces (GUI)**, particularly front-end menu selection screens etc. It will help you experiment with the navigation of your menu system and you can see it working before committing to the asset creation.

3D applications

3D applications are all very similar in what they do, but they all have a different interface and are generally used by artists. The most common applications used in the games industry, in no particular order, are 3D Studio Max®, Maya® and Softimage® XSi. There are others, which you will no doubt discover as you further your career.

These applications are often designed for many industries like the movies and commercials, not just the games industry. This is often why they fall short for games designers, by not including game-specific tools that allow designers to place and edit game content. The developer will write plug-ins and additional tools to compensate, providing the user with the ability to manipulate and export their worlds.

Environment designers will also use them for prototyping purposes. If you have a powerful enough PC that can handle a 3D application then start learning. Some application companies offer a version of their software, often for students and learning purposes, that can be used for free, but anything you render is stamped and cannot be used for commercial gain. However, it is a great way to learn and if you have access to a PC that can cope with this, then it will put you in front of the next guy waiting for an interview who does not have that ability.

Custom world editors

When you begin work with a developer, you may discover they have their own custom world editor, such as UnrealEd®. Details of this particular world editor can be found on the Unreal website.

The developer will normally allow time for a new designer to learn how to use their software, but having some experience using a 3D application will give you an advantage and subsequently be less daunting.

Custom world editors allow the user to do many things. They generally allow the user to manipulate the game worlds, including building and shaping the world using polygons, texturing, placing lights, objects, actors, navigation information, cameras etc.

Why do development teams design and build world editors when there are off-the-shelf products available? There are several reasons, the primary one being that it gives the developers complete autonomy – they can design the tool to do what they want it to do, and it will build the game they want to build. Consequently you are not forced to use off-the-shelf software that doesn't quite meet your expectations. If you are planning a series of games then building your own editor is a good idea, but a secondary team will be needed to maintain and update it. The team will also need time to create the editor prior to building your game, which can be hard to swallow for many publishers and investors.

A consequential effect of having your own world editor is that the pipeline for building your world becomes very efficient. It allows the designers to build the worlds, test them and alter them quickly and re-test them, knowing it will work every time. Often the game engine will be built into the editor, allowing the designer to play the game from within the editor and immediately see the results of their work.

Creating your own editor also means it can become a valuable asset to the company, and can give the developer another source of income should he decide to license it to other developers, which is the case with the Unreal Developers Network.

Some games are published with their editors, allowing the players to build their own worlds specifically for that particular game, which is a great way to learn the art of environment design.

2D applications

There will be many 2D applications you will use, such as paint packages like Photoshop® and CorelDRAW® to create diagrams and illustrations for your documents. This could also extend to flowchart programs, but many designers simply use their word processors to draw simple shapes. In the real world of flowcharts, every shape has a meaning and the structure of flowcharts have a language all of their own, which, in my experience, has not really been used extensively in game design. However, a flowchart can be useful, particularly when designing a complex puzzle in your game. It can also be useful for plotting the entire game structure, environment structure, and you can use it to plot the behaviour of your creatures. Flowcharts can help you visualise the decision-making process of your game, but it is entirely up to the designer if he wishes to use one or not.

You may also be called upon to use a traditional pen, pencil and paper. If your design has some quirky ideas that are hard to grasp, then you may be called upon to sketch your ideas, but you will not be expected to be a skilled artist. I asked many designers what they use as tools as part of my research, and many of them said they used their art skills to communicate their ideas. This particularly happens in the ideas/concept and prototyping stages. Beyond that and it's defined digitally.

You will most likely draw your levels out on paper before they are built in the computer and for that, you will need basic art skills. You must also be prepared to make notes at the beginning of your journey, and I always carry a pen and notebook around with me to grasp those ideas when they appear.

Miscellaneous tools

I have seen designers use some very odd things to portray their vision. While working at Virgin, one designer used Lego to construct his environments so he could see it in three dimensions. This worked, to a degree, and was a great experiment, but it can take up a large amount of space and is not really very practical. It is much better to use a 3D application and create box maps to test your ideas before artists construct them.

Every game that has ever been developed in the past should be used as a tool. Use them for your research and study the good and bad points of all games. They are out there and you have access to them all.

The Internet is a great place for research and there are many sites where you can find information on games and game design. You can also use the Internet to retrieve information on developers and they often advertise job vacancies on their websites. I have included many interesting websites in the bibliography.

For the creative writers among you, a good dictionary and thesaurus will be an invaluable tool as you write your game design documents, scripts, dialogue and story overviews etc.

One of your greatest assets will be your innate ability to recognise gameplay and use it as a tool to create your designs. There are many designers that call themselves designers, but fail to understand the process and core of games, the components that really make them work. There are also various types of designer, which we will go into in more detail the next chapter, who are particularly good at a specific role within design, rather than visualising the whole game.

The people around you are your tools to some degree. They will provide you with feedback and because they share the same passion, they are more likely to be honest in their criticisms.

Game-making software

There are some tools that one can purchase that allow you to create games from scratch, with little or no knowledge of programming required. Although these can be fun and you can learn elements of game design using them, it is highly unlikely that a game made from one of these will get into retail. However, for some, the fun is not necessarily in playing them, it is in the making of these games, and that is an important part of any aspect of game development.

An interesting website that includes game-making tools is: **http://dmoz. org/Games/Game_Design/Development_Tools_and_Software/**

Summary

The underlying message of this chapter is to use whatever you have to, in order to convey your idea well and convincingly. There are no hard and fast rules, providing it works for your team and it serves its purpose well. Learn as much as you can from the people around you and don't be afraid to ask questions.

Learn to use your tools well, whether it is an office tool or a 3D application, and use them until you know their features and can use them with confidence. The time taken to do this is an investment in your future and your goals.

CHAPTER 22

Anatomy of a game designer

What does a game designer do? Is there more than one game designer on a project? If so, what do the others do? Let's begin by looking at the different roles a designer can perform within a team structure. Many companies have different names for different roles, so for clarity, I am going to include a short job description that defines the role in question:

- **Lead game designer**
  - Usually the visionary
  - Must be able to communicate and present
  - Creative and imaginative
  - Technically astute
  - Artistically astute
  - A good creative writer
  - Must have the passion
- **Environment designer**
  - A person responsible for designing environments
  - Designs and implements game content
  - Usually works to a brief and can use a 3D application
  - Reports to the lead designer
- **Script programmer/designer**
  - Creates scripts for game functions, although this does depend on the style of game
  - Reports to the lead designer
- **Game tester**
  - Usually under-valued
  - Tests gameplay and balance

I am going to go through each of those roles in a little more detail, starting with the lead designer, and his responsibilities and duties throughout the creative process.

Lead game designer

I have always maintained that making games is a team effort and design input from all members of the team is invaluable. Communication with the rest of the team is crucial to ensure that what you are creating is feasible and is being implemented into the design in the best, most efficient way. One team member may come up with just one idea, which could fundamentally enhance the game and subsequently, the experience for the player. However, there has to be a filter, a decision maker or visionary. The reason for this is simple. Because of the large number of people working on the game that have direct input to the content, they are generally all very creative in their own right, but may have different ideas about how the game should be. This can cause problems if there is no one person to make the design decisions and filter the feedback.

The lead designer will champion the game from start to end. The design team will be the people with the answers to any questions that may arise regarding the gameplay, but the lead designer will ultimately hold the vision. Producers are also close to the product, but not as close as the designers. Producers tend to realise the schedule and manage the assets rather than design the content.

A lead designer must be able to see the whole design and be able to sell it to the world if he is requested to do so. Everyone around him can only see a piece of the whole, they aren't exposed to the game rules like the lead designer and they may get interpreted differently depending on what is being viewed by the spectator. Therefore, a lot of trust is placed on the designer.

External games, such as real-life sports games and board games, illustrate this exposure perfectly. The spectator *and* the participant can enjoy an external game equally because they can see the whole of the game in front of them. With video games, it is enclosed and confined within the computer and what the spectator can see on the screen is all he can see of the game rules and condition. If you observe a spectator watching video games long enough, you will notice they soon get bored or confused and wander off. This is one of the reasons why a lot of trust is placed in the lead designer. He is the one who holds the entire vision of the game in his head, prior to it being inked and, subsequently, digitally realised.

When doing my research, I considered why spectators walk away and don't stand and learn more. There are several reasons for this and the obvious one is that people in general have very short attention spans, particularly when it comes to computer and video games. The spectator will often start watching a video game when the player has already started playing, therefore he doesn't know what is going on. He cannot see the whole game space and therefore it is out of context. In a football game for example, you can look at the score and pick up the game immediately.

Holding the vision

As I've already mentioned, the lead designer is the visionary or the creative thinker and holds the entire game design in his head until it spills onto the pages. He is only responsible for the design aspects of the game and not necessarily the visual content. He will spend the entire duration on one project at a time and will most likely initiate the idea in the first instance.

Communication

This is a crucial aspect of the lead designer role. Some teams can grow to around thirty people and the lead designer must harbour the ability to communicate the game and other aspects of development to anybody who requests information. Game development is a team effort and communication is certainly a prerequisite of a lead designer role.

Creative and imaginative

This is very important, and again, it is a prerequisite for a lead designer. You do need to have a good imagination to design games, but if your imagination is somewhat lacking right now, it can improve and grow over time, providing you exercise it. Lead designers often harbour the ability to invent new worlds, establish new cities, towns, villages and inhabitants, and all the objects that exist in that world. The games industry does not insist on original ideas time and time again, but it does require that you keep inventing new techniques and interactive experiences. Take an old game and reinvent it, give it a fresh lick of paint and try something new with it.

A good example of this is 'Black and White' by Lionhead Studios. It is a god-game like previous games by the same designer, but it's a new world imagined and realised by the designers. The game also has the added element of a pet, which brings new challenges to the game and a new dimension to the genre.

As a lead designer, you may be called upon to invent new languages for your world, new creatures and insects and it all has to remain in context.

Technically astute

Being technically astute can give a designer a huge advantage. Even though you may have technical bods all around you, you will benefit from understanding the technical limitations of your target platforms. There is little point designing something if it won't fit into the computer or it simply isn't capable of doing it. You could ask, which is advisable anyway, but it will save a lot of time if you did your research and understood your technical limitations. By knowing what your target platform can do, you will derive what is and isn't possible!

This can also be said about the technology that drives your game. The rendering engine, for example, will have its limitations. Knowing what these are, such as how many polygons it's capable of rendering, can be useful if your design requires there to be hundreds of characters parading across the screen.

It will also be beneficial for you, as lead designer, to understand a programming language and the way in which programs and games are constructed from a technical perspective. I have known programmers to design to their capabilities and not push the boundaries, which is not what you want when you're at the cutting edge. Understanding a language like 'C' for example, will allow you to know what the programmers are capable of and will give you a better understanding of the programming scope.

If reaching the predetermined completion date comes down to tight deadlines, you can assist in the scripting the game, which is almost always underestimated in schedules. When it comes to redesigning for another platform, this will give you a better understanding of how to alter your design and realign it for another market.

Artistically astute

Being artistic can help you put across your ideas more effectively. However, being an artist is not a prerequisite. In my experience, having an artist sitting next to you who can 'really' draw simply from scribbling for a few minutes, is truly amazing and is a must if you want to experiment with different visual ideas.

You often find that a designer will, in his career infancy, try to draw but fail miserably. Budding designers are usually very eager to get the images that are embedded in their heads out onto any medium they can lay their hands on, including paper. If you can't draw, don't worry, somebody around you should be able to, and will most likely do it very well.

If you have described your main character, but you can't draw, try and sit with an artist who has experience in the animation industry. The skills they have suit the initial stages of game design perfectly. An artist who can sketch and isn't afraid to brush aside a drawing that isn't working, is a true asset. If you have done a good job in describing your main character, you will probably find that an artist like that can see him better than you, and will draw him far beyond your expectations.

If you can't draw, you should educate yourself in what looks good and what doesn't. Learn about colour and learn the proportions of a human being. You'd be surprised how characters in games often look out of proportion. A designer should also learn how to illustrate his world into diagrams, in order to map out the game world in detail, prior to building the box map. These things are expected from a lead designer role.

A good writer

This is one of the biggest priorities of them all. You will be responsible for creating a mountain of documents and you will oversee the entire game design from idea to post-production. You will need to write letters, emails and reports. They have to be comprehensible and you must be able to get your message across using the written word.

I have read documents that not only didn't make any sense to me but were also riddled with spelling mistakes and bad grammar. Something like this simply reeks of an unprofessional outfit. If you did badly at language in school, go back to college and learn it again. There are several books on the subject and a mountain of websites that can teach you also.

Your documents will be a mix of informative writing, creative writing, technical and factual writing. You will probably spend 50 per cent of your time writing. Being good with your mother-tongue is the most important prerequisite of them all.

Must have the passion

If you have no passion for making games, then you should find another career. Designing games can be an arduous task and to sustain the rigorous journey through the creative process, you will need to love your job, love games and love everything about the process. This includes the long hours, the criticisms and the pressure of creating something amazing. The role of lead designer should not be taken lightly. When you have a hit, everyone wants to be responsible for it, but when you create a stinker, it will be your fault.

Assistant designer

Often, the lead designer will have an assistant whom he can bounce ideas off and vice versa. This person is one step away from being a lead designer in his own right and will have, or almost have, similar attributes and skills as the lead designer. To assist a lead designer, particularly one that is renowned for creating great games, is a job that any designer would give his right arm for. If you get to this esteemed position, you should regard the lead designer as a teacher or mentor, and learn as much as you can from him. Avoid becoming arrogant and do not make it your mission to prove the lead designer wrong; he is where is because he has worked hard and can make games – obtain his knowledge.

Environment designer

Environment design is, of course, only one aspect of game design as we stated in Chapter 9, but it can be very time-consuming, and perseverance is required to create that perfect digital space. The reason why it is segmented as a specific design role is because it requires a particular skill (modelling) and the time required to do this will give two or three individuals full-time work for ten months to a year on a project the size of a racing game or an action adventure, for example.

An environment designer is a person who can design and model gaming environments from a game design perspective, i.e. not from an art perspective. This person should be able to visualise a scene and recreate the space inside a computer. He should have spatial awareness and be able to work from a design brief and a set of rules that govern the environment. The design brief could be as little as a simple description, or it can be a fully realised two-dimensional drawing that needs transforming into that extra dimension using a 3D application. Having an architectural background combined with the knowledge of game design and how games work is a rare combination of skills, and is not necessarily something employers look for, but it would be advantageous if you were thinking of moving into this area of game design.

Environment design is a very important job and is an art form in its own right. One of the things a designer must understand is world space, i.e. what makes a scene feel claustrophobic and how to shape and mould big open spaces. If you're designing an adventure game, the rhythm of open space/close space can be crucial to the general feel of the game. The designer should be able to shape the scene to complement and work with the game design in preparation for the artists. Of course, the job of the artists is to make the environments look great, but your job will be to make it feel great for the player and subliminally guide him through the game.

Environments can vary enormously depending on the style of game you are designing. It could be as small as a singular room or arena, to a vast open landscape full of creatures and buildings. However, much the same process can be used for any game in order to test and feel the space of the environment, and feel it in the context of the design prior to an artist applying his layer. You do not need finished art to create gameplay, as we've already established.

Script programmer

The title of this role can be a little misleading. It implies that you need to be a programmer, but strictly speaking, you don't. I have scripted games in the past and although I began as a programmer I don't consider myself to be one, and I certainly couldn't write code for today's platforms. You do need to learn the scripting language, however, and you obviously need good game design skills to do this job.

To the non-game developer literate, a script programmer could be perceived as a regular programmer. Although the job is essentially a type of programming, the scriptwriter will use a simple language, or tool, that the game understands, rather than the computer. In other words, within a game there usually exists a scripting engine that interprets scripts to perform game functions. The script engine is the link between computer and scripts, as illustrated in Figure 22.1.

FIGURE 22.1   Script engine

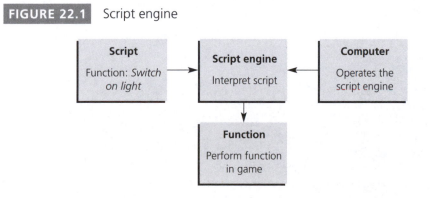

The programmers will write the script engine and the designer will write the scripts without any knowledge of the script engine code. However, the designer will need to learn the functions the script engine understands. Being able to create game content without knowledge of the core engine and without having to recompile the game engine can allow the designers to create content in isolation without using the time of the core programmers. For more information and an insight into game scripting, follow this link to UnrealScript: **http://unreal.epicgames.com/UnrealScript.htm**

EXAMPLE   **Script structure**

This example illustrates a typical, simple UnrealScript class, and it highlights the syntax and features of UnrealScript. Note that this code may differ from that which appears in the current Unreal source, as this documentation is not synced with the code.

```
//=====================================================
// TriggerLight.
// A lightsource which can be triggered on or off.
//=====================================================
class TriggerLight expands Light;
//-------------------------------------------------------------
// Variables.

var() float ChangeTime; // Time light takes to change from on to off.
var() bool bInitiallyOn; // Whether it's initially on.
var() bool bDelayFullOn; // Delay then go full-on.

var ELightType InitialType; // Initial type of light.
var float InitialBrightness; // Initial brightness.
var float Alpha, Direction;
var actor Trigger;

//-------------------------------------------------------------
// Engine functions.

// Called at start of gameplay.
function BeginPlay()
{
        // Remember initial light type and set new one.
        Disable( 'Tick' );
        InitialType = LightType;
        InitialBrightness = LightBrightness;
        if( bInitiallyOn )
        {
                Alpha = 1.0;
```

```
                Direction = 1.0;
        }
        else
        {
                LightType = LT_None;
                Alpha = 0.0;
                Direction = -1.0;
        }
}
// Called whenever time passes.
function Tick( float DeltaTime )
{
        LightType = InitialType;
        Alpha += Direction * DeltaTime / ChangeTime;
        if( Alpha > 1.0 )
        {
                Alpha = 1.0;
                Disable( 'Tick' );
                if( Trigger != None )
                        Trigger.ResetTrigger();
        }
        else if( Alpha < 0.0 )
        {
                Alpha = 0.0;
                Disable( 'Tick' );
                LightType = LT_None;
                if( Trigger != None )
                        Trigger.ResetTrigger();
        }
        if( !bDelayFullOn )
                LightBrightness = Alpha * InitialBrightness;
        else if( (Direction>0 && Alpha!=1) || Alpha==0 )
                LightBrightness = 0;
        else
                LightBrightness = InitialBrightness;
}
//---------------------------------------------------------------------------

// Public states.
// Trigger turns the light on.
state() TriggerTurnsOn
{
        function Trigger( actor Other, pawn EventInstigator )
        {
                Trigger = None;
                Direction = 1.0;
```

▶

```
                Enable( 'Tick' );
        }
}

// Trigger turns the light off.
state() TriggerTurnsOff
{
        function Trigger( actor Other, pawn EventInstigator )
        {
                Trigger = None;
                Direction = -1.0;
                Enable( 'Tick' );
        }
}

// Trigger toggles the light.
state() TriggerToggle
{
        function Trigger( actor Other, pawn EventInstigator )
        {
                log("Toggle");
                Trigger = Other;
                Direction *= -1;
                Enable( 'Tick' );
        }
}

// Trigger controls the light.
state() TriggerControl
{
        function Trigger( actor Other, pawn EventInstigator )
        {
                Trigger = Other;
                if( bInitiallyOn ) Direction = -1.0;
                else Direction = 1.0;
                Enable( 'Tick' );
        }
        function UnTrigger( actor Other, pawn EventInstigator )
        {
                Trigger = Other;
                if( bInitiallyOn ) Direction = 1.0;
                else Direction = -1.0;
                Enable( 'Tick' );
        }
}
```

Here is a section and an example script from the web page above, courtesy of epic games, **http://www.epicgames.com**

The key elements to look at in this script are:

- The class declaration. Each class "expands" (derives from) one parent class, and each class belongs to a "package", a collection of objects that are distributed together. All functions and variables belong to a class, and are only accessible through an actor that belongs to that class. There are no system-wide global functions or variables.

- The variable declarations. UnrealScript supports a very diverse set of variable types including most base C/Java types, object references, structures, and arrays. In addition, variables can be made into editable properties, which designers can access in UnrealEd without any programming.

- The functions. Functions can take a list of parameters, and they optionally return a value. Functions can have local variables. Some functions are called by the Unreal engine itself (such as BeginPlay), and some functions are called from other script code elsewhere (such as Trigger).

- The code. All of the standard C and Java keywords are supported, like "for", "while", "break", "switch", "if", and so on. Braces and semicolons are used in UnrealScript as in C, C++, and Java.

- Actor and object references. Here you see several cases where a function is called within another object, using an object reference.

- The "state" keyword. This script defines several "states", which are groupings of functions, variables, and code, which are executed only when the actor is in that state.

- Note that all keywords, variable names, functions, and object names in UnrealScript are case-insensitive. To UnrealScript, "Demon", "demON", and "demon" are the same thing.

At first glance, it may look complicated if you don't know what you are looking at, but you needn't worry, you can teach yourself one of many programming languages such as C, C++ and Java, which will stand you in good stead should you wish to become a scriptwriter.

Game tester

You might be thinking this is a very strange title for a designer, but game testing is one way into the games industry for many. The position is looked upon to be the most junior position in the industry, but in my experience, game testing is invaluable and we don't do it enough.

There are two types of game testers – one that plays the game to track bugs, and another that plays the game for balancing. Game testing for bugs is traditionally done at the end of development to track and eliminate bugs and erroneous quality issues. From a design perspective, testing should begin at the outset as soon as the game can be played. The tester should begin to play elements of the game, test them, try them out and see if he can break them. We have accepted the fact there will be bugs and we manage that aspect of development very well, but we should also accept the fact that not all of the design will work as anticipated, and manage that too. Some developers focus test, which is a great way of testing your product for the market place, as it exposes it to the target audience and to individuals who are not as close to it as the developers.

Some developers have gameplay testers who play the game as it is being built. This type of tester is looking for something different in a game, not bugs or erroneous quality issues. He is scrutinising the gameplay, the intuitive interface, searching for gaps in the rhythm and flow of the game, the puzzles that are too difficult and challenges that are not fair for the player. These types of testers are valuable to game development and I would consider them to be a type of designer. The reason for this is because they have an innate ability to detect gameplay that doesn't work. This you might think most people can do, and you would be right. But there is something different about these people – they can tell you *why* it is not working, which is a talent that is rare indeed. Artists have this ability also. Most people can see when something doesn't look right, but a good artist will tell you why it doesn't look right and know how to fix it.

Summary

Often a game designer will begin as a tester and work his way up to become a lead designer. You must learn the art form before you can use it and playing games well does not make you a game designer. Just like any career, it will take many years of experience and learning to achieve. The worst kind of designer is a pushy one who wants to walk before he can run and thinks his way is the only way. Creating games isn't like that and you must learn to work with other people on a single project for long periods of time.

Some designers can lurk in the shadows of programmers and rarely gain acknowledgement for their work. The exceptions are the programmer/designers who have migrated from programming to design, having had great success as programmers. Game designers can be compared to scriptwriters. Of course scriptwriters win awards and their name appears in the credits, as do game designers, but the movie director is usually the one that reaps the attention and praise. You must be ready to accept this fate.

CHAPTER 23

The final stretch

This is just a brief chapter, but something I felt was necessary to perhaps give you some guidance during the final stretch of the development of your game, and some direction beyond your first published game. Of course if you are working for a company, it will have its own plans on what is next for you, but you should keep check of your own personal goals and career and ensure you are continually growing as a game designer.

The final stages of your game can be a frantic place to be, particularly if something goes wrong. Your game will seem to be finished, but bugs will plague the producers, causing sleepless nights and sweaty nightmares! The moment your game goes beta, to the time it hits master is a hotbed of stress and frantic activity. If you can't program, there is little you can do but test any bug fixes that programmers claimed to have fixed.

No doubt the test department will have their blistering mitts on it. At this stage they will be testing for bugs and quality issues rather than gameplay issues. There is no time left to change anything now, it's too late for you. If you change one thing, the game will need re-testing from scratch to determine if the change affected other aspects of the game. The duplicators will be lined up, distributors will be waiting and retail will have a schedule to meet and an audience to please. It really is too late to change fundamental design elements now – so don't suggest it, even if you spot something that would make a huge impact – it's too late.

When the game lands on your desk in a shiny new case for the first time, and you can touch it, this is the moment you have been working towards. You feel like you've really achieved something amazing, which of course you have, because making games is not easy, as you will no doubt soon discover.

Marketing will be all over you like an infectious rash, so be ready for them. They may have already asked for screenshots for pre-release articles and press material, but now they will want even more. If you and your producer have planned your schedule carefully, you should have all the material they need at hand. For example, a complete walkthrough should be written by now. Screenshots will be in abundance and design documents will be final, complete and reflecting the finished game.

It's being duplicated – can I sleep now?

If there was one moment you thought it was going to end, it would be at the point where the game is being duplicated. However, the world wants to know about your game and you have to get out there and sell it to them. The industry press will want an interview with the designer and there are strategy guides to proofread. Oh, and let's not forget the other formats, they still need completing!

That's right – the other formats. Perhaps you have done cross-platform development? If that is the case, each platform will need completing and most likely will pop out at different times, not simultaneously. I have never worked on a game where all platforms are complete at the same time, particularly in today's market. There is simply too much paperwork and organising to do for each format. One of them would inevitably suffer if you were to try. Hopefully, the planner of your project will not have them all coming in at the same time on his schedule. If he does, give him a nudge and remind him that it isn't going to happen like that.

If your game is a PC game, and console versions have been planned, then it will undoubtedly need console realignment. You will have to modify the design to fit the target platform, and this could mean a new design document, a new interface and possibly actual design changes to the game itself. Consequently, this will have a rollover effect on the schedule for all departments including you as the designer, the test department, programmers and possibly some artists. The marketing will try and capitalise on simultaneous marketing for all platforms to manage the costs.

It's in the shops

Here comes the geeky bit. I have actually been in a game store when somebody picked up and bought a game that I had worked on. I wasn't there intentionally loitering, but it gave me such a buzz! The hard work suddenly becomes a distant blur and it is worth every agonising 24-hour shift, if only for this moment.

Savour this moment, because not all games get this far and it will be literally years before you get here again. However, if your game is a licence or has been extremely successful, the publishers may request a sequel. If this happens, be prepared for a short break and another onslaught of production. A sequel generally doesn't require as much work as the first, therefore less time is allocated and the rush of meeting deadlines is upon you once again. Hopefully, if you do go forward and create a sequel, you will take some time and deliver something new. Delivering a rehash of the first game is not good enough and you will lose your audience.

Re-evaluate the process

Your game is in the shops, you've recuperated, and you're ready for the next onslaught of digital mayhem. But before you do that, you need to take stock.

You should make time to look at the creative process of the game you have just created and you need to ask yourself several questions.

- Does your final game reflect your initial design goals? If so great, if not why not?
- Is the game fun to play?
- Is the game of a high standard compared to competing products?
- How successful is it?
- Was the creative process relatively smooth or were there some areas for improvement?
- What is next?

The first point is very important as it gauges your ability to realise the creative process. If your game falls short of your initial design, this is not a bad thing, providing it has no detrimental effect on the final product. If on the other hand, the game suffered for not including certain elements of the design, then you need to understand why those elements didn't make it into the game and highlight the effect it had.

Perhaps the decision not to include certain elements of the design was taken away from you, in which case, simply document that. It might have been that time had simply run out and there was no time left in the schedule, or a senior member of the team or upper management thought the game would do just as well without it. Whatever the reason, you must understand why the decision was made, make a note of it and move on. You must harvest experience from every game you design and then move onto the next. There is little time in this industry to become bitter and resentful. Remember, technology is relentless and games will be made with or without you.

Let's imagine for one moment that every element of your design did make it into the game, but it still fell short of a quality product. You must analyse why this happened. Perhaps the schedule was ludicrously short, which happens more often than I would like to mention. Maybe the content just isn't fun or maybe it was never tested and balanced adequately. Did you follow the process or did you skip a stage or two in eagerness? If it's because it's not fun, then how did it get past the play testing (not to be confused with game testing at the end of production)? Surely they would have spotted it at that early stage. If the design changed beyond recognition from start to end, why did it change? If it was fine at the start, what happened? Look into all of these things and learn from them; you will be surprised how much you can learn by looking back at the good and bad. You can even go so far as to make a bullet point list of do's and don'ts for your next game design journey.

Read what the critics have to say by all means, but don't take them person-ally. Some of them can be ruthless and often subjective. One man's meat is another man's poison. Extract the constructive comments and make a note for next time. One of the hardest things to do is admit you made a poor product, and most people will try and distance themselves from it. If you go from one product to the next, making the same mistake time and again, you will not last long as a game designer. Unfortunately, like most creative industries, you are only as good as your last game in this industry, so you must keep learning and evolving, or you will become stale.

One obvious way of determining your game's success is through sales, but not always. Even the best of games can sell few copies and badly designed games can do well. We all remember 'Rise of the Robots', one of the most hyped games in history, but it was no fun at all.

Licensed games can be a hit-and-miss affair, which is mostly down to the developer and publisher relying on the licence and not the content to sell the game. Whether the developers do this consciously or not, it does happen and can have a diverse effect on the industry as a whole, particularly if it does well. It simply sends a message to everyone else that they too can knock out a pile of digital mush and rely on the name to sell the units. Fortunately, punters are becoming savvy to this and will look at reviews and listen to their friends or even play before they buy, to get an opinion on the quality of a game.

When you are analysing your game and process, don't simply focus on the negative aspects; look at the positives too. If you did something that really made a difference, carry it forward with you to the next game and use it again.

Once you have analysed your process against the final product, write an evaluation document that highlights the positive and negative points of your experience. You can turn all the negatives into positives, in that you know not to do them again, and eventually, you will become a great game designer.

Summary

You've done it. You made your first game and you should feel proud. The end process of game development is the hardest time for most, and if you can get through it by helping rather than hindering, you will become an asset to the company you work for.

Designing games is an art form and a creative process is required, but you must always remember it is a business, and even though you may disagree with some of the decisions being made regarding your game, they are most likely made for financial reasons that are beyond your control. Providing they aren't design decisions, then you have to learn to accept them. If they are chopping chunks out of your game to bring it in on time, work with them to modify the game so it causes minimal damage and reaches its maximum potential, rather than push against the decision. I'm not saying you should fold on all decisions, you certainly should not, but if it is fundamental to the completion of the game, then listen and work with it. There will be many design decisions you can discuss diplomatically along the way without getting the team agitated.

If you have evaluated successfully with each design you do, you will no doubt begin to build a tome of techniques that will become invaluable to you as a game designer.

CHAPTER 24

How do I get in?

So, you've read the book and you're confident that you can become a top game designer. Good, because you can! Anybody can, you just need to learn how to do it, adopt the right frame of mind and attitude, get the experience and you're on your way. Reading this book is a positive step in the right direction but, as I said at the beginning, every game experience is different and comes with its own design challenges.

This chapter will discuss ways in which you can enter the industry. Currently there are few avenues, but things are changing as the industry matures. The Internet has made things a little easier to access most game development studios and publishers and the academic institutes are beginning to adopt the games industry as a serious career opportunity for students.

In the past

There was a time when you could sit at home, create your own game and send it to a publisher for publication. You had to be the designer, the artist and the programmer, but it was possible in the days of the Commodore 64 and Spectrum.

Of course, games were much smaller then, and it was possible to create them using the target machine, a simple compiler like Zeus, and a disk drive to store your code. Dpaint was the standard art package and that was all you needed; game design was rudimentary, but this allowed for some very interesting ideas and creative freedom. It cost little to make games in those days and most developers were doing it while keeping their day-job, unless of course they were extremely successful at making games.

My first game 'Starforce Fighter', a budget game for Mastertronic, on the Commodore 64 made me two thousand pounds. A quarter of that went to the sound designer and that was the first game I made any money from. To achieve that, I had to learn how to program even though I didn't do particularly well at maths in school. But I had a goal in mind – I wanted to be a game designer more than anything else: I studied maths again and self-taught myself 6502 assembly language, and the inner workings of the CBM 64. I also learnt by studying how the current successful coders of the time did it. I even went to the extent of writing to respected programmers like Andrew Braybrook of Uridium and Paradroid fame, and to my utter amazement, he replied and gave me some great advice and tips.

I created my own art for my games, but I was a naturally talented artist. I had taken art at school and college and was a reasonably good artist before I began to make games. The design aspect was a hit-and-miss affair for me at that time. It was as much experimental as anything else in the games industry, but it was a time when some fundamental design seeds were being sown.

Needless to say, those days have long since gone and you can't make games like that today. Technology has advanced so much in the last two decades that it requires large teams and huge corporations to fund, develop and publish computer and video games. It has grown from its humble beginnings into a thriving, global, multi-billion-dollar industry in a relatively short space of time.

PCs are now your only real avenue into coding and that can be a minefield at the best of times. The CBM64 and other 8-bit systems were small enough and manageable enough to enable one person to write a whole game; you knew what bits and bytes did what and they were relatively easy to program compared to today's beasts.

Education considerations

Can the subjects I study at school or college help with my career as a game designer? Actually yes they can, more so than you think. Like any other job in the world, gaining knowledge will greatly improve your chances of becoming a successful designer. Think about the games that are out there and their settings, for example. There are games based on the Second World War, there are games with a mediaeval theme context, games set in ancient Egypt and others that are set in space. Some games might ask you to run an economy, while others might ask you to manage a theme park. To create these worlds you need to have the knowledge on the theme and setting of the game in question, otherwise it becomes incomprehensible to the player – particularly if the player already knows a great deal about the game's subject, which is highly likely because that might be one of the reasons why he bought it in the first place.

The diversity in the type of setting your game can have is unlimited and any history, geography and economics lessons you might consider will no doubt go some way to enriching your design potential. Of course, the themes and settings of any game require substantial research. Therefore, learning as much as you can at school will give you a head start when it comes to creating your masterpiece.

Designers need to possess a broad skill set: English is a prerequisite for any designer and without a good knowledge of the English language you may not get far. There are of course some people who can communicate and use language that would convince an elephant it could fly, but lack the ability and creativity to produce the content for gameplay, so you need that balance.

Also a designer will use maths in his design, albeit basic maths – to calculate and manage a real-time strategy game, for example. You don't have to be a mathematician or even go to the extent of becoming a programmer, but maths in one form or another will be used when you design your game in any genre.

My advice to you is to study hard at school because, as in most jobs in this world, you will use what you learn. I can hear you all crying out 'but it's only games, they are supposed to be fun', and you are right, they are fun, but to make them fun requires a broad base of knowledge and a huge dollop of hard work. The games industry is demanding and not for the faint-hearted.

There is one component of game design that is not part of the national curriculum at any school level, as far as I know, and that is gameplay. You can be taught media studies and technical drawing, art, science, maths and English, which can help when designing games, so why not gameplay? Perhaps it's because the element that we call gameplay is not tangible; or is it the attitude that game development is not a 'real' job?

At college level, it is a different story – there you can learn the skills required for the games industry. Some colleges have recognised a gap and offer courses for school leavers and mature students that will teach them the skills required to enter the industry, as artists, programmers, designers and producers, at junior level.

Below is a list of courses you might consider, covering a broad range of skills that are used in the games industry from programming to art and design. I have also tried to include institutes all over the UK.

Note: All of the following links below were functional at time of writing, but they are regularly updated, and although the links may go out of date, you should check with the relevant college or university to see if the course still exists.

West Cheshire College
http://west-cheshire.ac.uk
- BTEC National Diploma in Interactive Games Technologies

St Helens College
http://www.sthelens.ac.uk/education/details.asp?p_id=3A2011
- Foundation Degree in computer game production

Salford University, Manchester
http://www.salford.ac.uk/course-finder/details.php?course=368
- BSc (Hons) Computer and Video Games

This course is supported by the European Leisure Software Publishers' Association (ELSPA), and a range of companies across the industry. Follow the link for more information.

Scotland has a rich talent base for game development and can boast a strong heritage in computer game development:

The University of Abertay in Dundee
http://www.abertay-dundee.ac.uk
- Computer Games Technology BSc (Hons)
- BSc (Hons) Computing (Games Development)

Bournemouth University – National Centre for Computer Animation (NCCA)
http://ncca.bournemouth.ac.uk/
An internationally acclaimed computer animation course has been run at Bournemouth since 1989
- Computer Animation – MA/MSc/PGDip
- Computer Animation (Effects) – MA/PGDip
- Computer Animation – MPhil/PhD

Bolton Institute
http://www.bolton.ac.uk
- HND Computer Games Software Development
- BSc (Hons) Computer Games Software Development
- BSc (Hons) Leisure Computing Technology
- Visual C++ Windows Programming – Level 1
- MA Creative Writing

Bolton Institute also offers various short courses in web design and 3D computer modelling on different levels that can assist in your career direction in computer and video games.

University of Bradford
http://www.eimc.brad.ac.uk/
- Interactive Systems and Video Games Design – BSc (Hons)
- Computer Animation and Special Effects – BSc (Hons)

Essex University
http://www.essex.ac.uk/ese/
- Computer Games and Internet Technology – BEng/CGIT (3-year)

University of Hull
http://www.mscgames.com
http://www.graphicsmsc.com
- MSc in Games Programming
- MSc in Computer Graphics and Virtual Environments

Leeds Metropolitan University
http://www.lmu.ac.uk/ies
- BSc (Hons) Computer Entertainment Technology (F/T, P/T)
- BSc & BTEC/HND Computer and Digital Product Technology (F/T, P/T)

University of Lincoln

http://www.ulh.ac.uk

- BSc (Hons) Games Computing (Software Development)
- BA (Hons) Game Design (Hull – 3 years)

Liverpool John Moores University – International Centre for Digital Content

http://www.icdc.org.uk/magames/

- MA – Digital Content

Liverpool John Moores University – School of Computing

http://www.cms.livjm.ac.uk

- MSc (PgDip, PgCert) in Computer Games Technology

London College of Music and Media

http://www.tvu.ac.uk

The Thames Valley University has a vast array of courses that are pertinent to the games industry, too numerous to list here.

University of Middlesex

http://www.cs.mdx.ac.uk

- Computer Science (Graphics and Games) – BSc (Hons)

University of Teeside

http://www.tees.ac.uk

- BSc (Hons) Computer Games Programming
- BA (Hons) Computer Games Design
- BA (Hons) Computer Animation
- HND Computer Animation
- HND Computing (Software Development)

University of Wolverhampton

http://www.wlv.ac.uk

- Computer Science (Multimedia Technology) – BSc
- Computer Science (Games Development) – BSc

There are more than likely to be many more than this and if you don't see your local university or college listed here, call them and ask them if they host any of the courses mentioned above. This list will be updated for subsequent books and for my website, so if any institutes wish to be added to the list, please contact me.

Career paths

First you must decide what you want to do and what area you would like to focus on. This being a book on game design, it would seem logical to concentrate on just that area, but I am going to discuss various roles and opportunities with the industry.

I will begin by saying that the industry is very competitive and the people currently within the industry can also struggle to find a position, so don't be knocked back by rejection, if you have something to offer, somebody somewhere will spot it and give you a chance, so keep at it if its what you really want.

Retail

If you are starting out, you could begin at retail. I know you have to stand in a store and sell products to the marauding crowds, but it could be worth your while. This is where the games end up after all, and you will garner information directly from the audience themselves. You could observe who are buying what games, and you will undoubtedly hear many of the complaints people have when they bring their games back. This alone can be valuable information, particularly if you create a log of such complaints.

No, I want to be a designer

If you want to be a designer, it is almost impossible to simply walk into a designer role from never working in the industry at all. This never happens, or at least it has never happened in my experience. The designer role is probably the most sought after role in the industry and is probably the most misunderstood. In order for you to truly understand what a designer role is; you need to do your research. That may include getting a job that is not necessarily your dream job, but merely a means to an end. You might also want to ask yourself, what type of designer am I?

Something else you need to be aware of. If you think that sending in a game design that you have sweated blood over, and that you believe will be a number one hit will get you a job, think again. No matter how good it is or how good you think it is, it will only join the same pile as another design that has the same aspirations. Games aren't made like this. They're not books and they're not created by just one person. Publishers and developers will never make a game from a design that has been sent in from a member of the public, for many reasons. For one, it has massive legal implications, but more importantly, they already have qualified designers that have a stack of designs they want to make. In fact, everybody in the games industry has a game design inside them, so the chances of yours even being read, let alone developed, are pretty much zero.

Besides that, publishers are only interested in products that they can 'see' will make them money, a game that is a valuable commodity to them. The bulk of these are mostly licensed products or sequels, but there are a few original titles making their way onto the store shelves. These however, have been proven during rigorous pre-production and prototyping stages and are generally designed by a reputable designer.

My advice to somebody who wants to be a designer would be to use what you know, i.e. how to play games, and enter through an alternative route.

Well, actually, I want to be an artist

An artist, eh? What sort of artist would you like to be? What are your strengths and weaknesses? There are many types of artist in the industry and if you're lucky, you may be multi-talented. Art director, lead artist, 3D environment artists, 2D concept artists, 2D character designers, 3D character modellers, 3D computer character animators, cut-scene artists and special effects artists are some of the specialist art fields in the game industry.

It is a little easier for an artist with real talent to get a job than it is for a designer. Providing you can show and prove your talent to the prospective employer, you should get some interest if they are specifically looking to recruit. I used to receive mountains of CVs, discs and videos when I was Creative Director at Virgin Interactive. But I had very little time to spend opening envelopes and wading through the piles of paper and CVs. The best way to prove your worth is to design a well-presented self-booting, interactive CD with your best work enclosed. Send a well-presented cover note with the CD, and make sure they are aware that it is self-booting.

Make sure that when the disk boots, they see something that will encourage them to look closer – your best work should be sitting on their screen staring back at them. Make an impression immediately. Don't be clever and think that a neat quirky interface will make you stand out; it will simply irritate them if they don't have much time. I once received a CV wrapped in a bar of chocolate that had been specially printed and wrapped like a real bar of chocolate. It must have cost a fortune. Needless to say, the only difference it made was to my waistline, nothing more than that.

Note: Please check all data you send for viruses. The companies you send discs to will undoubtedly be protected, but it can cause major headaches if you provide a disk with a virus attached.

Design a menu system using something simple like 'MS Frontpage' for example, but keep it neat. Access to your CV and the rest of your work should be unambiguous and easily accessible. Don't make it hard work for them, because if you do, they will switch off and move onto the next, if indeed they are specifically looking at all. Only send your best work, you don't need to send the whole two years' worth of course work and every piece of art you have ever created, you're only as strong as your weakest link and a lot of what you do will be sub-standard. Does that come as a shock to you? No one can create perfect work one hundred per cent of the time, it's just not possible! It's a human thing!

Did I say artist? I meant programmer

Good programmers are more likely to get through the net than anyone else. Great programmers are few and far between and even if you have no experience, but can prove you have the potential, you will get some interest.

There are as many specialist programming roles as there are artist roles, maybe more, including lead programmer, junior programmer, tools programming, AI programming, core graphics programming, games programming, audio programming etc. The same advice can be given to programmers: demonstrate your ability in an economic and professional way. When you send in your CV and your examples, be creative with your skills, but do not hinder the viewer. If you show your true potential and you have something to offer, they will be interested.

Or is it production I want?

This is probably one of the stickier ends of game development. A producer is responsible for delivering the game to the duplicators on time, bug free and within budget. If he fails this arduous task, it will most likely cost him his job! There are various levels of producing and I would advise you to learn every aspect of game development very carefully and thoroughly before you step into a role where you are responsible for two or three million dollars-plus worth of project. Unless you are an extremely confident person/project manager, it can be a stressful place to exist in game development.

You have heard the expression, you can't please all the people all of the time – well, in this role, this is virtually what you have to do. Manage the project, manage the development staff and keep them motivated and focused, appease the management and feed marketing. It is a huge juggling act that is certainly not for the weak-hearted. If you are less creative, but still love games and like a serious challenge, then this is probably the job for you.

Again, like a designer, this is probably one of the more difficult routes into games development. Going through QA can be a good route, and you will get to see first hand the stressful life of a producer. To get a taste of what's to come after a stint in QA, you could assist a producer to get first-hand experience of a producer role.

If you become a good producer, then it can be an extremely rewarding role and just as satisfying as creating the assets themselves.

General advice

Target your audience. How many times have you read that line in this book? Well, the same is true when you are looking for a job in the games industry. If you particularly like a specific genre, find out who makes them and target them. You are more likely to sound convincing to them if you get an interview, than if you know nothing about their products at all. You will ooze passion and they will notice. Some people are not fussy about the type of game they work on, which is fine, but be sure to do some research on the company before you go for an interview. They will ask you why you approached them and simply saying 'I want to get into the games industry' is not a good answer. Be prepared!

Who to approach in the industry

This is a tricky one, but most publishers have a human resource department, which deal with applications that are sent to them. If it is primarily development you want to get into, you should try and approach development companies rather than publishing companies. Although some companies have both a publishing arm and a development studio, there are many more development studios than publishing companies. Your application will most likely be diluted at a publishing company.

A tried and tested way of getting into the industry is to start on the ground floor – game testing. As I've said before, this is an important role for the development cycle of a game, so no job in this industry is too menial. Many people progress through to producers or game designers using this route and I know several people who have done this.

There are no defined qualifications for game testing, except that you obviously need a passion for games. Having an understanding of how games work and being able to demonstrate how a particularly bad game could be improved will also help you get a job like this. Being able to communicate this information in your interview will stand you in good stead. You will be required to work long hours, play the same game for three to four months at a time and describe (using the written word) bugs and problems you find with the software.

Testing can be good experience. Apart from your routine job of bug hunting, you may be required to travel to developers at home or abroad, which will give you insight into how games are developed. You may even be asked for feedback and play a role in the final product.

If you are successful in getting a job game testing, you can then begin your career climb to senior tester, lead tester and possibly move onto an assistant producer or assistant designer role. Once you are in the industry, you can plan your career carefully and you will have insight to guide you.

The best people to contact from this perspective are QA managers in publishing companies. Send them your CV and a cover letter showing your interest with regards to a QA/testing position. If they have no vacancies, they will let you know and they will keep you on file.

What the experts say

I asked many veterans of the games industry if they would like to contribute some advice to budding game designers. Here is what the experts say.

Chris Taylor from Gas Powered Games says: My advice is to get an entry-level job inside one of the larger publishers, and if money isn't an issue, inside a small startup. Learn the business inside and out by identifying smart and knowledgeable people who are 'teachers' that you can spend a lot of time with each day. Learn to listen and appreciate the fact that you are a student who will eventually get a chance to do the things that you have always wanted to do, but you need to put in your time first before you will get that opportunity. It took me 15 years to get to where I am today, and if I could go back, I wouldn't change a thing ... it took me this long to figure this stuff out!

Louis Castle from Westwood Studios says: As for advice to those seeking to get into the industry as designers, I think a love of gaming, lots of analysis and really strong communication and debate skills are a great place to start.

I have to concur, but I will also add that a solid educational foundation will certainly help you once you are in the industry. The games industry evolves at such an alarming rate that you constantly need to project forwards and try to imagine what people will want to play in 18 to 24 months, particularly if you are a designer. You will need to be innovative and create challenges that are as yet unseen in the world of video games. This is your challenge as a designer.

Societies and organisations

The **International Game Developers Association (IGDA)** will have some useful information for you, particularly on their 'breaking in' web page, http://www.igda.org/breakingin/

Here you will find advice from many industry veterans that will help guide your way through the foggy fringes of game development.

There are various industry events that happen annually that are not open to the public. However, if you know a particular company is going to be there, ask them to invite you along to show what you can do. If you can attend one of these events, it will give you a taste of what the industry is like and the kind of people that work in it.

For example, the **GDC – Games Developers Conference:** http://www. gdconf.com/ and http://www.gdc-europe.com/ happens twice a year and is run by developers for developers. The first date in the year is in the US, San Jose, CA around March. The second is in Europe, London around August / September. If you follow the links above, you will find all relevant information regarding those events.

The other two big events in the year are **E3**, Los Angeles, CA and **ECTS**, London, England, two major conventions attended by most of the big companies within the industry vying for business http://www.ects.com and http://www.e3expo.com/.

These events are for the industry as a whole and you will find a variety of companies there from the people who make peripherals, to publishers and developers. You will also find recruitment agencies reeling in the wandering talent that they can drop into their books.

Job agencies

There are many job agencies that serve the industry, like **OPM Response Ltd**, for example. Some are better than others, but all serve you, their assets. There are a few things you need to be wary of when it comes to agencies. They will have specific requests from within the industry, and they will most likely have hundreds, if not thousands of individuals on their books. They can be slow with feedback, if it's forthcoming at all, so don't think that just because you sent your CV into them, they will automatically get you a job. You still have to do the interview and you still need to have the talent you claim you are selling. When you approach them, treat them with the same respect as you would any other company in the industry, and don't rely on them. You don't have to pay them – they get their money from their clients who are the people looking for staff.

Here is a list of the agencies I have had experience with:

OPM Response Ltd – http://www.opmresponse.co.uk/

Aardvark Swift Interactive Consultants – http://www.aardvarkswift.com/

Answers Recruitment – http://www.answers-recruitment.com/

Datascope Recruitment – http://www.datascope.co.uk/

GamesRecruit – http://www.gamesrecruit.co.uk/

Interactive Selection – http://www.interactiveselection.co.uk/

Pelican Consultants – http://www.pelican-consultants.com/

You will find many jobs on these sites, which may also help decide what area of expertise you wish to pursue. If you go to their respective websites, some of them have hints and tips that may also be of use to you.

Summary

I hope this book has been as good a journey for you reading it as it was for me writing it. If you believe you were born to make games, then you probably will. A path exists for you; all you have to do is find it. It won't be an easy path to follow and sometimes you will wonder why you ever started it in the first place. Occasionally you may be filled with self-doubt, but you must persevere, it will be worth it, and a career in video game development can be a rewarding experience, financially, personally and professionally. Whatever you choose and whatever path you take, I wish you luck in your choices and hope to play your games someday.

Glossary

AI	Artificial intelligence
Avatar	A moveable icon representing a person in cyberspace or virtual reality graphics (*Concise Oxford English Dictionary*)
CBM64	Commodore 64
Cross-platform	Simultaneous development across multiple entertainment systems
DIR	Directory
Feature creep	A constant implementation of game features during production
Feedback	Visual and audio information delivered to the player from the game
FMV	Full Motion Video
FPS	First Person Shooter
Garb	Avatar clothing
Genre	A French word for 'type'
GUI	Graphical user interface
HUD	Head Up Display
LAN	Local area network
LOF	Line of Fire
LOS	Line of Sight
Melee	A word used to describe hand-to-hand combat
MUD	Multi User Dungeon
MMORPG	Massively Multi-player On-line Role Playing Game
NPC	Non-Player-Characters
OSD	On Screen Display
QA	Quality Assurance
RPG	Role Playing Game
RTS	Real Time Strategy
Splash screen	A title screen or other informative screen preceding a demo or prototype, for example
Stats	Statistics
Stream data	Pulling data from a disk while the game is in motion
UI	User interface
URL	Uniform Resource Locator – the address of a place on the Internet
USB	Universal Serial Bus
VDU	Video Display Unit

2D	Two-dimensional
3D	Three-dimensional
8-bit	Eight bits or a byte
16-bit	Sixteen bits, or a word, or two bytes

Bibliography

Books and games

Dungeon Siege; Gas Powered Games
Chris Taylor and his team have created a landmark title and an evolutionary product in the world of RPGs. It exemplifies a well-balanced game that provides a unique experience and opens up role-playing games to a much wider audience.

> http://www.gaspoweredgames.com/index.shtml
> http://www.dungeonsiege.com/index.shtml
> http://www.dungeonsiege.com/ds2.shtml

Black and White (PC)
Devloper: Lionhead Studios
Publisher: Electronic Arts
http://www.lionhead.co.uk/index2.html
http://www.ea.com/home/home.jsp

Luigi's Mansion (Nintendo Gamecube)
Publisher: Nintendo
http://www.ninetendo.com/index.jsp

Tetris:
Publisher: The Tetris Company
http://www.tetris.com/index_front.html

Robert McKee *Story*, published by Methuen, 1999
An insightful look at the substance, structure, style and principles of story and screenwriting. I have read many books on story construction and this is one book that I can highly recommend.

Christopher Vogler *The Writer's Journey: Mythic Structure for Writers*, 2nd edition, published by Michael Wiese Productions, 1998
This is another book for writers and storytellers. As games drift towards the movie industry at a relentless pace, the techniques used by storytellers and scriptwriters will become more appropriate, and game designers can only learn from their techniques.

Steven D. Katz, *Film Directing: Shot by Shot*, published by Michael Wiese Productions, 1991
Games and movies are both visual mediums and both use camera techniques. This book starts with visualisation and follows through to camera movement.

Steven D. Katz, *Film Directing: Cinematic Motion*, published by Michael Wiese Productions, 1992
Yet more tips for camera techniques that designers could adopt for their games to provide a deeper experience for the player. This book covers staging for multiple subjects and choreography in confined spaces, among other topics.

Periodicals

This is a list of retail and trade magazines that practitioners read, or will have read at some point in their career:

MCV (UK) is a weekly trade magazine that covers news, future trends and jobs.
http://www.mcvuk.com

Develop (UK) is targeted at the development community rather than the industry as a whole.
http://www.developmag.com

EDGE (UK) is a retail monthly magazine that can be found in most high street magazine sellers. Covers a broad range of topics including previews, reviews and news from all aspects of the games industry. It is also a regular stop for anybody searching for a job in the industry.
http://www.futurenet.com/futureonline

Game Developer Magazine (US) is a great monthly magazine for developers. It gets deep into the nitty gritty of game development and tackles the more advanced elements from every aspect of making games. A must-have mini-bible for all game developers.
http://www.gdmag.com/homepage.htm

Websites

Gamasutra (US),
http://www.gamasutra.com
A web-based magazine, again targeted at game developers. Covers many topics including news, features, companies, jobs, discussions and forums.

http://www.dperry.com
A very useful website with articles, industry information, jobs and a forum, by an industry veteran who knows a thing or two about making games.

http://www.game-research.com
Another useful website where you will find research into games and many other interesting links to the games industry.

http://www.triplejump.net
A source of reference for my Draughts/Checkers text.

http://www.tradgames.org.uk
The on-line guide to traditional games – history and useful information.

http://www.mobygames.com
A great site for research purposes. They have an extensive database of games on new and old consoles and computers.

Index

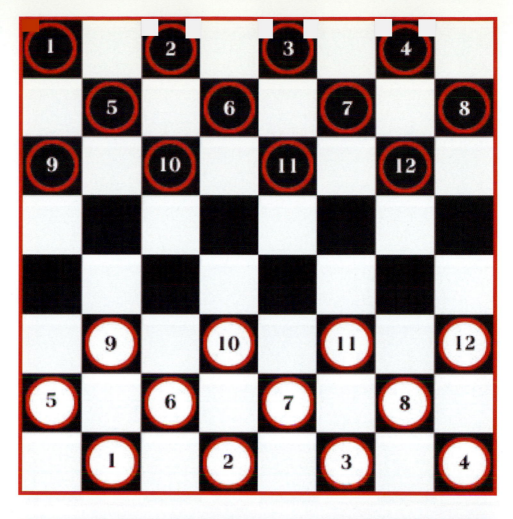

Figure 1.3
Draughts players'
pieces

Figure 1.4 Tetris
player's pieces

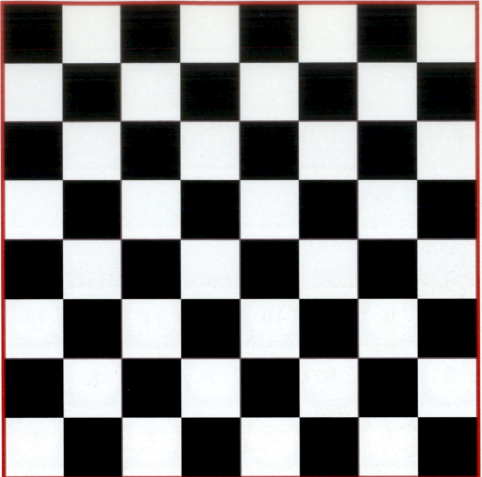

Figure 1.1
Draughts playing field

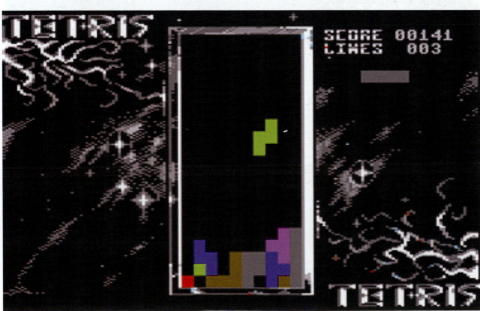

Figure 1.2 Tetris boundaries

Figure 14.1
Dungeon Siege
characters

Figure 15.5
Dungeon Siege
re-configurable keys

Figure 15.2 Dungeon Siege drag and select

Figure 14.2 Norbot

Figure 12.2 Game within a game

Figure 13.1 Dungeon Siege map system

Figure 10.1
Dungeon Siege
navigational device

Figure 12.1 Little
computer people

Figure 8.4 Norbot power cell

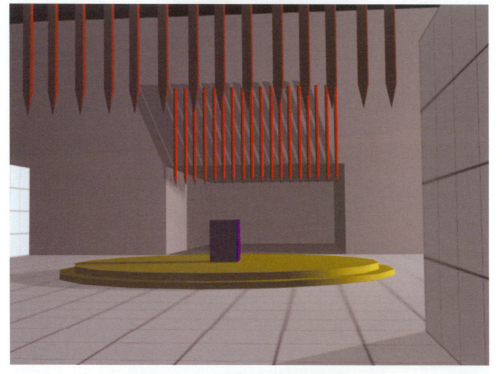

Figure 9.2 Boss arena box map

Figure 8.2
Dungeon Siege
weapon value

Figure 8.3
Dungeon Siege
weapon value

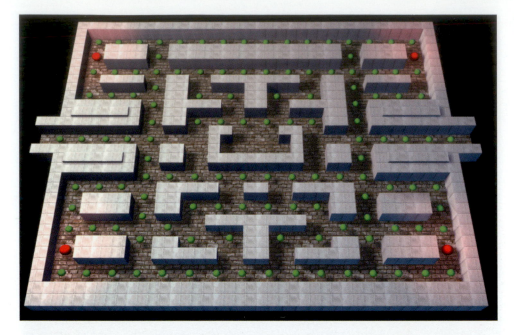

Figure 7.1 Maze environment

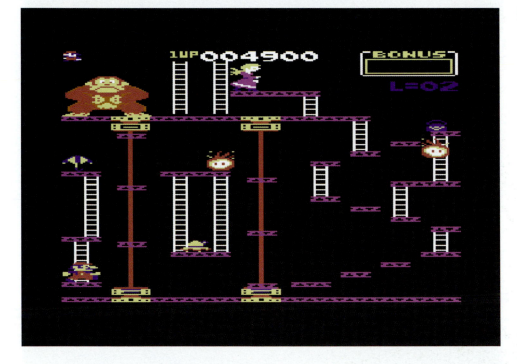

Figure 7.2 Donkey Kong

Figure 6.2
Dungeon Siege
avatar at conception

Figure 6.3
Dungeon Siege
avatar at completion

Figure 6.1 Dungeon Siege visual feedback

Figure 2.7 The
Hobbit (C64)

Figure 5.1
Dungeon Siege

Figure 2.5 Command and Conquer

Figure 2.3
Dungeon Siege
characters

Figure 2.4
Dungeon Siege
inventory

Figure 2.1
Boulderdash

Figure 2.2
Command and
Conquer